Creating and Sustair Arts-Based School Reform

Taking a close look at the issue of the arts and school reform, this book explores in detail how the incorporation of the arts into the identity of a school can be key to its resilience. Based on the A+ Schools Program, an arts-based school reform effort, it is much more than a report of a single case—this landmark study is a comprehensive, longitudinal analysis of arts in education initiatives that discusses the political, fiscal, and curricular implications inherent in taking the arts seriously.

Offering a model for implementation as well as evaluation that can be widely adapted in other schools and school districts, *Creating and Sustaining Arts-Based School Reform* will inspire arts educators to move from advocating more arts to advocating the arts as a way to reform schools. Administrators and policy makers will see how curriculum integration can be used to revitalize and energize schools and serve as a springboard to wider reform initiatives. Researchers and students across the fields of arts education, school reform, organizational change, and foundations of education will be informed and enlightened by this real-world scenario of large-scale school reform.

George W. Noblit is the Joseph R. Neikirk Distinguished Professor of Sociology of Education and Chair of Culture, Curriculum and Change in the School of Education at the University of North Carolina at Chapel Hill.

H. Dickson Corbett is an Independent Educational Researcher conducting evaluations of school reform initiatives.

Bruce L. Wilson is an Independent Educational Researcher engaged in longitudinal research and evaluation projects focused on improving teaching and learning conditions in schools with populations of high poverty.

Monica B. McKinney is Associate Professor, School of Education, Meredith College.

Creating and Sustaining Arts-Based School Reform

The A+ Schools Program

George W. Noblit,
H. Dickson Corbett,
Bruce L. Wilson,
Monica B. McKinney

Routledge
Taylor & Francis Group

NEW YORK AND LONDON

First published 2009
by Routledge
711 Third Ave, New York, NY 10017

Simultaneously published in the UK
by Routledge
2 Park Square, Milton Park, Abingdon, Oxon OX14 4RN

Routledge is an imprint of the Taylor & Francis Group, an informa business

Typeset in Gill Sans and Sabon by
Swales & Willis Ltd, Exeter, Devon

Library of Congress Cataloging in Publication Data
Creating and sustaining arts-based school reform : the A+ schools
program/George W. Noblit . . . [et al].
     p. cm.
Includes bibliographical references and index.
1. Arts–Study and teaching (Elementary)–United States–Case Studies.
2. School Improvement programs–United States–Case studies.
1. Noblit, George W.
LB1591.5.U6C74 2008
372.5′044–dc22   2008021721

ISBN10: 0–8058–6150–5 (hbk)
ISBN10: 0–8058–6149–1 (pbk)
ISBN10: 0–203–88735–2 (ebk)

ISBN13: 978–0–8058–6150–1 (hbk)
ISBN13: 978–0–8058–6149–5 (pbk)
ISBN13: 978–0–203–88735–6 (ebk)

Contents

Preface

This book is an examination of how to create and sustain arts-based school reform. It is based on studies over 8 years of the A+ Schools Program in North Carolina (now in Arkansas and Oklahoma as well). The A+ Schools Program is the largest arts-based school reform effort in recent history, and the only one to have had significant research funding attached to it. With almost $1,000,000 total funding from the Thomas S. Kenan Institute for the Arts and the Ford Foundation, we have thoroughly studied both how to implement and how to sustain over 10 years a school reform effort that involves increased arts instruction and arts integration, a network form of organization, and a creative process of school reform that instead of mandating specifics asks people to think creatively about the process. The result has been a highly successful reform project with strong school-level buy-in and adaptation to local needs. Finally, the schools also found they were successful on high-stakes tests as well.

We first look at the moves to establish and implement the pilot program in 25 schools in North Carolina, and then examine why the A+ Schools Program has been sustainable now over 10 years and has expanded to 42 schools in North Carolina and to two other states. This explanation includes both the unique model of school reform employed and the dynamic power of the arts to improve the lives and learning of students and teachers.

This book makes a unique contribution in several ways. First, it describes how to create and sustain arts-based school reform, and as such has great significance to both the arts and to school reform. There are few studies of sustainability of any reform efforts let alone an arts-based model. Second, the focus is on how a creative process of reform, led by cultural artists, offers lessons about how the recent school reform era could have unfolded but did not. The focus on creative problem-solving, on both/and rather than either/or decision-making, and on developing a wide range of social networks to facilitate the reform all are unique in the literature. Third, a spotlight on the particular role of the arts in making schools more meaningful places for both students and teachers ends up showing that the arts enabled the schools and teachers to make a moral claim. Here the claim to doing the right thing for kids enabled the A+ schools to deal with high-stakes accountability successfully—retaining both the full curriculum regardless of what was tested and a focus on student development and learning.

Acknowledgments

The story of A+ that we tell in this book is the result of 12 years of work by a large team of researchers.[1] We gained access to this story first through the evaluation of the 4-year pilot of the program. This was followed by 2 years of writing and light fieldwork as we produced the evaluation reports. All of this was funded by the Thomas S. Kenan Institute for the Arts. These data became the basis of the first five chapters that follow. The Ford Foundation was interested in the unusual sustainability of the program and funded an additional 2 years of research, and a first draft of this book. The results of the research funded by Ford are reflected in Chapters 7 through 9. Reviewers for publisher Lawrence Erlbaum and Associates suggested revisions of the initial draft of the book to enable it to speak to a wider audience, and we thank them for their guidance. The research team continues to work with A+ in many ways, including being involved in a recent National Endowment for the Arts (NEA) grant to consider the results of the research in North Carolina, Oklahoma, and Arkansas, and some of what we have learned in this process is included in Chapter 9.

We are indebted to the evaluation and research team that made this book possible. We also thank the Kenan Institute, the Ford Foundation, and the NEA for their support. We need to be clear that this book does not necessarily reflect the views of any of those who have funded aspects of it. Nor does the book reflect the views of the entire research team. While we have not had any major disagreements, we are too diverse and too thoughtful to be represented in any one work. We remain colleagues and friends who plan to continue our dialogue in future publications as well. The authors here also acknowledge that what is good in what follows belongs to the larger team and any errors are solely those of the four of us.

About the Authors

George W. Noblit is the Joseph R. Neikirk Distinguished Professor of Sociology of Education in the School of Education at the University of North Carolina at Chapel Hill. He specializes in the sociology of knowledge, school reform, critical race studies, anthropology of education, and qualitative research methods. His most recent book with Jane Van Galen, *Late to Class: Social Class and Schooling in the New Economy* (State University of New York Press) received a Critic's Choice award from the American Educational Studies Association.

H. Dickson Corbett is an independent researcher who spends his time studying reform in low-income school settings around the country. His most recent work has been published in *Listening to Urban Kids* (State University of New York Press) and *Effort and Excellence in Urban Classrooms* (Teachers College Press) as well as journals such as *Educational Leadership* and *Theory into Practice*. He received his PhD in Education from the University of North Carolina at Chapel Hill and now resides in Southeastern Pennsylvania.

Bruce L. Wilson is an independent researcher who is engaged in a range of longitudinal research and evaluation projects, all of which focus on improving teaching and learning conditions in schools with populations of high poverty. The primary goal of this work is to produce information that will be useful to schools and agencies helping schools as they refine the work they are doing to improve learning for all students. The results of this work have been published in a range of books, journal articles, and reports. His academic training was at Stanford University where he earned an undergraduate degree in Sociology and a PhD in Sociology of Education.

Monica B. McKinney received her PhD in Education from the University of North Carolina at Chapel Hill. She is currently Associate Professor in the Department of Education at Meredith College in Raleigh, North Carolina. Her teaching and research interests include school reform, geography of schools, and qualitative research methodologies. She is a recipient of the Pauline Davis Perry Award for Research and Publication.

Chapter I

Introduction

The arts in schools can play a central role in both improving teaching and learning. The A+ Schools Program and its original 24 implementing schools are testaments to that. This book illustrates the ways in which these public schools used the Program to help larger numbers of teachers and students become more engaged and more successful teachers and learners. This Introduction sets the stage for this story by highlighting three conclusions, three critical sources of support, and six core commitments that guided both the program developers and implementers.

The A+ Schools Program is remarkable in many ways. First, it is built on the assumption that a curricular area that is often devalued in education, the arts, can be the basis of whole-school reform. A+ has shown that the arts and arts integration can invigorate entire schools. As a fourth-grade teacher explained:

> The A+ training and going through that week really pulled us together as a team and gave us an opportunity to see how much better we could be. We used to have really wonderful things going on in isolated classrooms, but what was going on in one classroom did not affect the rest of the school. Now whatever is going on in one classroom has a tendency to go out to the whole school or be a part of something larger that impacts the whole school to make a larger experience for all the children.

Second, the A+ initiative has proven to be powerful, value-added school reform. It enables schools to accomplish that which is being demanded of them in terms of accountability and student achievement and provides students and teachers with a meaningful and engaging approach to education. The arts and arts integration simply make classrooms and schools more desirable places to be. As one parent explained:

> Before A+, school was not a place that I, my children, or the teachers wanted to be. Now we are all excited to be here. It creates a place

where teachers want to be, and everyone is involved in the learning process.

Third, A+ has proven to be a sustainable reform both in individual schools and as a larger reform initiative. Regardless of the hype that has gone into school reform over the past 20 years or so, school reforms tend to have a short half-life in schools—implemented one year, waning the next and replaced with a competing reform the third. National reform organizations have a longer half-life but the schools they work with come and go. A+ has demonstrated that arts, arts instruction, and arts integration with other subject areas can gain a remarkably lasting foothold in education, and did so because it directly altered the educational experiences of teachers and students alike. As a student explained: "Everything is connected. It's neat how our teacher puts everything together. It's like a big-ole-knot of work. It's easier for you. We do a lot of work in one day, and it doesn't seem like work." This amazed even casual observers, such as one caregiver we sat next to during a school production:

> My granddaughter cries if she can't come to school. She really loves it. My daughter even uses it as a threat. Can you imagine that?! She says, "... if you don't clean your room, you can't go to school tomorrow."

The Thomas S. Kenan Institute for the Arts initiated A+ less as a reform "model" and more as a philosophy of instructional change. Kenan hypothesized that the most effective way of enabling the arts to gain an enduring foothold in the curriculum would be to encourage all the 24 schools that participated in the pilot phase to adapt the concept of arts integration to their unique contexts. This dual emphasis on a commitment to the arts and flexible implementation caused the A+ Program ultimately to look different in each of the schools.

The schools' efforts, however, were not without guidance and support. While the schools were figuring out what arts integration meant in their individual situations, they benefited from three vital sources of reform-related support for their efforts. These sources of support are a network that provided ideas and problem-solving, a sponsoring organization that secured support and funding, and extensive whole-school professional development. Let us elaborate on each.

A Network for Ideas and Support

All of the schools participated in an evolving network of schools that served as a forum for intensive professional development (especially in the summer institutes), the exchange of ideas, and joint problem-solving. Educational reform networks have become increasingly popular as schools and educational reformers have come to realize the complexity and severity of organizational capacity issues in sustaining school-based reform. In their study of "school family networks" in California, Wohlstetter and Smith (2000) found that connecting schools and networking them as a family unit provided the needed capacity to support large-scale systemic change:

> Reforms focused at the level of individual schools are dependent on the organizational capacity and the human capital of that school alone. Past research has shown that some schools can improve but that most do not have the capacity to support that change. Networks give schools the missing capacity. By bringing their collective expertise to bear on reform, school family networks can plan for complex and coordinated solutions, tailored to fit their particular situation that neither the district nor individual schools muster the capacity to address.
>
> (Wohlstetter & Smith, 2000, p. 514)

Such networks, then, are de facto organizations themselves that provide a supportive environment within which individual schools pursue their reform goals. More about how the A+ network supported schools will be explored throughout the book, but especially in Chapter 3.

A Sponsoring Organization

The Kenan Institute worked at the state level to secure and maintain a continuing source of program funding and recognition. In order to realize their vision of a fully arts-integrated curriculum, schools needed to hire additional arts personnel, particularly dance and drama teachers, and increase their music and visual arts teachers from part-time to full-time assignments. Large amounts of consumable art supplies also had to be purchased and continually replaced. The Kenan Institute lobbied the North Carolina General Assembly to provide the funding that would enable full implementation in each of the 24 schools, with the bulk of the state funds paying the salaries of additional arts personnel. Kenan was successful in obtaining state funding, but the General Assembly appropriated only half of what was needed. Kenan and the schools themselves decided that they would be funded on a sliding scale, with the poorest schools receiving more funds. While the funding levels never reached originally intended levels, schools enjoyed a degree of security in knowing that the program, even at the reduced level, had achieved line-item status in the yearly educational budget at the state level. Kenan, and increasingly, the network itself, worked consistently throughout the pilot to build and maintain a coalition of A+ supporters. The goal of this political activity was to build the Program's legitimacy at the state level and ultimately institutionalize it as a part of North Carolina's approach to educational improvement.

Extensive Whole-School Professional Development

Each school took part in extensive reform-wide professional development activities. This component included an initial 5-day residential teacher-training institute for the entire staff of all participating schools. The training addressed interdisciplinary teaching, hands-on experience in the arts, and strategies for administering the Program. Though shorter in length, staff returned to the summer institute each year for follow-up sessions. Also, regional and school-based workshops, mostly using staff from other A+ schools around the state, occurred during the school year.

Research has increasingly found that the key to successful school reform is the use of professional development aimed at developing the capacity of teachers and schools to improve instruction (Corcoran & Goertz, 1995; Fullan, 1993; Pink & Hyde, 1992). Structural changes alone have been shown to have little impact on improving practice without an emphasis on "changing norms, knowledge, and skills at the individual and organizational level" (Elmore, 1995, p. 26). As Hawley and Valli (1999, p. 129) note: "School improvement cannot occur apart from a closely connected culture of professional development."

A+ assumed that effective professional development required a blend of teacher knowledge and experience with research-based strategies, reflecting a growing number of reform initiatives that viewed teachers' knowledge as integral to changing schools. As Richardson (1994, p. 6) writes:

> The conception of teaching underlying these projects rejects the dominant notion among many educators and policy makers that the teacher is a recipient and consumer of research and practice. Rather, the teacher is seen as one who mediates ideas and constructs meaning and knowledge and acts upon them.

From this change perspective, teacher learning is linked to larger change efforts such as democratic schooling, school reorganization, and to viewing teachers as potential leaders and activists (Cochran-Smith & Lytle, 1999). To this end, A+ focused on professional development and utilized the network to link schools to share information and sustain the Program.

Throughout the A+ pilot, reform-related activities occurred at multiple levels of the state's educational system—at the building level, at the network level, and at the state level (Gerstl-Pepin, 2001). Through the frequent interactions that occurred within and across these levels, the schools heard common messages about what arts integration might look and sound like—and about the importance of the arts. Embedded in these messages were at least six expectations about the directions the schools might take. These *core commitments* are the common threads woven through the variety of creative approaches the pilot schools took to implementing A+.

First, *students should have increased exposure to arts instruction*, both in classes with arts specialists and through arts activities in their regular classrooms. The original goal of the Program was for all pilot schools to have full-time staff in four art forms (music, visual art, dance, and drama), enabling students to have an hour of arts instruction each day and exposure to all four of the arts each week. Because state funding for the pilot was lower than originally anticipated, not all schools managed to achieve this. Instead they split positions, combining dance and drama, for example, or meshed one of the arts into physical education (PE), or simply did without one.

Second, implied in the above description of increased arts, *schools should foster two-way arts integration*. This meant that schools had to consider how to infuse the arts into the core curriculum and the core curriculum into the arts. Rather than relegating the arts to a backseat or infringing on time to master the "basics," this idea tried to establish a complementary relationship between the arts and the major subjects. The arts were no longer considered a distraction from the core curriculum. On the contrary, two-way arts integration provided opportunities for students to encounter the central ideas of the curriculum more frequently and more diversely, increasing the chance for all students to master content at a deeper level.

Third, *teachers should tap students' multiple intelligences*. Through the arts, and in line with Howard Gardner's seminal work on multiple intelligences (1983, 1993, 1999), students in A+ classrooms would have a variety of ways beyond books, lectures, and pencil-and-paper tests to access important ideas and to demonstrate what they had learned. Professional development provided participating educators both a philosophical grounding and practical strategies for using this theory. The idea was to attract students who previously had been unengaged in school and to enable all students to draw on their individual learning strengths. In reality, acting on this idea required teachers to place a heavy emphasis on hands-on activities.

Fourth, *schools should adopt an integrated, thematic approach to the major ideas in the curriculum*. Rather than thinking of content as discrete pieces of knowledge separated into distinct disciplines, this core commitment emphasized ideas organized around a few themes that cut across content areas. Thematic units represented an opportunity to connect arts instruction to that in the other disciplines. Not only did such units offer room for arts content to be included but also they lent themselves to students' being able to express what they were learning in creative ways.

Fifth, *schools should increase professional collaboration.* Arts integration presented a vision of teaching and learning quite different from what the schools had in place. While participating teachers had experimented with using the arts from time to time, they found that coordinating integration throughout a school required teamwork, planning, and professional development. Thus, Kenan felt that the schools would have to break down the traditional isolation of teachers and have them working together more than they had in the past.

And, finally, *schools should strengthen their relationships with parents and the community.* To create rich arts-integrated learning experiences, schools might need more resources than they currently had, both artistic and otherwise. Thus, Kenan suggested that schools draw on the talents and resources of parents and community institutions, including area cultural resources, local colleges and universities, and the media.

Schools, of course, not only had to weave these expectations into the fabric of their local communities but also into mandates from the state. Thus, A+ participants had to ensure that they still covered the North Carolina Standard Course of Study and prepared students to succeed in North Carolina's new high-stakes accountability program (i.e. the ABCs standardized testing program). The A+ Schools Program, rather than imposing a rigid model of reform, instead exposed school staff to a series of philosophical and instructional ideas and then encouraged local interpretations and innovations to suit the schools' idiosyncratic contexts. Control of the Program, therefore, devolved to the schools.

In combination, the above features of A+ distinguished the initiative from traditional arts-based education approaches in two ways. First, it placed the arts at the center of instruction of the standard curriculum. By making the arts the focal point for instruction, the Program combined the "arts-for-their-own-sake" and the "arts-as-instruments-for-facilitating-content-acquisition" justifications (see Chapter 2 for a full explanation of this distinction). Thus, A+ called for both a strengthened arts curriculum and an integrated approach to instruction. Second, it established a network among participant schools that fostered development of the Program. This loose consortium of educators enabled the schools to learn from each other and to reinforce the value of implementing A+. This network also reinforced the centrality of ground-level creativity in shaping the reform, while at the same time it provided a way to involve officials at the district and state levels.

This Book

It all began with a phone call from Dick Corbett and Bruce Wilson to George Noblit. They called to say that a request for proposal was being released for an evaluation of an arts-based school reform program and to ask if we wanted to put together a team to bid on it. We did and now many years later, we have put this book about our collaboration to bed. Yet A+ remains strong and we have assumed a new role within A+, now less as evaluators and more as consultants helping A+ think through its needs for knowledge production as A+ both sustains itself and expands to new venues. As this book comes to life, a new story is being written.

Chapter 2

An Unusual Development

We have been witness to an unusual development: arts-based school reform. For some 12 years, we have watched and studied an educational reform effort that violates all types of usual understandings about school reform and about learning. School reforms have become *packages* which are purchased and are to be implemented with fidelity. Schools adapt to them rather than adapt the reform to their needs. Further, in an era of accountability, most educators have come to believe that focusing on the tests, on skills, on discrete answers to questions, and on test taking itself is what they must do. Learning has become conflated with the measures used rather than the processes used to acquire and deploy substantive knowledge. It may come as no surprise that the artistically inclined would break out of the common understanding and seek innovative approaches to educational reform, creating a different model of reform and of teaching and learning. Like all artistic endeavors, the A+ Schools Program both draws from that which comes before it and breaks from those traditions. Unlike some forms of art, which seek to separate themselves from everyday life, the A+ Schools Program sought to engage everyday schools in creating an unusual reform initiative. This unusual development had powerful effects on the schools involved, and this book is intended to examine these effects. We will do so by relating what we learned through evaluating and researching the program and these schools. The lessons are many and are complex. Implementing and sustaining school reform is not easy. Schools wax and wane in their efforts to educate children, often as the result of factors outside their control. Yet the story we will tell in this book is largely a success story, even with the issues that continue to confront the A+ schools and the critiques we will offer. Telling a complex story, however, requires some grounding. Creekside Elementary School, as a case example from the A+ Schools Program, did this for our research team; and we believe it will allow the reader to see what A+ was all about. So, we start the book with a case study. To set that case in a larger context, we also provide a brief history of the A+ Schools Program. Those sections provide the backdrop for what will be accomplished in this book—a nuanced story of reforming schools with the arts.

The Struggle at Creekside Elementary

Creekside Elementary School was in trouble. It had committed teachers and students who needed an education as much as they needed a stable and supportive home life. Yet it was a school that was out of sight in the city—out of sight; out of mind. The school district was moving towards an "open choice" policy that would allow parents to choose the school their child would attend. The policy would likely lead to a resegregation of the schools, critics argued, but the press of white and more wealthy parents was inexorable. To compete, and competition was the order of the day, Creekside had to become something it was not—a school somehow distinguished. Part of this was to succeed at the impending high-stakes accountability system the state was imposing, but this would not be enough as the school had its history and location working against it. It was not and had never been a middle-class school. Its students were largely of color and they had little success with the conventional curriculum. It was the type of school that the school district hoped would disappear in the competition for students.

Creekside Elementary was desperate for a miracle. When we first met the principal of the school in the early summer of 1995, she was excited that they had been selected as one of the pilot schools for the A+ Schools Program. She hoped this was the miracle she and they needed. High-stakes testing had just been legislated and A+ had just announced it had not received the full state appropriation it had anticipated. The meeting was of representatives of the 24 selected schools[1] to celebrate their inclusion but it also became the first instance of the schools being involved in the design of the A+ Schools Program. At this meeting, they were asked to decide how to proceed given the reduced funding. Options were discussed but basically were two: reduce the number of schools so that each could have the funding level originally planned upon or keep all the schools at reduced funding provided by the state. The initial celebration became a tense moment. Some schools offered that they could proceed largely with their own funds; others needed all the funding they could get. Creekside was in the middle. The district would provide funds to prepare the school for the local open choice competition to come but even more so Creekside needed to be distinctive and the superintendent saw the arts as one way for the schools in his district to develop. It needed A+ for its ideas, its professional development process for teachers, and especially its image as the arts-based school reform in North Carolina. After some debate, it was decided that all schools should be retained in the pilot, and funding should be allotted by need as well as effort. Creekside Elementary was in!

Creekside Elementary was, and is, located in a largely lower-class neighborhood just outside of the downtown area of a small North Carolina city. It is a kindergarten through grade 5 school with approximately 500 students located just outside the downtown center. The two-story school building itself is about 50 years old but is generally well kept. A detached gymnasium and a newer structure housing the school's kindergarten classes were added during the 1970s and 1980s. An auditorium is shared with the middle school next door and numerous trailers supplement the main structures.

Many of the students who attended the school came from poor families, with a large percentage of students receiving free and reduced lunch (the number ranged from 70% to 76% during the pilot period of the A+ Program and has now increased to about 80%). A large housing project was a few blocks from the school, and there were several hotels within a short distance where families in transition lived. The school population was, and is, among the most challenging in the county. Ninety-two percent of students tested under No Child Left Behind in 2003 were considered "economically disadvantaged." Approximately 65% of the school's students were African American, about 20% were white, and 10% were Hispanic.

In addition to having large numbers of families in need, the school had documented widespread incidence of child abuse and neglect. A larger number of children qualified for Title I services than the school could provide, and discipline had been a lingering concern of teachers and administrators alike. Moreover, the school had a large transitional population, with as much as 50% of its student population turning over in a school year. At Creekside Elementary School, low test scores and a large Title I population made success in the ABCs a difficult task. Moreover, the school felt that it was not meeting the needs of its students, and this continued as the A+ Schools Program was first put in place.

During the first year of the A+ Program, Creekside followed the original model of the A+ Schools Program, hiring additional arts staff and putting in place structures to facilitate grade-level planning and increased efforts to use more arts-based, hands-on instruction in the classroom. A trainer from the A+ summer institute became the school's full-time curriculum coordinator, and the focus at Creekside became a more concerted effort to follow the state curriculum. In a rising tide of other priorities, however, the focus on A+ became more difficult for the school in the second year.

Creekside lost many of its teachers when it switched to a year-round schedule at the beginning of year 2. Because of the school year's early start, the Creekside teachers were unable to attend any of the summer institutes that year, and a special training session just for Creekside was postponed. As a result, many of the teachers hired in the second year knew little about the Program. Several more teachers left the school after year 2, leaving the school with a majority of teachers hired after the A+ Program began.

At the end of year 2, the school was categorized as low performing in the ABCs accountability program, despite a concerted effort to prepare students for the end-of-grade tests and what the school's leadership felt were respectable gains in actual test scores by their students. The designation of "low performing" under the North Carolina ABCs accountability program (with 40.9% of the school's students performing at or above grade level in math and 48.2% doing so in reading) dealt a further blow to the belief that the A+ Schools Program was serving their needs well. There was the departure of even more teachers after the second year.

Also at the end of year 2, the principal hired two new specialists, giving the school a strong and energetic arts team. The principal also hired an additional arts specialist to serve as half-time coordinator of the A+ Program, and the Kenan Institute scheduled a summer institute that the teachers could attend. Throughout these early years (and to today), arts specialists planned their lessons to correspond with the grade-level curricula. Grade-level teachers planned together, but with so many new teachers unfamiliar with the A+ Program, arts integration in the classroom was more sporadic.

As year 3 began, the Creekside principal was hopeful that new life would come from the A+ Program. During the first semester, there was more emphasis on helping newer teachers understand the A+ Program, and there was collaborative planning in grade levels to start the year. By December, however, it became clear that the effort that the school was putting toward improving the test scores of its third, fourth, and fifth graders was not resulting in the kind of gains on "practice" tests that would be necessary to avoid retaining the low performing label in the ABCs program. The stakes were high, at least as threatened, with schools twice named low performing eligible to be taken over by the State Board of Education. Frustrated that the current arrangement of arts instruction was ineffective for the ABCs, and certain that the school had yet to see the true potential of integration of arts into the curriculum, the principal decided to "think outside the box" and change the format of the program.

Beginning in January of year 3, the arts teachers each worked with a third-, a fourth-, and a fifth-grade teacher for 90 minutes of daily, collaborative instruction in math, the testing area and grade levels in which Creekside needed the most gains in order to move from the list of low performing schools. Along with 90 minutes of math, teachers in these grades were to spend 90 minutes on reading and 60 minutes on writing daily, with the rest of the time devoted to science, social studies, and exercise. Students in kindergarten, first, and second grade no longer had arts classes, but they received an additional physical education class each week, and teachers were encouraged to continue incorporating the arts into their instruction. Many of the new teachers taught at this level, however, and arts integration was not systematic or pervasive.

The new arrangement was stressful at first for nearly everyone involved, and the upper-grade teachers struggled to make the most of the opportunity to team-teach. In many cases, arts teachers tried at first to integrate their art form, but mostly by the end of the fourth quarter, arts teachers were serving as tutors to students who needed individual attention. There were some notable exceptions, however, leading to some strong examples of integrated instruction. The drama teacher relayed, "it's so integrated that sometimes it's hard to tell who's doing what." As a whole, the math lessons resulted in dramatically reduced discipline problems in the upper grades, as well as dramatically improved test scores, as the school went from "low performing" to "exemplary growth" status.

As Creekside planned for the fourth year, the teachers looked to build upon the strengths of this new arrangement and to make it less stressful. Formal PE classes returned at all levels, and the lower grades added a limited series of classes with the arts specialists. With the upper grades, year 4 meant creative experimentation within the 90-minute teaming format. At the beginning of each quarter, arts teachers rotated through the classrooms at each grade level, giving students nine weeks of intensive exposure to each of the four art forms.

During the 90-minute blocks, the teachers had the option of team-teaching the whole group or splitting the classes in half and offering intensive, focused instruction for 45 minutes to smaller groups of students. Often this allowed the arts teachers to have students work on elaborate projects, and the daily contact meant that the students could finish multiple projects. Most of the time, teachers integrated with math, but they were also able to have students do creative work that was not necessarily integrated into the math curriculum.

The school found that teaming leads to the greatest amount of creativity in instruction when the teamed teachers developed an easy working relationship. Teachers in this situation were able to communicate freely about their work, identify students' particular needs, and design creative instruction to promote students' understanding. While the teachers did not articulate an explicit connection to multiple intelligence (MI) theory, this instructional creativity is certainly consistent with MI approaches. Teaming also broke the patterns of isolation in discrete classrooms and provided instructional flexibility. An unexpected result of teaming was that the arts teachers learned more of the grade-level curriculum, and classroom teachers have been more fully exposed to the potential of arts instruction. The principal added, "teaming ended the we–they stuff" and "destroyed the barrier" between grade-level and arts teachers in the building.

By the end of the fourth year, Creekside had found that team teaching led to not only repeatedly improved test scores, but also to more creativity and flexibility in instruction, better relationships and communication between teachers, increased knowledge of the Standard Course of Study for the arts staff, and better exposure to the arts for grade-level teachers. Creekside also believed that the educational gains of its students went beyond test score performance. The school had developed a model of A+ that worked for it and had developed a substantive identity for itself based upon the A+ Program and the arts.

Since then, the district has continued to support Creekside Elementary, picking up the cost for the additional arts teachers when A+ funding ended. The school has tinkered with and refined its model but has not drastically changed it. Success of the school is still defined in terms of test scores, which seem to permeate everyone's thinking, but given the improvements they have seen and the stakes involved, this is not surprising. The school has continued its climb, going from 70.2% to 87.1% of students scoring at or above grade level in math from 1999–2000 to 2002–2003. Similarly, scores in reading during the same time period rose from 60.4% to 74.7%. Teachers remain committed, however, to the integration of arts and the use of hands-on activities and the school's website touts "Welcome to Creekside A+ Arts Academy."

Arts Integration at Creekside Elementary

The arts are clearly an important part of the curriculum at Creekside Elementary. During our visits, we observed each of the arts teachers. Music reinforced fifth graders' understanding of fractions as groups of students composed and then performed for each other rhythms based on whole notes, half notes, quarter notes, eighth notes, and sixteenth notes. Student groups wrote their compositions on the board and then played their creations on claves, maracas, drums, and other percussion instruments. Mathematical concepts such as reducing and converting were reinforced as the teacher asked questions such as "who can reduce 4/16 for us?" Dance supported third graders' understanding of units of measurement as groups of students choreographed dance movements that corresponded in size to measures such as cup, pint, quart, and gallon. The dance teacher began by showing students real-life examples of each of the measures and then proceeded to illustrate the relationships among the measures in graphic form on the board. She then began modeling how movements of varying sizes can be used to represent the measures and how repetition of the movements can create "gallon-sized" dances. The smaller the movement, the smaller the measure and the more times it needed to be repeated to reach a gallon. Once the class had worked through several examples, students broke into groups and created their own gallon dances using various combinations of movements.

The art teacher worked with fourth graders creating Greek vases out of clay. In the process, she discussed symmetry and shape as well as metric and standard measurements. We also observed her having a first-grade class draw lines that corresponded to the way different types of music made them feel as they listened. They then reviewed concepts such as horizontal, vertical, diagonal, zigzag, wavy, dotted, and dashed. The drama teacher connected to an ongoing unit on plants and flowers in a kindergarten class as he read a story about a flower to them and discussed how the flower may have felt as various things happened. Students then curled their bodies up like seeds, slowly opening up and growing until they were standing and fully-grown. All the while, he reminded them to show him with their faces how they were feeling. These observations were supplemented by stories of many other lessons throughout the year. For instance, the drama teacher explained that he often supports students' understanding of word problems by developing ways to act them out. It is clear that the arts teachers at Creekside focus their integrative efforts on supporting the mathematics curriculum, but there is also evidence of more sweeping curriculum integration in the areas of science, reading, and social studies.

The arts teachers are not doing it by themselves. There were also numerous examples of the arts being incorporated into the classroom. During our visits, students sang songs related to their various areas of study. Fifth graders sang the 50 states song they sing every day and performed their multiplication rap for us. First graders sang a couple of songs related to a unit they were doing on sea life. They also showed us pictures they'd been drawing in conjunction with their studies. Second-grade students demonstrated their knowledge of the life of the bumblebee and the process of pollination through both song and paintings made by creating different "pollen" mixes with paint. Students in an exceptional children classroom acted out different characters in a story as their teacher read. Other activities that were related to us included acting out events from history, developing and deciphering pictographs in language arts, creating bio-mobiles representing different eco-systems in science, and incorporating song and movement into a unit on the Oregon Trail (students learned Sweet Betsy From Pike in addition to discussing and measuring distance around the track, learning that the trail was about 2,000 times around it). One teacher commented, "arts are the driving force of A+" and this seemed evident in many of the classroom activities. Furthermore, many of these examples were tied to "thematic units" that integrated multiple core subjects along with the arts into larger explorations, such as the Oregon Trail discussed above, which in the end integrated social studies, math, science, language arts, and various arts.

The school is also proud of its extracurricular arts events. Creekside has an after-school Arts Enrichment Program that combines additional core subject instruction with time for kids to do "arts for arts' sake." For instance, a group of after-school students has painted an impressive mural in one of the hallways in the school. One of our visits occurred after end-of-grade exams at the school and the day before its A+ celebration. There was both a sense of relief that testing was over and an excitement over the next day's events. Several of the classrooms we visited were working on their presentations: a kindergarten class was practicing their graduation song and a group of fourth graders was working with the dance teacher rehearsing their dance. This integration of the arts into the school celebrations is everyday practice at Creekside. For example, the school includes arts productions in quarterly awards programs. These programs honor good behavior (A+ citizenship) and good grades (A+ academics). A fun family picnic day, a field day, and a student talent show provide further venues for artistic expression.

What Is Sustained at Creekside Elementary?

Creekside Elementary continued to actively use its arts-infused A+ identity. The school's A+ banner remained displayed prominently in the main hallway and a framed poem hanging in the waiting area outside the principal's office read:

> We're the bulldogs, green and white. We've got bookworms and math puzzles.

> We've got spelling bees and writing prompts. We've got a science lab and drawing skills. We've got plays to create and dances to learn. We are the prisms sparkling and bright at the A+ Arts and Science Academy of Creekside Elementary.

Visitors to the school's website were welcomed to "Creekside A+ Arts Academy" and an "Arts" link on the homepage revealed individual information pages for each of the arts teachers.

Creekside also continued to maintain a full complement of arts staff with four full-time arts teachers in art, dance, drama, and music. The music teacher, who was also the school's A+ coordinator, had been with the school since 1996. The others were newer to the school, as well as to the profession, with less than three years' experience. Creekside teachers admitted that they were concerned when the previous arts teachers left, but believed talented individuals had replaced them. In their view, the new arts teachers were "high caliber" and "generally willing to promote academics along with their field of art"—a necessary viewpoint given the school's emphasis on using the arts to achieve greater learning in other subjects. Accordingly, the A+ Program had not lost any momentum, but had instead, according to them, gained "new perspective" as a result of turnover in the arts staff.

Creekside had also maintained its focus on collaborative teaching, which has, in turn, facilitated a focus on arts-infused, integrated instruction. The principal explained: "We have had and still have teachers who love integration and love the arts. Even teachers without natural affinity like it." While all students experienced integrated lessons in social studies and the sciences, reading comprehension and retention provide focus in kindergarten–second grades and math provides a similar focus in third–fifth grades. Teachers continued to work through the contradiction between their desire to integrate and a mathematics pacing guide developed by the state's Department of Public Instruction to help schools make sure they cover all the appropriate concepts. The pacing guide does not always accommodate the natural connections Creekside teachers wish to make. Nevertheless, the arts have brought the curriculum to life. The arts teachers provided more support to the classroom Standard Course of Study because classroom teachers do not have the expertise to provide the technical support for the arts. But the classroom teachers did incorporate artistic activities in their classrooms even when arts teachers were not there, and "in terms of moral, ethical, teaming support, it's equal" as one staff member put it.

The school's continued focus on collaborative teaching also sustained communication and helped build a sense of connectedness and inter-dependence among the teachers. While some grade levels said they were "closer" than others, most of the teachers we spoke with did not believe that the school would enjoy the same level of communication without A+. The principal added that this communication is two-way and that A+ had created a community of teachers because they've been forced to talk with each other in order to know what's going on. Because everyone worked together and everyone shared, "everyone gets to know everyone here."

How A+ Was Sustained at Creekside Elementary

The school's high levels of communication and collaboration helped create a support network for new and continuing teachers alike. Teachers were finding their comfort levels with the arts through different activities over time. One teacher, who was new to the school last year, reported that she had trouble seeing where she could incorporate the arts. After work-ing with her grade-level teachers and with the arts teachers for a year, however, this year she had "a picture." Another teacher expressed appre-ciation for having the dance teacher at the school. It was easier for her to think about how to do art, drama, and music in her own classroom, but struggled more with dance. Working with the dance teacher made her feel more open to dance and more comfortable incorporating it into her classroom.

More formally, a mentoring structure was in place for bringing new teachers on board. All new teachers were trained and introduced to the A+ philosophy through attendance at the annual summer conferences and supported through a first-year teachers' group. Additionally, each new teacher had a mentor for three years. Outgoing teachers have provided lesson plans and advice, particularly to the incoming arts teachers. The dance teacher was a student teacher who taught at Creekside and liked it so much that she stayed. Continuing teachers also talked about the A+ summer conference and its role in professional development. In addition, the A+ fellows (the professional development staff of A+) brought a team to the school so that the staff could look at curriculum and plan collaboratively. The principal explained that Creekside has provided other in-house professional development for classroom teachers related to collaboration and the arts. MI training—brain research and learning styles—are part of the School Improvement Plan.

Scheduling also helped sustain A+ at Creekside. Whereas scheduling of the arts in most schools has students going to dance on Mondays, drama on Tuesdays, and music on Wednesdays, arts teachers at Creekside saw the same third, fourth, and fifth graders every day for a quarter (except in February and March when they rotated 2 weeks in and 2 weeks out because of testing). K–2 classes followed a 2-weeks-on/2-weeks-off rotation all year. Arts teachers spent three or four periods with third–fifth graders (45 minutes each) and two periods (40 minutes each) with kindergarten–second graders and received an extra planning period during one quarter. They liked this rotation schedule because it gave them better rapport with the students and allowed them to work on bigger, more meaningful projects. They believed students become more comfortable, less nervous, and therefore were able to create some wonderful things. Classroom teachers agreed that the concentrated arts classes were good; students could complete whole projects and maintained their excitement. An early elementary teacher observed her students retained information better when they were in the arts rotation.

The sustainability of A+ at Creekside also could be attributed to community support and collaboration in many forms. Because Creekside served a generally poor population, the school maintained a clothes bank for its students and their families and, in conjunction with the nearby middle school, provided other social services to the surrounding community. Community connections related to the arts included taking students to perform at various community events as well as inviting local artistic organizations (i.e. Shakespeare festival, local symphony, a local arts conservancy) to the school. In local displays of student artwork, the pieces produced by students at Creekside stood out because of their curricular connections. This brought positive attention to a school that counter-balanced negative perceptions. Teachers reported that there had been a lot of community support in the form of donations of art supplies, sponsors for children, volunteers in the school who helped with holidays, etc. Last but not least, the school had an annual A+ reception featuring arts-based presentations and performances by the students.

The positive attitudes and enthusiasm of the teachers were very important factors in sustaining the A+ Program and the school's focus on the arts. As the principal explained: "We have confidence that we can make it work." The teachers corroborated this interpretation and gave themselves credit for sustaining the arts. In fact, they believed it was up to them to make it happen. As one teacher said, "teachers sustain the arts here." While all agreed that they needed to stay testing focused, they also believed they were given the freedom they needed to do what they wanted artistically as long as they could show connections to the tested curricula. Classroom teachers credited arts teachers as a big support. Without them, productions would have been smaller or would not have happened at all. They believed the arts teachers extended the curriculum and made Creekside unique. In fact, one teacher came to Creekside because she had a friend at another A+ school and she saw the potential.

The teachers' belief that A+ is good for students was at the heart of their positive attitudes toward the Program. Teachers found that student behavior was better because the arts are aesthetically pleasing and are loved by the students. This in turn helped the students get into their schoolwork more and kept them more interested. One teacher stated that many children at the school do not know how to deal with or shut down their rage. She credited the arts teachers and volunteers for giving these students an outlet for their emotional self-expression. Other teachers viewed the Program as providing an outlet for talent and energy. Teachers also believed that A+ is more in tune with what their students need academically. Instructional subject areas are integrated and connected as they are in real life. They maintained that this helps students become critical thinkers and makes them more confident. Students benefited from attending community events not only because they got to experience various artistic displays and performances, but also because they learned to be audience members as well as performers. In other words, they learned social etiquette as well as to appreciate art. They also learned the mechanics of artistic performance and began to notice things such as set design. These teachers believed that it is important to expose students to the arts at a young age and were pleased by the foundations laid in kindergarten, first, and second grades that prepared students for fairly complex work in the upper grades.

Teachers saw students who moved from low performing status to become at, or above, grade level and credited the arts and the A+ Program. One teacher even did an action research project on the effectiveness of A+ in her classroom. She did two weeks of traditional teaching and two weeks of arts-integrated, MI lessons and used an established test to measure the results. She was quite impressed; only two students had higher growth during traditional instruction. The rest had nearly double achievement growth with arts instruction over traditional. For her, this was proof of the effectiveness of A+.

The Future

Given the amount of teacher turnover and the challenges presented by the state's testing program, Creekside Elementary School has faced an uphill battle to keep the arts alive and strong. The school has found success, however, as evidenced both by what has been sustained and by the mechanisms in place to sustain it. The future undoubtedly holds successes and hurdles both anticipated and not. A few of the "known" hurdles involve the ubiquitous areas of teacher turnover, testing, and funding.

Though Creekside has gathered a group of teachers who believe in the school's approach, faculty turnover will continue to present the challenge of acclimating new teachers to the school's hands-on, collaborative approach and of teaching them how think about A+. Currently, the school's teachers appear to have the focus and the desire to maintain their efforts in this regard. The principal relates: "We are seeing teachers becoming more comfortable . . . we have teachers who love integration and love the arts . . . even teachers without a natural affinity like it." Also working for them is their continued involvement with the summer A+ professional development conferences. This support enables the teachers to continue to be creative as well as focus on the state curriculum.

Creekside is very conscious of how well (or not) its students perform on the state's end-of-grade tests. Teachers are concerned that the tests' emphasis on discrete, finite answers differs from the multiple answers and alternative approaches toward problems that the students experience in the A+ and MI-based instruction. They are also concerned about the amount of time spent assessing students each quarter. The principal is unapologetic that the bottom line is test scores, and given today's political climate, there seems to be no other logical stand. While concerns over testing led to the school's unique approach toward drawing upon the arts to enhance instruction, they also led to a somewhat utilitarian view of the arts. This is not to say that the administration and teachers do not recognize multiple values of the arts as shown above, but it does mean that if test scores do not continue to rise, they may be pressed to search for a different approach.

Tightening budgets represent another area of concern for the school. Creekside teachers are dedicated enough to search yard sales and stores such as Goodwill for things they can use in the classroom. They receive a small amount of money that can be used to buy art supplies and other materials, but many of the teachers pay for materials themselves. Having enough money for the extra arts positions remains an ongoing concern for the principal but to date the district has come through with its support of the arts. In fact, the district has added another arts magnet elementary school and students can continue their arts-focused education at one of two middle schools. The new magnet school is supported in part by a federal grant, an option that Creekside Elementary is also looking into.

Other A+ schools facing the low performing label in the ABCs program have enlisted their arts teachers to help prepare students for state testing. While some have used limited teaming to help with reading instruction, Creekside is the only one of the A+ schools to restructure its A+ Program around the teaming concept. Unconventional thinking fostered creativity in instruction and taught unexpected lessons of cooperation and mutuality between arts and classroom teachers. In other schools, test preparation has led to decreased amounts of arts integration and limited creative instruction. Creekside is an example of a creative approach that has yielded substantial results. A+ was certainly not the miracle they thought they needed in the beginning, rather A+ has proved to be a way to work through the difficulties associated with education in a way that has engaged and changed teachers and teaching. It has also meant students have a richer curriculum and do better on tests as well. The experience of Creekside demonstrates that it is amazing what schools can do with the arts when they are a part of a wider effort that nurtures ideas, prepares teachers to meet the challenges ahead of them, and allows and helps schools adapt a reform to their circumstances.

A Brief History of A+

To fully understand A+ one must move beyond individual cases and grasp its larger development over time. Understanding the A+ Schools Program historically is one way to perceive the challenges and accomplishments it represents. Gerstl-Pepin (2001) has written a history of the A+ Program that explores how it came to have its unique status as an alternative public sphere in educational reform in North Carolina and the nation. In her account, A+ had elements of a grassroots movement and through creating an alternative discourse about reform, A+ "provided a space for citizens to come together to dialogue and to strategize about how to reform and improve schools" (p. 9) through the arts. Her argument is not that A+ was a populist movement but rather that school reform in North Carolina was typically top-down and coerced. A+, in contrast, emerged from an amalgam of cultural arts activists, educators, philanthropic organizations (most notably the Kenan Institute), and others. It was not a people's movement but neither was it a government program.

A+ was first conceived by Ralph Burgard, based on his observations of arts-based schools in South Carolina and Georgia. This led to his spearheading an effort to create two arts-based schools in Southeastern North Carolina. These efforts drew the attention of the newly formed Kenan Institute for the Arts, which adopted as its inaugural project the development of the A+ Schools Program. As the idea developed in discussions with arts activists and educators (1993–1995), A+ came to be conceived more broadly than simply more arts in schools; A+ was to be about educational reform. A series of planning committees (including a program committee, a policy committee, and a creative committee) was formed. These committees involved educators, arts people, local politicians, and community members from around the state—people often left out of discussions about educational reform. Their discussions generated ideas about how the Program should be designed, eventually leading to the six core commitments described in Chapter 1 (increased arts offerings, two-way arts integration, a focus on multiple intelligences, integrated and thematic curricula and instruction, increased professional collaboration, and stronger relationships with parents and community) and a belief that schools entering the Program needed to commit for the full four-year pilot period.

A+ gained considerable momentum when the governor expressed his official support for the Program. Planning continued and a request for proposals process led 48 schools to apply for A+. A selection committee chose 25 schools, one of which did not implement A+. The schools represented a mix of urban, suburban, and rural schools; a mix of elementary, middle, and high schools; and from the three geographical areas of North Carolina (the mountains, coast, and piedmont). Yet in 1994, state elections resulted in the Republican Party taking control of one house of the General Assembly and vowing to reduce spending.

While the Republicans led an assault on education spending, they also pushed through legislation to reduce the size of the State Department of Education and to begin a high-stakes testing program (the ABCs). Funding for the A+ Program was reduced to $500,000 a year (one-third of the original proposal), just as A+ began the first summer institutes to help prepare teachers for the curricular and instructional challenges of A+. The Kenan Institute solicited outside funds and invested considerable funds of its own to reduce the impact of the lost state funds, but was unable to fully address the shortfall.

The first summer institutes in 1995 focused on curriculum mapping for arts integration, for networking across the schools, and provided an opportunity for A+ to be talked about away from the press of local and state pressures in education. As above, even with the funding reduction, the 24 schools voted to keep all schools in the Program. This meant, of course, that some schools had better local resources to fill in the funding gap than others as A+ began implementation in 1995–1996. As a result, first-year implementation varied across schools even more than anticipated. With high-stakes testing looming, early indications of student success and indications that A+ was a powerful platform for developing external support for schools both from the community and from funding sources kept the schools in the Program.

In year 2 of implementation (1996–1997), a protracted state budget battle ended with level funding for A+, and again Kenan had to develop alternate funding sources for the summer institutes and other activities. The state initiated the ABCs in its first incarnation (but it wasn't until the summer of 1997 when scores were publicly released that the schools saw what was fully in store for them). A+ was also building its own network structure and developing its A+ faculty (later called fellows) who were responsible for planning and coordinating professional development opportunities. The initial professional development staff for the summer institutes had been mostly arts expert-based. Yet it was also clear that the schools themselves had remarkable teachers and ideas as to how A+ could be done. These teachers were invited to serve as "idea champions" (Gerstl-Pepin, 2001, p. 35) both in their schools and Program-wide.

The ABCs pressed teachers to teach to the test and this threatened A+ in many schools. As a result, A+ began an effort to develop an alternative assessment process and successfully sought Goals 2000 funding to develop an "enriched assessment process" that was compatible with A+. The 24 schools continued to implement A+ as they learned more about what was possible, but the accountability press coupled with principal and super-intendent changes meant most schools had accomplished "pockets of success" (Gerstl-Pepin, 2001, p. 37) rather than widespread implementation. Yet as the A+ faculty came to be drawn increasingly from the teaching staffs in the A+ schools, new "idea champions" began leading A+ in the schools. Further, teachers also reported the arts were giving students new interest in school and learning as well as being attractive to parents.

By 1997–1998, A+ continued to receive level funding from the state, but also had to deal with the aftermath of the first state released test scores for the public schools in August 1997. It was as if a "bombshell" (Gerstl-Pepin, 2001, p. 43) had been dropped on schools. The focus on growth shook even schools that traditionally had higher achievement scores. A+'s emphasis on enriched assessment was the prominent project of the year. Yet the Kenan Institute also led another shift as well. Now that the schools had some experience with A+, it was decided that the A+ faculty of teachers should become the brain trust of the Program. In the early years many decisions had been made by Kenan, but it was increasingly clear to Kenan that the A+ faculty were the creative core of the Program and less likely to be reactive to the pressures of accountability and other challenges to the arts. Moreover, this brain trust was also serving as leaders in the A+ schools themselves, linking the wider Program more strongly with local school efforts.

Summer institutes were shortened in year 3 from 5 days to 2 days at a central location and a second 2-day on-site workshop at the individual schools. In this way, the summer institutes were both about introducing new ideas to the schools and about adapting these ideas to the local school context. An Assessment Institute was also held at the end of March 1998 where schools shared their unique enriched assessment processes. Many things were remarkable about this meeting, but most important was sharing how other A+ schools had linked A+ type assessment with standards for the ABCs. Instead of seeing A+ and ABCs as opposed, most schools had figured out ways they could work together. This came at a key point since pressure from school districts to increase test scores reached new heights. Teachers began to worry that creative teaching would no longer be valued. In the end, A+ was increasingly seen as a way to use the arts to promote learning in other subjects. Yet teachers also lamented what the ABCs were doing to students and their learning, and the network and meetings associated with A+ enabled teachers to dialogue and develop a strategy of "playing the game" (Gerstl-Pepin, 2001, p. 53) with testing while valuing the creativity A+ had helped them develop in teaching.

The fourth year (1998–1999) marked the official end of the pilot period and began on a positive note. The previous year all the A+ schools had met their expected growth on the ABCs. This, plus a concerted effort by Kenan to develop bipartisan political support, resulted in state legislators visiting A+ schools and being impressed by what they saw. A+ also became one of two state reforms that qualified for federally initiated comprehensive school reform grants. The transition to seeing the A+ faculty as the brain trust also matured. Renamed the A+ fellows, the teachers were asked to take part in planning for A+'s future. Enriched assessment also continued to be an emphasis for professional development and regional meetings, and by the end of the year each school participated in an on-site workshop on enriched assessment. This effort had been so impressive that districts were also asking for workshops for their non-A+ schools to help with new promotion standards based on test results. A+ also began to connect with other national reform projects including the National Writing Project and the Chicago Arts Partnership in Education. A+ had also begun to expand the number of schools within North Carolina.

Gerstl-Pepin (2001) ended her history with the end of the pilot period. Yet A+ continued to develop and change. In the years since the pilot, A+ has expanded to other states, most notably Oklahoma and Arkansas, and added schools in North Carolina to total over 40 A+ schools as we write this book. The original contract districts signed with Kenan promised that districts would increasingly assume funding necessary for the Program, but this did not occur. A+ schools have had to develop new funding streams for their Programs and have had to make decisions about how to cover a range of arts in rather creative ways. We will discuss the impact of these changes in Chapter 6. The Kenan Institute also changed its commitment to A+ and in the end A+ was "spun off" to the University of North Carolina at Greensboro with transitional funding. A+ has become a self-supporting reform initiative. The A+ schools see the uncertainty of this but have also weathered many storms and much uncertainty in the past. Their participation in the planning and in the network helps them understand the challenges ahead. No doubt A+ will change as a reform program and in each of the schools, but this is its history as much as its future.

We can see the history of Creekside with A+ in this history of the wider Program. The challenge of high-stakes testing, and the emphases on the state curriculum and local adaptation, interacted to allow Creekside to develop its approach to integrating the arts in math in the grades where the test scores had been lowest. Creekside's embracing of A+ allowed it to claim a niche in the "choice" initiative in its district and to be seen as both successful and different from other schools. Yet as experience with A+ matured, Creekside wanted the arts more intensively involved in the education of all its students. Creekside created an enriched assessment process that fits their needs and lets them also embrace the arts in a way that made sense to them. They have been very active in the network and are a success story that many recount as indicative of what is possible with A+. Creekside remains a strong supporter of A+ as it makes the transition to a national reform effort. Schools who may be interested in A+ but have concerns about testing are sent to Creekside as one example of how A+ can be adapted. Creekside's story also sets the stage for the rest of this book. It helps demonstrate that A+ is an unusual case of the arts in education. While Creekside's story is a promising sign in and of itself, it also bridges to a set of themes that cut across other A+ schools. These can serve to guide other arts and education efforts and will be discussed throughout the book.

Reforming Schools with the Arts—An Outline for the Book

The story of Creekside Elementary is not a typical story of an A+ school. Indeed, given the nature of this reform effort, there are no "typical" stories. Each school has its own story, and in this book we will share many of these stories even though we cannot possibly tell all 24 stories that we know. Thankfully, while there are 24 different stories, there is a set of themes that enables us to focus what follows and to better communicate the overall lessons of the A+ Schools Program. These themes can be seen in Creekside's story and allow us to introduce what is to come in this book.

Creekside's story is about an unusual form of arts-based educational reform. As we came to know more about arts education and particularly efforts to use the arts to reform education, we came to see that A+ was indeed an unusual development. As we discuss in Chapter 2, the arts have a history of being relegated to a secondary status in the school curriculum. It is outside the core subjects and all too often seen as a frill. There are many reasons for this including the American penchant toward utilitarianism but reading the history of arts education leads us to conclude that proponents of the arts have contributed to this secondary status as well. Being stuck in a battle over whether it should be "arts for arts' sake" or "arts in service of learning other subjects," has limited the thinking about the role of arts in education. After reviewing the history of arts education reform, we then note that A+ took a "both/and" approach to this dichotomy. This set it apart from other efforts. However, A+ also represents another unusual move in arts education. It envisioned the arts not just as about curriculum but also as a way to promote whole-school reform. Indeed, it was this last move that led to our being awarded the initial evaluation contract. Our competitors knew much more about the arts and arts education, but we were researchers who specialized in studies of school reform. This also led to an inside joke in the evaluation team. The contract was for a 5-year study and we knew quite well that reforms tended to have waned by then, often as early as three years. We later told the Kenan Institute we figured this meant we were to have 2 years of funding without anything to evaluate. The story of Creekside shows how wrong we were to underestimate the power of this arts-based reform initiative. It is now 12 years since we started work, A+ is going strong and expanding, and we are still working with A+ in various ways. Some joke.

The Creekside story reveals how central the nature of the reform initiative was to its continued development. The A+ Schools Program began with an initial idea but did not push the fidelity to the idea in ways education reformers often do. Clearly, the Kenan Institute wanted the reform to move ahead and to have the schools push themselves into new areas of development. As artists, the Program staff saw their job was to be creative and to help the schools and educators be creative as well. We explore this story in Chapter 3. We wish to be clear, however, that the story is one constructed via a set of relationships, what came to be called networks in the parlance of school reform as well as sociology. Thus the story of what the Program did cannot be separated from what the schools did. Both learned from the other and adapted their initial understandings. One of the key learnings on both sides was how A+ was unlike the top-down reforms schools were used to implementing. Fidelity to the reform was not as important as figuring out what could be done best with the arts in what situation. Thus implementing A+ was as much about learning and creative organizational action as it was about doing what one promised in the proposal that got a school selected. We use a set of stories from some of the other schools to show how the relationship between the schools and the Program was mutually adaptive. We also discuss which of the original ideas were set aside in the process, and which hopes went unfulfilled.

As noted above, we were cynically prepared to write an examination of the demise of A+, even while we hoped for the best. In the early years, the challenges occupied the minds of everyone involved. Creekside and all the A+ schools faced challenges, including teacher and administrator turnover and the competing pressure of high-stakes testing. Turnover and competing reform initiatives are the usual culprits of the demise of school reforms, but did not do A+ in. The lesson is important. It is not that A+ escaped common threats to reform. It is rather that they survived them. We have concluded that this was the case because A+ had a set of what we came to consider "protective factors," including the A+ network, multiple leadership roles within each school, and stable—albeit reduced—funding. These enabled A+ to adapt, to innovate, and to persist. We present a series of examples in Chapter 5 that demonstrate that adaptation is key to reform persistence but that adaptation itself is embedded in network organization, shared leadership, and continued availability of resources.

It is well-established by now that school reform is about cultural change as much as it is about restructuring the organization (Pink & Noblit, 2005). This was clearly the case with Creekside. They came to use A+ as the way to think about how to respond to challenges. We begin Chapter 6 with a set of other cases of schools that exemplify different types of school identity with A+. We use these to set the stage for a discussion of the three ways A+ was embedded in school identity: affiliative, symbolic, and substantive. We view these identities as *levels*—each builds upon the preceding level. Achieving a substantive identity is to be viewed as quite an accomplishment but many A+ schools were able to achieve this. Yet it is also true schools are not destined to stay at one level or another. The schools we studied moved in and out of these identities. It may be obvious that the lowest level of school identity with A+, affiliative, is the easiest to sustain and the highest, substantive, takes considerable work to achieve and sustain. Yet we would argue a key point missed in the literature on school reform, whether arts-based or otherwise, is that of maintaining the distribution of identities throughout the history of the reform such that each school can see itself in relation to others. This is decidedly difficult when fidelity to a reform is less emphasized as one cannot use a checklist of characteristics to evaluate where one is. Nevertheless, we think schools did understand that, with A+, depth was key, and that was about how embedded A+ was in the school's identity and culture. Creekside was different than many but everyone was clear that A+ was deeply a part of their school's identity.

Implementation is very important in getting school reform in place and having the desired effects, but all too often implementation becomes the goal, supplanting what the implementation was to achieve. Implementation is the first step in getting arts-based school reform in place but it is not sufficient to sustain the reform over time. The inside joke of the evaluation team was based in this understanding; many reforms get implemented but do so in ways that do not lead to lasting change. Such efforts do little to generate evidence that these efforts are worthy sustaining in the face of continued challenges. Creekside found out that A+ could be used to respond to challenges and in the process learned to make A+ their own. They then generated evidence that A+ worked for them in ways nothing else ever had. In this, they learned how to use A+ to manage change itself. Since there are few cases of sustained reform of any type, and especially of arts-based school reform, we devote Chapter 7 to illustrate *what* sustainability looks like. As should be evident by now, the A+ that was sustained looked different in different schools.

Creekside Elementary also gives hints at *how* reform is sustained in A+ schools. Clearly, the protective factors discussed in Chapter 5 are implicated in sustainability. Yet our study of sustainability suggests that there is more to this. There is a close match of what has been sustained and how it been sustained. This simultaneity is worth consideration. That is, A+ has focused on processes and the schools have done likewise. In creating and adapting processes to local school needs, the schools have created mechanisms that embed A+ in the decision-making of the school, in the culture of the school, and in the management of change. Yet there is something special about the arts that contribute to the sustainability of A+. The educators we talked with and observed were clear that they were doing something morally better for children. That is, the arts make teaching and learning interesting and inviting. Thus A+ is sustained, at least in part, by the belief that the school is doing something good for students (and for teachers, the community, and society). As the old adage goes, there is nothing more powerful than the belief that you are doing what is morally correct. Chapter 8 illustrates that point, exploring how A+ was sustained.

We have used the Creekside example in many venues, and people see both the promise and peril of school reform in it. School reform itself must be recreated every day in schools. It can never be presumed to have been accomplished and thus one just ride along on the laurels. Similarly, at the program level, A+ is always being recreated. In this, there are many *promising signs* we will discuss in the final chapter—for A+, for educators, for arts reformers and policy makers, and for arts researchers and evaluators. Here we will reengage the limitations of A+ and that which was left on the wayside as the reform effort adapted and matured. Yet we will also discuss where A+ is now. As part of the effort to expand the effort, A+ has generated a set of essential understandings that guide but do not overly constrain schools. A+ has expanded into two other states, Arkansas and Oklahoma, and others are in the process of coming on line. This has led to the establishment of other research teams that have much to offer to our understanding of creating and sustaining arts-based school reform. The results of these studies, and ours, were recently shared at a national conference on the research on A+ schools funded by the NEA. The growing knowledge base itself is a most promising sign and helped inform our final chapter.

Chapter 3

Arts in Education

From Threatened Curriculum to a Way to Reform Schools

As a team, we had much to learn about the arts. True, each of us had our own connection to the arts and as adults we had a different relationship with the arts than we had when we were in school. In our youths, we had the usual but sporadic required courses in the arts—mostly visual art and music. For some of us, this led to some artistic inclinations that have extended over the years. In other cases, school art classes led to a sense that mastery would elude us forever. We did not experience arts classes that actually built capability over time or that were integrated with other content so we could see how the arts were a form of learning or representation or even a part of a well-lived life. All of us grew up knowing, however, that popular music was something attractive. Some of us played in bands and so on, while others just knew it was "their" music. Here is where we learned that some forms of arts were seen as dangerous. It was not just that some artists painted nudes, and that was clearly risqué if not outright forbidden. It was also that the music we grew up with was actually associated with strong beliefs about what is right and what is wrong. Rock and roll led to dancing that was licentious and thus should be avoided. Jazz, blues, rhythm and blues, and soul music was about black people and this was an association many adult, and not so adult, whites wished to avoid—even though they had danced to jazz bands in their days. Still later in our lives, these forms of music were explicitly attached to politics as we learned just how dangerous the arts could be when expressing ideas that others wanted suppressed.

As adults, we have developed different connections to the arts. We do "artsy" things, such as play music and certainly dance. All of us have more appreciation for the arts as can be seen in our homes and offices and our all too occasional visits to museums and art galleries. It can also be seen in our families. We have spouses and children active in various forms of arts and, with the insight that comes with the years if not with explicit instruction, we now recognize the art in everyday life—in carpentry, landscaping, and all sorts of what would have been called in our youth vernacular art, and in school had been demarked as "industrial" or "manual" art, which we all understood as being prepared for industrial work rather than for creativity.

Our own histories with the arts were a template, albeit all too unconscious, for our work with A+ schools. We had been hired to evaluate the Program because we were experienced in the supposed "hardball" arena of educational policy and school reform. We were one of a number of interfaces with politics that A+ needed. They had others articulated as well. The Kenan Institute was a player in the politics of knowledge in North Carolina, and had facilitated state funding even if at a reduced level due to a switch in the dominant political party. As noted earlier, they had myriad networks of foundations, arts organizations, key influentials, and so on. Yet they could not solely rely on politics in the wider scene of educational reform. They sought an evaluation that would hopefully legitimate the Program as effective. We were practiced at explaining how evaluations do not always, or even often, deliver the results people wanted. Yet there was something compelling to us about A+. A+ was a little like rock and roll in our youth. It was going against the grain. It planned to invert the hierarchy of subjects in school by making arts primary. It was bucking the all too narrow definition of learning that under-girded high-stakes testing and accountability systems that were then just emerging. We met the people involved and felt the growing enthusiasm, even in the face of challenges that we knew had daunted other school reforms. We observed classrooms and saw kids at work building the volcano that was the basis of the science unit, dancing mathematics, and making music with social studies. We were clearly being pulled in by the Program. In the ultimate evaluation of rock and roll tunes of our youth, it was as if A+ "had a good beat and you could dance to it!"

We, of course, also learned a lot about the arts in education along the way. We did the usual literature review and were able to meet and talk with many knowledgeable people simply because the Program and its extensive evaluation plans had attracted the attention of those who were, and are, players in the national arts and education scene. We owe these people much as they invited the naive in and educated us in ways we cannot fully express. We can say we were more than a little impressed by the openness of these experts to newcomers and to their willingness to engage in debate as well as collaboration. Through them we largely learned what follows: an understanding of how the A+ Schools Program builds upon the history of arts and education and, as importantly, how it is different. Just as nothing emerges totally new in the affairs of humans, nothing is left unchanged as well. We did learn that in the arts this adage has a particular edge to it. That edge is the way the arts are as dangerous as they are reassuring. The next section sets the stage for that perspective by offering a brief history of arts education in American schools.

Arts, Power, and Change

The arts are intimately connected to culture. However, culture is not an innocent anthropological concept. Rather culture is intimately tied to issues of power. For example, in nineteenth-century American life, the advocacy of arts education was tied to the specific interests of a gentleman class—white male, property owners (Stankiewicz, Amburgy, & Bolin, 2004). In this, the arts were to improve the upper classes by allowing them to escape the materialism of everyday life and allow these men to appreciate a more aesthetic view. There was a general distrust of the arts as overly sensuous and early art education efforts took pains to separate their view of art education from this "problem." They focused on disciplining art through an emphasis on technique and principles of criticism and this was in turn rhetorically connected to promoting a "republican social order" (Stankiewicz et al., 2004, p. 35).

By the mid-nineteenth century, art was becoming democratized through its inclusion in schools (Wakeford, 2004). The arts for everyone however did not mean that the arts were to have the same meaning for everyone. There was work in a growing art industry for the working classes, and the middle class began to see the arts as part of a project to improve their status. This was met by the upper class seeing arts education as a way to preserve their "cultural authority" (Stankiewicz et al., 2004, p. 36). In this, the arts came to be attached to philanthropic efforts to improve the lives of others, including women and the children of the poor. This paternalism worked to insure that the arts were seen both as a vehicle of the elites and a mechanism of social ameliorization. Wakeford explains, however, that the arts in the common schools were seen a very particular way:

> The philosophical origins of mass arts education, therefore, were imbued with a belief that the arts were not mere ends in themselves, but rather, that they were implicated in the development of sophisticated mental faculties with both academic and practical applications. Nonetheless, the democratizing calls of common schools movement, driven by a populist belief in education's mandate to provide marketable skills and knowledge to all, held the arts in a hesitant half-embrace. During most of this era the primary rationale for arts curricula circulated around ideals of cultural and moral refinement, based on the notion that appreciation of artistic form, or recitation and memorization or moral texts through song, could foster a sense of beauty, harmony, and social order . . . Thus, as the common school movement advanced, deeper links between the arts and learning remained attenuated.
>
> (Wakeford, 2004, p. 85)

While art, especially drawing, had been a part of schooling since its earliest days, it was not until the 1870s that art (as drawing) became legislated for public schools, first in Massachusetts and then in other states and cities. Free drawing was the emphasis of these early efforts but as industrialization spread objections of educators to vocational education gave way—manual training gave way to industrial arts. Industrial education came to have an arts emphasis, especially in emphasizing crafts as a way for workers to find enjoyment in their work. Here some of today's tensions with the arts can be seen. The arts were simultaneously argued to be about preparing people for work, for the inculcation of a certain notion of "taste," and as part of an effort for social reform (Stankiewicz, et al., 2004). The danger of the arts in the latter also became part of a project of what came to be called the "aesthetic movement" which, according to Stankiewicz et al. (2004, p. 45), "placed artistic values over ethical ones. Its central idea was art for art's sake, a celebration of universal form and style apart from the historical, social, and moral contexts in which works of art were created or used." This movement was part of ensuring that by the time that arts educators had conceptualized their unique role, visual art education had become a mechanism for the reproduction of social stratification, and a way to control the population.

Music education took a somewhat different tack, but was also caught up in the multiple goals for the arts in education. Post-Civil War music education was dominated by vocal music which, was "heralded as a source of mental discipline and moral development" (Wakeford, 2004, p. 86). He continues:

> Its advocates defended music for both its intrinsic and extrinsic values: through the artistic power of song, students' character could be strengthened and their emotional sensibility enlivened. But, also, it could aid their skills of pronunciation of the English language, and develop their memory.
>
> (Wakeford, 2004, p. 86)

Being about mental discipline, morality, and correct diction meant that music was, in the end, similar to the visual art education in being about social reproduction, even if the claims were less practical than visual arts education.

In the early twentieth century, the visual arts continued to be in service of other ends. On the one hand, the visual arts were part of preparing people for work in the constantly changing industrial workplace. White (2004, p. 57) notes that such programs, which began with a focus on specific types of industrial work, became more associated with "design, aesthetics and consumerism." This also formalized a gender distinction with industrial arts for boys and work and household art for girls within the home. On the other hand, the visual arts were also seen to be about healing and fledging programs of art therapy were promoted for the disabled and for soldiers returning from World War I. (This was once again emphasized post-World War II.) Finally, the visual arts were also seen as part of civic development and community awareness, as civic organizations deployed an array of arts for the community projects in the 1920s and 1930s that were part of sustaining and expounding mainstream values.

Music education, alternatively, by the turn of the twentieth century was not about developing practical skills as was the fate for visual arts education. Music rather moved toward being a formal school subject and created music appreciation courses that were more historical and dedicated to teaching a formal approach to understanding music. Wakeford (2004, p. 98) argued that these courses were focused on students learning to discern features of music and memorizing these. Performance was neglected as music became an abstract and theoretical discipline, promoting one version of teaching the arts for arts' sake.

The progressive movement contained many contradictory elements but in this seemed to create an early articulation of arts integration. Dewey and others saw the manual arts as an excellent example of experiential education but also developed the idea of a "correlation" between production in the arts and learning of other disciplines. Wakeford (2004, p. 88) saw this as more than just early arts integration: "Here, the distinction between 'doing' and learning began to erode, which portended pedagogical developments to come later in the Twentieth Century." While in the wider education system the arts continued to be both about practical application and about a moral uplift version of arts for arts' sake, the progressive movement argued for "creative self-expression" in which "meaningful distinctions between the arts dissolved" (Wakeford, 2004, p. 89). Music education moved away from its earlier formalism and incorporated instrumental music, orchestras, and bands into the curricula (Keene, 1982). Visual artists began to emphasize expressive drawing and a wider range of arts projects, including printmaking, mural, and sculpture (Wygant, 1993). These moves were important in many ways such as in their foreshadowing of the modernist movement in art. Educationally, they also signaled that the arts were about cognition of a particular type involving subjective perception and expression. These moves not only promoted what we now call integration of the arts with other disciplines, but also called for collapsing distinctions between school subjects (Wakeford, 2004). These moves also asserted what was to become a mantra of arts integration—that the arts are ways to maintain students' interest in a subject.

It was with the advent of the Cold War that the federal government began to show an interest in the arts, and this ironically was the result of the efforts of scientists who argued for a joint emphasis on science and the arts (White, 2004). This, however, was marked by the emphasis on the disciplines and thus the result was a focus on arts professionals and aesthetics as the discipline grounding for the arts. In this shift, "critics caricatured progressive education as a laissez-faire pedagogy that fetishized individual creativity and self-expression at the expense of educational standards and the appropriate prioritization of math and science curricula" (Wakeford, 2004, p. 94). The disciplinary move led to an array of responses that came to fruition some 20 years later. On the one hand, it set the stage for the Getty's *Discipline-Based Arts Education*, which we will discuss in more detail later. It also created a backlash that led to promoting programs that involved students in artistic production, and what now is a mainstay of many state and local arts councils—the visiting artist programs in schools that both teach arts and emphasize arts integration as well. This backlash also included efforts such as that of Project Zero at Harvard to articulate the arts as a mode of cognition (Wakeford, 2004). It has been this effort that ultimately led to Gardner's (1983, 1991, 1999) theory of multiple intelligences, which A+ found to be a useful metaphor in their efforts, but we are getting ahead of ourselves.

The challenge of the Cold War and the disciplinary emphasis that resulted, it must be remembered, also was taking place in the context of the struggle for civil rights in the United States. The federal government and state governments were consumed with fighting a rear guard action to maintain segregation, both de jure and de facto. In Southern schools with de jure segregation, the Brown v. Board decision was first stonewalled effectively for some 15 years. When it was clear that the federal courts were going to order systematic reassignments of students to desegregate the schools, there were massive protests by whites and in the end the schools were desegregated largely on terms favorable to whites. The Northern states originally viewed the issue as one involving only the Southern states with legalized segregation. Yet with the passage of the Civil Rights Act of 1964, it was clear that many Northern school systems could be seen as having de facto desegregation. If they had what came to be termed "racially identifiable" schools or classrooms then they could be cited by the U.S. Office of Civil Rights and federal funding threatened (Noblit & Johnston, 1982). This promoted widespread changes in educational policy and practice that would be argued to be counter to efforts to promote what was rhetorically termed "excellence" in education. Thus school desegregation and issues of race came to be seen by some as eroding academic standards. In different ways, those promoting the arts as production and cognition and those promoting educational equity were both seen as part of eroding academic quality.

Generally, the National Commission on Excellence in Education's (1983) report, *A Nation at Risk*, is taken as a backlash to school desegregation and efforts to promote a more equitable society as well as schools. In an interesting shift of responsibility from business to education, the schools were seen to be responsible for a perceived lack of economic competitiveness. Regardless of questions about how the schools could be held responsible for the failures of business, this report ushered in a lengthy period of school reform that is only now reaching its endgame with the accountability movement. This reform era presumed the failure to be the result of a weak curriculum with low standards, which can be remedied by a focus on basic skills, more focus on science and math, and higher and enforced standards. While there is a contradiction between high standards and basic skills that has never been addressed, this reform era has also politicized education and its practices in many ways. The arts in education have been caught up in this politicization as well. Wakeford (2004) argues that the recent reform era framed the debate so that "'learning' was inflected in opposition to pedagogy that revolved around 'doing'." In such a context, it seemed that the only alternative was to argue the arts were disciplines much like other school subjects, repudiating the argument about the uniqueness of the arts.

The Getty Center for Arts Education moved on this front in the early 1980s when it created what came to known as discipline-based art education (DBAE), which critiqued the then existing production emphasis of arts education and argued that art criticism, the history of art and aesthetics, needed to be central in the arts curriculum. In 1988, the NEA issued a report, *Toward Civilization: A Report on Arts Education*, that endorsed a discipline-based approach and took a broader view of the arts disciplines. Yet in doing so, the report explicitly linked such an approach to the Reagan administration's politics. The disciplinary approach was to foster a particular view of American culture and promote students' acceptance of that view. This politicization of the arts led to two different efforts (Wakeford, 2004). One was to promote more open-ended goals for arts education fostering students' thinking skills. Gardner's (1983) argument that multiple intelligences exist and are represented in different forms of activity is an example of this effort. The second was to promote a form of arts integration that focused both on more arts content and on the use of the arts production to promote learning in other school subjects. A+ is a prime example of such learning through and with the arts efforts in that it asked for expanded arts offerings and arts integration. Yet it must be emphasized that the A+ Schools Program is unique in its whole-school reform approach, linking the arts to learning and to educational change.

This brief history of arts in education should make three things clear. First, the major ideas that characterize even new initiatives have historical antecedents. The new in arts and education is built upon a history of ideas that may not be known to the wider public or even to artists and educators. Second, these ideas exist in relation to one another and are often seen as being in opposition. This is not unusual in education (see Noblit & Dempsey, 1996) but it makes the case that educators and the public need an understanding of history to know why particular efforts are interpreted to have specific meanings. A good case in point can be Getty's DBAE. DBAE was an effort to legitimate the arts in education as distinct disciplines but now is being interpreted as having been a conservative effort to promote nationalism. This is a result of the subsequent NEA report and not DBAE itself. Those who do not know the history of arts in education may well make this mistake, and in doing so misunderstand DBAE and what it was trying to achieve. As we develop below, examining DBAE is also useful as a way to understand what A+ offered.

The third way this history is useful is to remind all of us that given the contested history of arts in education there have been many justifications for the arts in education. The arts have struggled repeatedly to find a permanent home in schools. The history of arts education is one of fits and starts, contracting and expanding as the demands on public schools' money, time, and energy ebb and flow. The problem is not so much lack of appreciation of the arts but priorities. Despite the similar pronunciation, the arts quite simply are not part of the three "Rs." They are not "core" subjects. Their instructors are not "regular" teachers. Most states include the arts in their mandated courses of study but not in their testing programs. No matter how valuable people perceive dance, drama, visual art, and music to be, they remain add-on programs. Consequently, arts advocates justify the presence of the arts in a school's instructional program often in reaction to this marginalization of the arts as subjects in schools. In the history above it is possible to discern at least seven arguments for giving the arts a place in the public school curriculum, which proponents combine in various ways (e.g., see Fiske, 1999; Longley, 1999). For us, these include:

- The arts are worthy of attention for their own sake, primarily because they inherently enrich those who participate in and appreciate creative endeavors.
- The arts enable moral and social development.
- Learning about the arts is an essential ingredient of becoming culturally literate.
- The arts can be an instructional tool that more effectively allows students to acquire and process content in "core" subjects. A more concrete variation of this rationale boasts of the arts' capability of raising achievement test scores in one or more of these subjects.
- The arts are a vehicle for tapping into the multiple intelligences prevalent among students, thereby giving children the opportunity to learn in the style that best suits them.

- The arts increase students' interest in school, particularly those who have previously been unengaged, and this increased interest yields a concomitant benefit in motivation to learn.
- The arts enable students to develop "workplace" skills and understandings—such as critical thinking, teamwork, creativity, and communication—that instruction in major subjects habitually neglects.

As elaborate as this list is, they are all reducible to an essential question: Are the arts to be justified for the creativity they involve or for their utility in other domains? The list above shows that since the arts have been unable to defend the former as the primary justification, much effort has been put into the latter. The politics of defending the arts has also led this to be framed as a dilemma. That is, creativity versus utility. In the next section, we want to explore the recent history of this seeming dilemma by revisiting that history, especially that of DBAE, as a way to understand what A+ uniquely represents as an art-based school reform initiative. In this, the history of arts in education becomes an explanation of why we found A+ so interesting. In the last section of this chapter we discuss another major dilemma facing local educators as they struggle with what value to place on arts education. This involves whether to follow mandates from above about the best ways to embrace arts education or to create that model themselves out of their own experiences and knowledge.

Negotiating a Role for the Arts: Resolving the Creativity/Instrumentality Dilemma

The arts have always presented a dilemma for public education in the United States. It is true that in any society, the arts are a major part of the expression and development of a culture. In the United States in particular, the multiplicity of cultural groups has meant an eclectic mixing of artistic forms and aesthetic styles. Creativity is valued, and novel, creative art forms are celebrated. At the same time, the culture in the United States is pragmatic. Americans tend to be very instrumental in orientation. We value achievement, determination, and efficiency. In everyday life, it often seems that creativity and instrumentality are opposed. We are impatient with creativity, particularly if it takes time away from getting things done. Then again, if we place too high a value on instrumentality, we remain unsettled. We find that getting things done most efficiently can also be hollow if what is accomplished is not creative, novel, or artful.

This seeming dilemma between creativity and instrumentality is perhaps most evident in our schools. Traditionally, public education has had numerous goals. For the new millennium, we expect our schools to contribute to the vocational, intellectual, creative, political, and moral development of children. With so much to accomplish, schools tend to become fragmented, with courses and requirements tacked on to the existing structures of schools inherited from previous generations. For teachers, the creative task has become how to fit everything into the school day—to "cover" material quickly and move on to the next topic. Among other purposes, the goal of fostering creativity tends to become lost, while other, more instrumental goals take over—at least for a time. In this environment, the arts, although they have long been considered essential to the development of creative abilities, remain a low priority. In times of fiscal difficulties, the arts are pushed aside to allow more time for the pursuit of subjects seen as "basic"—subjects that serve more immediate and more clearly instrumental goals. Or, in cases of space constraints, the arts find themselves without appropriate spaces for students to make artwork, to sing and play music, to explore drama, or to move with dance.

Throughout the United States, the arts and arts education have found themselves beleaguered and undervalued. Typically, at the margins of the school curriculum and ever vulnerable to being eliminated, arts educators have for several decades sought to raise the profile of their subject matter in the curriculum. As discussed above, there have been two major approaches: one to increase the creative potential of arts instruction, and the other to demonstrate the instrumental benefits of art instruction. A major goal for arts educators has been to improve the quality of arts instruction nationwide, fostering greater creativity and appreciation for the arts (Eisner, 1990, 1998b). Other educators, as well as researchers and policy makers, have addressed the impact of the arts on student learning and skill development (Catterall, 1998; Darby & Catterall, 1994; Fiske, 1999; Pelavin Associates, 1994). Still others have combined these notions to explore their fundamental implications for teaching and learning (i.e. National Advisory Committee on Creative and Cultural Education (NACCCE), 1999; Parsons, 1998). These various discussions have contributed to a wide variety of approaches that schools have taken to incorporate the arts into curriculum and instruction (Herbert, 1998; Hoffman-Davis, 1999).

One national approach has been to define the arts as "basic" to the curriculum. In its most widespread incarnation, this notion took the form of DBAE, an approach to visual art education with roots in the aesthetic theories of educational philosophers in the 1960s and 1970s, notably Harry Broudy and Eliot Eisner. DBAE gained prominence in the early 1980s through adoption by the J. Paul Getty Trust. It has been an effort to treat the visual arts as a discipline—similar to other academic disciplines that traditionally are more highly valued in education (Wilson, 1997).

More precisely, in DBAE, art was seen as being made up of four disciplines: art production, art history, art criticism, and aesthetics. Through the Getty Education Institute for the Arts, located in Los Angeles, DBAE became an influential form of education in the visual arts. School districts throughout the Los Angeles area adopted the program and trained teachers in how to use the four disciplines, and the Getty Institute sponsored a series of regional institutes throughout the country that have further explored the potential of DBAE in different contexts. The results have been widely documented (e.g. Dobbs, 1998; Hamblen, 1997; Silverman, 1997; Wilson, 1997; Wilson & Rubin, 1997), its philosophies widely debated (e.g. Arnstine, 1990; Catterall, 1998; Clark, 1997; Eisner, 1990, 1998a; Parsons, 1998), and its link to educational reform analyzed (e.g. Fullan, 1994; Wilson, 1997). Educators and researchers have adapted its principles to other art forms as well, most notably to music education. Other efforts have taken a similar approach to arts education, particularly in the visual arts, including programs based at and affiliated with the Lincoln Center Institute in New York. Programs affiliated with the Lincoln Center Institute incorporate contact with artists and arts organizations in multiple art forms for educational experiences and teacher training. The institute is informed by the educational and aesthetic philosophies of Maxine Greene, and evaluation of the Institute's programs was through Project Zero at Harvard University (Csikszentmihalyi, 1997).

The Getty Institute and the Lincoln Center projects expanded to a national scale through regional institutes and affiliations with local arts and arts education organizations. As DBAE expanded into regional institutes, teachers and university educators elaborated the original notion of visual arts to incorporate the four disciplines within the visual arts (art production, art history, art criticism, and aesthetics) to different settings and goals (Hamblen, 1997; Wilson, 1997; Wilson & Rubin, 1997). As the regional institutes proceeded, schools branched out from focusing just on arts education and began to integrate other areas of the curriculum and collaborate with a wider range of teachers and members of the community. DBAE evaluators distinguished these new forms of DBAE with terminology such as "Second Generation DBAE" (Hamblen, 1997). Authors of recent research reports have placed great value on collaboration and integration, pointing to schools' innovations as a potential future direction for DBAE implementation (cf. Parsons, 1998).

Throughout its development as an arts reform, DBAE has had its critics and commentators. Some of the major criticisms are that DBAE is too prescriptive, that it values Western art and aesthetics above others, that it contributes to the fragmentation of the curriculum into separate disciplines, and that it places inordinate emphasis on art history and criticism to the expense of creativity (Arnstine, 1990; Catterall, 1998; Noddings, 1994); others are concerned that the focus on district-wide reform is inappropriate (Jackson, 1987). Some criticisms arise from specific instructional programs associated with DBAE or materials distributed at DBAE institutes. Other criticisms address more specifically the particular philosophical basis of the initiative and its orientation toward school reform. DBAE proponents have responded to commentators by noting that DBAE is adaptable to local goals, that teachers are encouraged to develop their own curricula, and non-Western art and aesthetics are incorporated (Clark, 1997; Eisner, 1990, 1998a; Wilson & Rubin, 1997). In any case, recent changes at the Getty Institute have meant that DBAE has lost significant sponsorship.

There are some significant differences between DBAE and the A+ Schools Program. First, and most significantly, the philosophies that underlie the A+ Schools Program are a more loosely grouped collection of theoretical dispositions about the arts and student learning. The Program does not advocate a particular aesthetic view or stress the importance of the arts having disciplinary components. Schools acknowledge Howard Gardner's (1983, 1991, 1993, 1999) MI theory for its metaphorical grounding of the multiple approaches to instruction that arise from integrating the arts. Unlike schools based specifically on Gardner's MI theory, the theory has served as a philosophical allusion for grounding arts integration. Few schools have delved substantially into the specific instructional implications of MI theory that groups affiliated with the Harvard Project Zero have (e.g., Krechevsky, 1991). Instead, A+ schools have followed four related instructional themes: enhanced arts instruction, arts-integrated instruction, collaborative planning, and thematic unit development. Associated with these instructional themes is an additional theme—community and parent involvement—that in most cases has less impact on instruction but is nevertheless significant.

Second, the A+ Schools Program has been from the beginning a holistic approach to instructional innovation, with arts integration the focal point for delivering not only meaningful artistic experiences but also innovative instruction across subject matter areas. In contrast to DBAE, the emphasis on professional development in the A+ Program is less on the development of aesthetic sensibilities and critical dispositions and more on curriculum and instructional design. The A+ Program gives individual schools a greater opportunity to take the philosophies associated with the Program and create a defining metaphor for the entire instructional program.

Third, the A+ Program begins with recognition of the contribution of the four art forms of visual art, music, dance, and drama to instruction. In contrast, DBAE was primarily a program for improving the instruction of the visual arts, although other educators have applied its philosophy to other forms as well. The inclusion of all four art forms is intended to expand the abilities and opportunities for children to learn. It also places within the school building up to four arts specialists who are available for collaboration with classroom teachers. In this sense, the A+ Program requires a larger pool of personnel resources, a constraint that DBAE avoids by using existing visual arts or music personnel, coming perhaps from initial concerns in the Los Angeles area about arts positions being eliminated in schools.

Fourth, the A+ Program makes the individual school the focus of reform. While DBAE advocates have also acknowledged that a solely top-down approach to school reform is ineffective (Fullan, 1994, 1999; Wilson, 1997), DBAE planners chose to focus on school districts for greater impact on arts education (Eisner, 1990). As a reform focused on the entire curriculum, the A+ Schools Program begins with individual schools that are prepared to effect cultural changes to implement arts integration. At the same time, A+ recognizes the importance of district-level support for the Program, and similarly to DBAE, encourages opportunities for community connections and collaboration.

Finally, approaches to arts education that conceive of the arts as disciplinary have been helpful toward strengthening the quality of art education. However, the underlying pursuit is legitimating the arts in education, and this limits the discussion to the place and significance of the arts in opposition to the rest of the curriculum. This replicates the dilemma of creativity versus instrumentality, even if the role of the arts is articulated and made more important. The A+ schools initiative represents a different approach to this dilemma. Instead of trying to resolve the dilemma via a victory of creativity over instrumentality, the A+ Schools Program has resolved the dilemma by not opposing either creativity or instrumentality. A+ schools are about both creativity and instrumentality. Further, substantive identity schools found this to be effective in their assertions of identity. They embrace and value the arts, but they also use the arts as the focus of school reform. While arts and education initiatives often see arts as instrumental in promoting learning in other subjects (Winner & Hetland, 2000), A+ has been about using the arts to reform schools. At the same time, we will argue that creating school identities around an arts reform is not easy. Moreover, the schools and the A+ network were faced with another dilemma: the bottom-up/top-down dilemma in school reform. Again, schools with substantive identities were able not only to negotiate their way through the dilemmas but were also able to use these negotiations as the basis for positive change.

Negotiating the Role of Advocacy in Arts-Based School Reform: Resolving the Bottom-Up/ Top-Down Dilemma

A second difficulty schools face in incorporating arts education into their programs is in how to make it happen in a school setting. When people have an idea they want to implement widely, the temptation may be to legislate, so that everyone has to follow suit. In educational reform literature, this is known as a top-down approach, and it is known to fail routinely. Broad, sweeping changes in education rarely happen. Top-down reforms tend to stifle creativity and inhibit local control (Fullan, 1991,

1994, 1999). That is partly because schools are places that have cultures, and these cultures are slow to change. External policies get reinterpreted, misinterpreted, modified, mediated, and otherwise ignored within the context of school cultures. What Weatherly and Lipsky (1977) call the work of "street-level bureaucrats" is school culture adapting outside influences to local goals and constraints.

In the case of arts education, legislation from above may swing the pendulum from creativity to instrumentality for a time, but schools are accustomed to these swings. At many schools, the constant state is compliance with befuddled amusement at initiatives imposed from above. Schools contend with federal, state, and district requirements for curriculum, often balancing seemingly competing priorities as they plan classroom instruction. In North Carolina, arts education has contended with the changing perceptions of the importance of creativity and instrumentality. In the 1980s, arts instruction was an integral part of the state's Basic Education Plan (BEP), when school districts hired arts specialists in large numbers. For several years, more schools had greater numbers of arts specialists than before. In nearly all cases, implementation added courses to the existing curriculum, and the arts competed for attention along with other parts of the curriculum. In subsequent years, with growing enrollments, tightening budgets, and greater local discretion, many of these positions were lost. When the A+ Schools Program began in 1995, many elementary, middle, and high schools in the state employed art and music teachers, but many of these teachers were itinerants visiting two or more schools each week. Although the state has maintained curriculum standards for all four art forms, few schools employed teachers for dance or drama, especially at the elementary- and middle-school levels as the state did not fund them. This state dominance in the curricula played out in school reform efforts as well.

The history of school reform in North Carolina has been essentially one of state control, and the selected schools were ill-prepared for a reform such as A+, one that facilitated rather than mandated innovation (Jehl & Payzant, 1992). In North Carolina (and many other states), the school reform era ended up meaning that the schools *must* reform. New standards were mandated. Districts were encouraged to have schools adopt reform packages. Yet there were two types of reform. One type was for all schools, such as new standards, curricula, testing, etc. and then there were reforms for schools that were deemed inadequate. Schools that had histories or reputations of high achievement, notably largely white, suburban schools, were insulated from these pressures, while schools with more diverse populations and histories of lower achievement were largely the schools targeted for reform. Thus school reform in North Carolina was largely seen as having a set of characteristics. First, it was for schools that were stigmatized as lower achieving. Second, it was a mandate for these schools. Third, local school input was limited (and then only some-times) to a choice of which reform the school would adopt. Finally, school reform was something to be implemented but schools had learned that the state and districts mandates had a relatively short half-life. Educators would speak of a 3-year cycle of implementation in the first year, work out kinks the second year, and adapt these efforts to the new reform mandate in the third year.

This type of cynical knowledge about reform efforts were what the schools brought to A+. While A+ wants schools to volunteer for the A+ Program and many did, there were also various levels of district and principal coercion. Some schools and educators had been part of the 18-month planning process, and thus knew more about, and had a role in shaping, the reform and had what we came to call "preexisting sentiments" for arts-based efforts at school reform. Nonetheless, schools in North Carolina "knew" how to do reform: they implemented it and that was that. They relished the initial summer institutes and found the teacher-led curriculum planning to be engaging, but they assumed that they would implement A+, that they would comply with what was required. They were ready for the type of reform the earlier DBAE promoted, but they were not ready for A+.

To implement in the way the schools understood it, they needed to know what was required. A+ did have some of this as a result of their more or less grassroots planning process: the four arts being taught, arts inte-gration, thematic units, community and parent collaborations, and so on. However, A+ did not tell the schools how to do all this. When the school principals and coordinators met in state or regional meetings and asked how they should proceed the stock reply from Kenan Institute staff was: "How do you think you should?" This then led to the schools discussing options and making adaptations to local contexts. This was evident even in the early stages of the Program. As we have already recounted, on the day the schools met to celebrate their selection, they had to agree on how to address the lower than expected state appropriation. The schools were faced with deciding to go with fewer, fully funded schools or to keep every school selected and work out a way to handle the funding. In this first experience with making key decisions about the nature of A+, they chose the latter. Yet this was insufficient for schools to change their under-standing of the dynamics of school reform.

The schools learned over time to play a fuller role in the future of A+, largely because the Kenan staff repeatedly posed this question to them. In this we see A+ approaching the top-down/bottom-up dilemma of school reform by embracing both instead of choosing between them. Clearly, A+ was both. The early planning process involved many constituencies and the general outline of the reform was then sent to the schools to plan their application. The summer institutes and later conferences had an explicit emphasis on curriculum planning and ways of doing arts integration that in turn asked the schools to develop their approaches and their curricula.

Perhaps the most challenging issue for the A+ Schools Program was its emergence simultaneously with high-stakes accountability in North Carolina. End-of-grade testing in the elementary schools or end-of-course testing in the secondary schools was designed to determine the school's overall reputation and whether or not the teachers will get a bonus for the school year. As this state mandate was being implemented, schools across the state began to consider how to best comply and protect themselves from public stigma and the threat of state and district intervention if test scores remained low over several years. In this environment, anything that does not contribute to preparation for testing is undervalued. Members of the evaluation team were observing other, non-A+ schools in North Carolina for other studies, and witnessed how the curriculum was being narrowed to that being tested. This was even encouraged by the state itself. The A+ schools were concerned about this and wanted to avoid this as much as possible. The A+ schools debated this issue extensively and decided that instead of inscribing accountability as the enemy, they would develop what came to be called "enriched assessment." Each school examined the curricula and instructional strategies it had developed with A+ and developed an assessment protocol (loosely following the ideas of authentic assessment—Wiggins, 1993) that better represented what they were doing with integrated instruction and then linked these assessments with those of the high-stakes accountability system, called the ABCs in North Carolina. They shared these protocols with each other at a state-wide conference. The schools had poster sessions that described their approaches and "talk and swap" quickly evolved into the media of the day.

Here we can see how the A+ schools developed a new way to work with reforms. A+ encouraged them to take charge of the future of A+ both in their schools and as a reform initiative. High-stakes testing was clearly a top-down mandate but the schools in the end decided to use A+ as a way to respond to it. They both protected their curricular approach and found a way to link it to this dire mandate from the state.

Conclusion

The A+ Schools Program is a unique initiative in the arts and in schools. Two dilemmas have structured the larger history of arts education and school reform: creativity versus instrumentality and top-down versus bottom-up. A+ decided to embrace both dilemmas. The arts should be both about arts for arts' sake and about improving learning in other subjects. The approach to school reform similarly should be both top-down and bottom-up. Importantly, however, resolution of the dilemma of creativity and instrumentality emerged as a creative response to the struggles to implement the A+ Program in the first place. The Program started out to promote the arts and art education with the prescription that this would also contribute to improved academic achievement. The Program involved a wide range of stakeholders in its development and had a foundation as the lead agent in the reform. Promoting local adaptation of the reform and inviting the schools into the deliberations over the nature and future of the Program both made A+ a more democratic reform and let the schools develop an approach to A+ that they were invested in sufficiently to use it to guide their local decisions as well as the decisions about A+ as a wider program. As a "democratic" reform, the A+ Schools Program responded to the challenges of local schools and communities and of state policy changes creatively. As a reform "written in pencil," it rewrote itself repeatedly both collectively and in the individual schools. In the next chapter, we will describe what this looked like in terms of several schools and the wider network organization A+ employed to develop the reform initiative.

Chapter 4

Turning the Vision into Reality

Creekside Elementary (presented in Chapter 2) provided an example of how one school decided to do A+. In this chapter, we describe the A+ Program as envisioned by its creators and illustrate some of the other ways in which that vision developed into reality through examples found in some of the A+ schools. The Kenan Institute for the Arts initiated A+ less as a reform "model" and more as a philosophy of instructional change. Kenan hypothesized that the most effective way of enabling the arts to gain an enduring foothold in the curriculum would be to encourage all the 24 schools that participated in the pilot phase to adapt the concept of arts integration to their unique contexts. This dual emphasis on a commitment to the arts and flexible implementation caused the A+ Program ultimately to look different in each of the schools.

The original intention of the A+ Program was for all schools to provide students with daily arts instruction and instruction in each of the four arts forms—visual art, music, dance, and drama—at least once each week. When the A+ Program began, the Kenan Institute had expected a much larger state appropriation than it actually received. Only about one-third of the planned finances were actually made available to the Program, however, so schools did not receive as much funding as they had hoped for or expected. The effect of this funding cut was that schools awaiting the funding had to scramble to find other resources to provide these arts experiences, not offer them as completely, or not be part of the Program. It is noteworthy that the principals of these schools worked together within the context of the A+ network to distribute the available resources in an equitable manner and that, of the 24 schools that participated in the pilot phase, no schools dropped out of the Program because of the decreased funding. (The 25th school was dropped by its district.)

During the first four years of the Program, we saw schools employing various strategies to deliver arts instruction. Nearly all offered daily arts instruction of some kind, but the form of this instruction varied by school and by semester or year with only a few schools finding it possible to offer instruction in all four arts continuously throughout this time period. With limited resources (either financial or personnel), typically dance and drama were the two arts forms either not offered or creatively offered in combination with music or PE. Some alternated between dance and drama or combined them into a single course. Middle and high schools typically offered a menu of arts courses that mostly covered all four of the art forms.

In addition to this variety in staffing arrangements and curriculum organization, we recorded how schools varied in the amount of arts integrated into their regular, grade-level or subject matter courses. Partly this reflected the pragmatics of launching a large-scale program with limited resources. Partly it was also by design or adaptation. We saw that schools differed as to the degree to which the arts courses reinforced the curriculum, differed as to how thoroughly the arts were integrated by teachers who were not arts specialists, and furthermore, how different definitions and orientations toward the arts were used. Underscoring the cultural nature of school reform, we also observed different orientations toward thematic planning, curriculum integration, multiple intelligences, professional collaboration, and parental and community involvement.

In many ways, this variability in implementation was to be expected. As stated earlier, rather than imposing a rigid model of reform, the Program instead exposed school staff to a series of philosophical and instructional ideas and then encouraged local interpretations and innovations to suit the schools' idiosyncratic contexts. Control of the Program, therefore, devolved to the schools. Though the approach of the Kenan Institute was to encourage flexibility in implementation, allowing each school to mold the Program in ways that made sense with existing beliefs and contexts, the schools did hear a common message about at least six expectations. These core commitments are: (1) an increased exposure to arts instruction; (2) two-way curricular integration in which the arts classes reinforce the regular curriculum and regular classroom instruction reinforces what is being taught in the arts; (3) tapping into students' multiple intelligences; (4) an integrated, thematic approach to planning and instruction; (5) increased professional collaboration; and (6) strengthened parent/community relations.

While the schools worked individually to implement the Program, they also worked together within the structure of a supportive, evolving A+ network that helped forge and maintain important connections between and among them. The network provided support in the form of professional development opportunities during the summers and throughout the school year. It worked with the legislature to help secure and maintain funding for the Program. It continually evolved to meet the needs of the schools, organizing an enriched assessment project and recruiting teachers from the schools to serve as A+ fellows. It brought various groups of participants (fellows, principals, coordinators) together in both regional and state-wide venues to share successes, to problem-solve, and to help determine the direction of the Program.

The following three cases help to illustrate how schools adopted and adapted the core commitments of the Program and made them their own. The vignettes also show how the schools' involvement in the network influenced their efforts. We have chosen to write the vignettes in the present tense in order to represent the schools as "live" settings and the ongoing nature of the A+ Program.

Entomon Hills Elementary School: A+ Provides a Fresh Start

It is a beautiful spring evening as a crowd of about a thousand people begins to gather at the local amphitheater. Tonight's gathering is a celebration—of the arts, of learning, of community. The large setting easily accommodates parents, relatives, and friends of those who volunteer, work, and learn in Entomon Hills Elementary School. The arts teachers have been here most of the day setting up numerous displays of student work and rehearsing with the groups of students who paraded through for their final practice runs before the big show. As the celebration gets underway, the stage is decorated with artwork and props created by students. The many exhibits and performances not only showcase students' talents in the visual arts, music, drama, and dance but also highlight the classroom learning that has occurred this year in other subject areas. Community partners (including the owner of the amphitheater who donates the space for this event) are honored and thanked for their contributions to the school. The evening ends as all members of the school community come together on stage in a unifying finale.

Entomon Hills Elementary is one of two elementary schools in the A+ Program designated as an arts magnet school; specifically it has an arts and science theme. The school is an urban magnet located in one of the most populous school districts in North Carolina and enrolls about 25% of its student body from neighborhoods surrounding the school while attracting the other 75% from throughout the county. The result is a student body that is diverse in race (about 50% of students are white) and income (about 50% qualify for free or reduced-price lunches). Entomon Hills Elementary as it exists today is the result of the opportunity to start over as a magnet school so a bit of history is in order.

Before becoming a magnet school, Entomon Hills Elementary served a working-class African American neighborhood. While it was well regarded by the neighborhood, the school district had struggled with ways to desegregate the schools in the sprawling county that includes a large city and several smaller towns. The school district concluded that converting the inner-city schools into magnet schools would be a way to attract white students without resorting to widespread busing. In its first incarnation as a magnet school, Entomon Hills had been a classical studies magnet. This magnet theme was not able to attract sufficient students from outside the neighborhood, however, because the curriculum associated with it was not regarded as unique. In many ways, the failure of this first magnet attempt led to the opportunity for the school to redefine itself dramatically. As the school began searching for a focus that would facilitate a fresh start, the A+ Schools Program was being developed. School personnel saw A+ as a way they could help themselves develop as an arts magnet. Several of its teachers participated in the planning meetings sponsored by the Kenan Institute and helped mold the A+ Program as well.

Unlike many of the other A+ schools, Entomon Hills secured additional funds through a federal magnet grant. The additional funds gave the school a clear advantage in its implementation of the A+ Program in that it was able to fully staff all four arts areas (dance, drama, music, and visual arts). Its magnet focus also meant that all teachers had to reapply and "try out" with a sample integrated lesson plan in front of a panel of teachers in order to work there (a practice that continues as part of the application process). Staffed by teachers hired specifically with the arts theme in mind, Entomon Hills is an example of a school that has incorporated all of the elements of the original A+ concept and consequently has initiated a holistic approach to the development of children. A full complement of carefully selected staff hasn't meant, however, that implementation has been all smooth sailing for Entomon Hills. Teachers have worked hard to develop a set of promising practices that support their program in both substance and spirit.

A fully staffed arts program has meant that students receive formal instruction in an art form each day. The school has a permanent arts display at a local hospital and each year auditions a singing and creative-movement routine in a state-wide competition. They also solicit famous people to send a photo and write a letter of support for the arts and for Entomon Hills and display them in the school.

As part of developing its distinctive two-way arts integrated curriculum, the school has struggled to schedule time to enable arts and regular classroom teachers to plan instruction together. By the third year of the pilot, grade-level teachers were not only completing "web sheets" detailing their upcoming curricular goals and providing them to the arts teachers, but they had also settled into a routine of reserving after-school time every other Wednesday so that grade-level and arts teachers could meet together face-to-face and work on planning. These meetings are the essential mechanism that has enabled two-way curriculum integration to occur. They have also led to team-teaching in one of the upper grades; an arts teacher and a classroom teacher teach together during literacy instruction.

Entomon Hills Elementary is one of the few schools that have delved deeply into MI theory. It found that an emphasis on MI was a necessary component of the integrated curriculum and instruction. In the first two years of A+, the school focused on developing a language of MI that was shared by teachers, students, and parents. This was successful, but they also realized that they needed to make MI a more formal part of the curriculum. By the third year of A+, according to an Entomon educator, "everybody started out at the beginning of the year with some kind of multiple intelligences plan." This has helped ensure that MI is used in all the classrooms.

The Wednesday meetings mentioned above have also been important for the planning and teaching of thematic units across the school. School-wide themes throughout the year help provide focus and help keep collaborative planning on track. Having a full-time A+ coordinator is also an asset in this regard. Teachers have learned that the integration of curriculum and instruction is crucial. According to one teacher, "the only way the program works is with 90% integration." They also have elaborated a number of assessment practices that support their program and have developed electronic portfolios as part of the A+ network's initiative on enriched assessment. Everyone understands that A+ is still "evolving" at Entomon Hills and that the level of effort that they put forward is necessary for the Program and school to work.

Regular, ongoing professional collaboration can be quite a challenge, but shared professional development opportunities help tie Entomon Hills' staff together. Each summer, virtually all of the teachers from Entomon Hills participate in the A+ summer institutes sponsored by the network, and the school uses local and magnet grant funds for additional professional development during the year related to A+. Staff meetings have also become staff-development opportunities. New teachers are given an orientation and mentoring support as well as A+ professional development.

The evolution of the A+ network has also been important to Entomon Hills, providing both extensive opportunities for professional development and the sense that the school is contributing to and benefiting from a wider collective effort to improve schools through the arts. Teachers from Entomon Hills are active as A+ fellows who play an important role in coordinating and conducting the summer training institutes. They travel to A+ schools throughout the year, working with teachers and sharing ideas. They provide leadership, along with other A+ fellows distributed throughout the network of schools, and are now seen as a key element in sustaining and expanding A+.

Entomon Hills has also actively and successfully harnessed the power of its community. Staff have developed several ways to get parents involved in the school: the school regularly stages "informances," which are relatively informal performances that display for the parents and staff what the students are learning in school and parents also give tours to visitors, serve on the school-improvement and publicity teams, chaperone and support field trips, and participate in the "helping hands group" that supports the school and instruction in a myriad of ways. Numerous partnerships have been created as well: the performing arts amphitheater, a theater company, several local businesses, and a university. These partnerships have provided the school with access to arts events, venues for the school's arts performances, resources to reward students, and volunteers to assist the school with its activities. The university partnership involves a public-relations course that has helped the school market its program.

A+ is working well at Entomon Hills Elementary but the school's earlier history also is testimony that it takes more than extra dollars to make an effective magnet school. In this case, it took a distinctive idea, committed staff, interested parents, and the commitment to implement the innovation with integrity. The staff says, "it is still exciting for us." They also "definitely see more creativity in the children—a greater willingness to get up in front of the group and being comfortable doing so." The principal noted he had "been in education for 30 years, and I have had more parents come up and say how wonderful the program is—more compliments than I ever had. They rave about how good their child is doing." As the principal explained:

> The only negative part is that we have done such a good job that parents rave about us, and we are beginning to get a higher population of ADHD and ADD [hyperactive] children . . . so we get kids who do not score as well [on tests].

This has meant that Entomon Hills has redoubled its efforts in both basic skills and A+. The staff recognizes that it has done a good job with A+, but this leads to other worries as well: "We're concerned about what will happen when the kids leave here. Where will there be A+ middle and high schools?" In 1999–2000, one of the community's middle schools joined the Program. This as much as anything is testimony to Entomon Hills' success with A+.

Albany Woods Elementary School: Bringing it All Together with A+

A fourth-grade class works on a batik project during art class for several weeks. The project ties into their year-long study of the regions of North Carolina. Groups of students make batik prints of the various regions and then the prints are sewn together to form a map of the state illustrating major geographical and cultural features such as the State Capitol and the Outer Banks. Students explain that they are using what they have learned in their classrooms about state geography and state history to design their prints. They add that while doing the prints themselves, they learn about color mixing and perspective. The students explain how their curriculum is connected. As one states, "pretty much everything we do in art has to do with North Carolina because that is what we are studying this year." Another adds, "all year we have been learning about North Carolina through different art forms and then we show what we learned through singing it, dancing it, and drawing it."

Albany Woods Elementary serves several small communities near the coast of Eastern North Carolina. Its student population is more than 90% white, however social class backgrounds vary. On average, about one-third of its students receives free or reduced-price lunches. The local tourist economy has been growing, and a nearby military base has been expanding. Albany Woods is more typical than Entomon Hills among A+ schools in that it is a school that implemented the major themes of the A+ Schools Program without the benefit of starting over. Yet this school has found a unifying focus around the A+ Program, has had strong parental involvement, and has forged a community identity around A+. This context necessitated compromises, but it has led to innovation that is significant and sustainable.

Albany Woods has a tradition of responding to state-reform initiatives, but unlike many schools that simply submit to state reforms, Albany Woods seeks them out for what they can contribute to its instructional program. It regularly volunteers to be included in pilot programs for the state and often anticipates reforms before they are mandated. In recent years, it has worked with innovations involving site-based management, technology, block scheduling, school and schedule management programs, community involvement, peer tutoring, and alternative assessment. It has also tried several programs designed to improve literacy. The many initiatives could be fragmenting, but Albany Woods has worked to align its various teaching reforms. For example, staff have embedded A+ in their use of developmentally appropriate practice, which shares with A+ the use of instructional themes, hands-on instruction, and alternative assessment. Albany Woods Elementary saw A+ as an opportunity to build on what they had already done. A+ has enabled them to staff the arts more fully, to fund necessary professional development, and to purchase supplies with which they can integrate instruction.

Unlike the example of Entomon Hills, most of the elementary schools participating in the A+ Schools Program did not have a deep reserve of resources to tap into. Following the lead of the network with its federal Goals 2000 grant to support the Program's enriched assessment project, Albany Woods has supplemented the meager funds it has received through the A+ Program with monies from a Goals 2000 grant and other small grants. These funds have helped to fully staff the arts (the school previously had offered only part-time music and part-time art) and have supported a variety of initiatives. The school now boasts a student art gallery located outside the media center, a keyboard lab, and has its own TV production room and daily news show run by the students. Introducing the A+ focus on the arts, has, in the words of one teacher, increased "access to the specials and their expertise to support and build on what we are doing in the classroom."

Albany Woods has found it difficult to schedule sufficient common planning periods for the arts and regular classroom teachers, a problem confronted by the other A+ schools as well. While schools have overcome this hurdle in various ways, Albany Woods has begun to use teacher journals in which teachers record pictures, key words, topics, and ideas they are working on their classrooms. These journals rotate at least weekly between the arts teachers and classroom teachers. This communication process supplements the planned integration of lessons and enables teachers to adjust to the needs of students as units proceed.

Further, Albany Woods has found that the MI concept has been helpful in its curriculum. MI is evident throughout the building, and in the languages of teachers and students. Albany Woods has also found the eighth intelligence, the naturalist's intelligence, to be ideal for arts-integrated science and math curricula, and the teachers have developed new curriculum guides that reflect this form of intelligence.

In addition to their focus on curriculum integration, teachers at Albany Woods have also emphasized curriculum alignment with North Carolina's Standard Course of Study. Working together and following A+, they have mapped the yearly curriculum. In so doing, they emphasized connections across the curriculum and designed themes to fit with the Standard Course of Study. A grade-level teacher relates,

> one of the best things that's come out of it is being able to interact and plan . . . with other teachers . . . Now when I plan, I make sure I include more movement. I've always included music and art, but now I make sure I incorporate the other intelligences as well.

Since teaching integrated lessons and units is complex, the school has created a process where professional development involves a guest (often an A+ fellow) or staff member teaching a lesson repeatedly in the morning so that many teachers can observe the lesson. In the afternoon, students are dismissed early so that teachers can examine the lessons they've witnessed. They ask questions, discuss reactions, and consider how they could use similar techniques in their instruction. This process is an effective addition to the A+ summer institutes in that it involves a direct translation into classroom practices. It also serves as a regularly occurring mechanism to help orient new teachers to the school's vision of A+.

Participation in the network has been beneficial for Albany Woods in a number of ways. As mentioned above, the school was able to draw upon the model provided by the network in its application for a Goals 2000 grant. In fact, a proportionately large number of schools in the network applied for, and received, Goals 2000 monies for various A+ related projects during this time. While the summer institutes have been well attended by the teachers and many of the teacher assistants, it is the A+ Assessment Conference that stands out as most useful for the teachers at Albany Woods. Sharing with others the ideas for enriched assessment that they had already developed and, in turn, learning what other schools were doing related to assessment provided a unique professional development experience.

Like most schools in the Program, Albany Woods has also experienced principal turnover. Early on, the viability of the school's A+ identity became attached to the principal who led the school during the planning, application, and early implementation phases. The school district came to regard him as someone who could change schools, and he was transferred to a school that was in difficulty. While principal turnover is often associated with the demise of school reforms, this was not the case at Albany Woods. The new principal was met by a contingent of parents who explained that Albany Woods was an A+ school, and it was expected that the new principal would continue the A+ Program and build upon what had already been achieved. The new principal decided that the school's identity was powerful, and she committed to the reform.

Not all parents in the community were of a like mind, however. In an interesting turn of events, the school's increased focus on the arts, and its A+ identity, became an election platform issue for one of the county's candidates for school board. This parent—and his backers—took up the "back to basics" rallying cry, deriding the school for its perceived lack of focus on the three Rs. The pro-A+ faction won at the ballot box, however this event did serve as a reminder to the school of the importance of communication. While parent–teacher conferences have always occurred, teachers now recognize that these annual conferences are a good opportunity to explain what is going on in the classrooms, to highlight how the arts promote learning in "basic" areas, and to emphasize multiple intelligences. For instance, teachers can review a picture drawn by a student, revealing it to be a representation of the water cycle that also demonstrates what their child is learning. Meeting in this way promotes understanding of the school's A+ Program while teaching parents about MI theory and alternative assessment.

A+ has given Albany Woods an identity that had been elusive, despite all the previous efforts to improve instruction and learning. This identity has had many effects. First, it has given teachers, students, and parents an organizing concept. Before A+, the many innovations were seen as needed to address the needs of the children, but the sheer number of reforms made it hard to keep a coherent focus. With A+, these reforms could be articulated as part of the larger A+ approach. Second, A+ is also distinctive in that the school can claim to be different—and better—than other schools. The A+ identity is evident in parent–teacher organization meetings, during which children perform. The performances, in turn, have increased parent attendance. Third, being an A+ school has also made it easier to get media coverage, because the performances and art displays are perceived as more newsworthy than everyday school events. Fourth, the A+ identity and its attendant activities enhance the school's public-relations efforts and link the school to the arts council and community arts events. The identity is sufficiently distinctive, positive, and well recognized that a local realtor has advertised homes in the attendance area by indicating that the children will be able to attend an A+ school.

West Hollow School: Adapting A+ to Fit the Community

> We formed a committee to discuss the idea; we want to build a log cabin, including an amphitheater cut into the side of the mountain. It's a cheap way to get a theater. The cabin will be classroom sized. It will have a fireplace area for storytelling, archival space for things like the looms and the rag-rugs. We want to build it to the right of the art room, make it extend from the Envirothon trail. It would be a sort of welcome center. There will be a front porch with rocking chairs and a garden with heritage seeds. We want the local farmers to donate the seed strains they've cultivated through their farms. We can tell stories about the area and the families who live here. We can invite the other fourth graders in the county, and our kids can teach them what they've learned. We've found a lot of success with kids teaching kids. The Appalachian Studies class will develop the archives, probably videos and tape recordings. Also as partners, some of the engineers from TVA can help the students design the structure for the log cabin. The idea is to focus on the heritage and issues within a 100-mile radius of the school. (Teacher)

As the only A+ School enrolling students in grades K–12, West Hollow School has had unique challenges in its implementation of the A+ Schools Program. The small size and geographic seclusion of West Hollow and the surrounding area contributes to a community of people who described themselves variously as "close-knit," "conservative," and "proud." As the center of the community, West Hollow School has a role tied closely to the community's past and future. The school is located along a winding, two-lane road that runs through a valley in Hollow County in the

Appalachian Mountains. The school unites several small, rural communities in one Pre-K–12 building that houses about 425 students. For grades Pre-K–8, there is typically one teacher per grade, with 18 to 28 students per grade. Another K–8 school feeds into the high school, giving the high school a population of about 200 students.

Much like other rural areas in the South, poverty is evident throughout this community, with few service businesses or employment opportunities. A mining company and a hydroelectric operation once employed hundreds of workers, but they have cut back substantially on their employment in the past 25 years, and few new manufacturing industries have filled the void left in the labor market. The community has seen a growing number of retirees moving into the area and anticipates an increased tourist market in the years ahead. Other new residents commute to jobs in distant urban areas, the closest being about 75 miles away. Some in the community anticipate a change in culture if more outsiders move into the area. In addition to losing industry and jobs, the community faces losing its high-school graduates unless there are promising employment opportunities in the area. The school's response has been to help create employment opportunities, and A+ advocates at West Hollow want the A+ Program to be seen as contributing to the school's larger goals.

West Hollow has developed a "hands-on" orientation to curriculum integration, using a broad definition of the arts to encourage wider participation by the faculty, students, and community in the process of integrating instruction. At the same time, hands-on instruction at West Hollow—through the A+ Program as well as other, complementary initiatives at the school—serves the larger goals of preserving the community and providing for an economic future.

In shaping A+ to meet the needs and desires of its community, West Hollow has defined the arts very broadly to include mountain crafts and vocational arts that are hands-on but contribute in a different way to the creative process. Focusing on "hands-on" enables the school to incorporate many different kinds of activities into its A+ efforts as well as to accommodate the differing needs of its elementary, middle, and high-school populations. Students at all levels receive some arts instruction, though funding levels have not been enough to fully staff all four of the arts promoted in the Program. Students do, however, have numerous opportunities to participate in creative initiatives such as the drama club, the award-winning conga band program, wood shop, and the choral music program in the upper grades. These popular and well-executed examples of arts instruction began before the A+ Program, but have a new meaning and prominence with A+. West Hollow also frequently brings in visiting artists, such as storytellers and mountain musicians, and artisans such as blacksmiths, weavers, and stone masons, to do demonstrations and instruction. In this way, teachers have been able to integrate arts without having to have particular expertise themselves. These visitors, and various field trips, also serve to add an element of cultural diversity to the curriculum.

The school has tried numerous methods for facilitating curricular integration through enhancing communication among teachers. Various meeting times and scheduling revisions have been attempted, but none have been sustainable. While periodic staff development meetings provide forums for sharing of curriculum and discussing possible connections, communication among teachers is often dependent upon personal initiative. Curricular maps and webs have been helpful, particularly at the secondary levels where teachers have traditionally been more isolated. Teachers also utilize visits from artists and other local events to make connections across curricular areas. Because West Hollow has K–12 students together in one building, teachers have the additional advantage of linking instruction across multiple grade levels. High-school students have gained from opportunities to teach younger students what they have learned. This is particularly notable in the area of life science, with use of the school's nature trail, but also in other courses. Though many of the connections that teachers make, particularly at the secondary level, tend to be links rather than instances of true collaboration, teachers' interest in communicating with each other, despite the difficulty, suggests a sincere interest in making the curriculum connect across subject areas and into arts classes. In interviews, most faculty say that despite time constraints, the A+ Program has given them more incentive and interest in communicating with each other. One teacher relates:

> I have been able to tell a huge difference in teacher communication. Yes, it's not as good as it could be, but it's so much better than it was. And it's not that we disliked each other. It's just that A+ has given us a reason to make time.

West Hollow's definition of A+ as hands-on has, to some extent, brought about a natural incorporation of multiple intelligences. Teachers have also done some professional development with learning styles. Though this facet of the Program is not primary for West Hollow, the school has developed a planning format that encourages teachers to consider what multiple intelligences are being addressed (through both instruction and assessment) in each lesson. Teachers and students alike are being encouraged to try different ways and different things in their teaching and learning.

West Hollow has implemented several large-scale, school-wide themes, including an Olympics theme just before the Atlanta Olympics, as well as an ecology theme. In the latter case, growing out of the initiative and interests of a small group of teachers, K–8 teachers planned across grade levels and incorporated such activities as enhancing the school's nature trail and implementing a school-wide recycling program. More common are smaller-scale themes, particularly at the elementary level, that help tie curricular areas together and provide focus.

Large-scale activities such as those just described require teachers to go above and beyond the professional collaboration generally accommodated by the school's schedule. Such planning depends upon teachers' relationships with each other and their willingness to go above and beyond. Some of the specialist teachers are also particularly energetic at pursuing this level of communication. For West Hollow, however, collaboration is much more than teachers talking with one another within the building. After experiencing involvement in the A+ network, seeing both what it could and couldn't do for them, West Hollow proceeded to partner with several other Appalachian schools to apply for, and receive, a Rural Challenge grant through the Annenberg Foundation. Rather than diverting their attention from A+, this grant, which focuses on preserving local heritage, blends nicely with the school's arts as crafts and community focus.

It is important here, to discuss briefly the network's influence at West Hollow. Because most of the schools in the network are elementary schools, West Hollow and the other schools with upper-grade configurations have struggled to make some network activities applicable to them. The relevance of discussions about integration, assessment, and planning is affected by the different structures and expectations found in grades 6 through 12. These middle and high schools have worked together, however, to develop strategies that work for them.

Because it is located within a close-knit community, West Hollow School is made up mostly of people who have been committed to the community for generations. Many of the younger teachers are former students and numerous artisans in the area offer their time and energy to teach their crafts and trades to the next generations. As is typical of schools elsewhere, West Hollow sees more direct parent involvement in the classroom at the elementary level than at the middle and high-school level. Band and chorus concerts and basketball games are big community events, however, and support of these and other programs is strong. As the tie that binds this community together, West Hollow recognizes its role in the community's past, present, and future.

Taking advantage of its strong community identity, West Hollow sought participation in the A+ Program, not so much to reform itself but to expand on the ideas that it was already pursuing. People at West Hollow disagree about the extent to which participation in the A+ Program has changed the school, and some contend that nothing substantively has changed. Most teachers who contend that nothing much has changed also told us that faculty communication and collaboration have increased and that students have been exposed to more arts activities. It is likely that, in this close-knit community, ownership of whatever instructional innovations that have come from participation in the A+ Program is more important than identifying themselves as an "A+ School" or even a significantly changed school.

The process of adapting A+ to its own community context and goals has taught West Hollow a most important lesson. West Hollow has grown beyond the mentality of simply implementing a pre-packaged reform and has learned how to use reform for its own ends. This realization contributed to West Hollow's winning an Annenberg Rural Challenge Grant for "place-based" education. West Hollow has gone from being an out-of-the-way, even out-of-the-loop, rural school to a school that is a player in national reform efforts.

As West Hollow finishes its fourth year of participation in the A+ Schools Program and its first year of the Rural Challenge program, it finds itself in a position of having gathered ideas and resources from outside agencies and reformed them to its own local goals. The school is now working with a nearby K–8 school on the ideas behind the A+ Schools Program, and it is collaborating with several nearby high schools on its Rural Challenge program. Participating in the A+ Schools Program helped it be creative in the use of arts but more importantly allowed it to create its own generative reform process.

Conclusion

As we have seen, the A+ Program is an approach to comprehensive school reform that views the arts as fundamental to how teachers teach and how students learn in all subjects. Its central tenet is that arts integration creates varied and rich instruction, thereby increasing the probability that students will be able to acquire and process information in ways that suit their learning strengths. Its focus on facilitating success for all students leads to numerous instructional and organizational changes in schools, from a belief in multiple intelligences that influences both instruction and assessment, to integrating the curriculum and planning thematically. The Program recognizes that teaching and learning in this way requires new kinds of professional collaboration and community participation. It also recognizes that each school must adopt and adapt these various components to fit its own unique local context and culture.

As it accommodates individuality, however, the A+ Program also understands the power of working together to create and sustain school reform. In working together, it develops a shared culture for the Program itself; one that values not only the arts, but also shared decision-making and an inclusive community. Right from the beginning, this culture was established as principals were asked to make important decisions about participation in light of reduced funding. New principals (such as those at Entomon Hills and Albany Woods) are able to connect with other principals and learn from them at regularly held principals' meetings. A+ coordinators from each these three schools (and all the others) are likewise able to learn from one another, share successes, and brainstorm solutions to problems. The A+ fellows provide leadership in implementation not only within their own schools but also in other A+ schools through their work with the summer institutes and other professional development activities they help with throughout the school year. The work of the enriched assessment project drew upon the knowledge and creativity of all of the teachers in the network and provided an important boost for the Program when an increased focus on test scores might have otherwise stymied their efforts. By providing opportunities for ongoing communication among the schools and through taking its direction from the needs of those schools, the network became and continues to be an effective support system for the schools.

Chapter 5

Reform Persistence in A+ Schools

Given the historically marginal status of the arts in American education, the litmus test of whether they have become ingrained in a school is what happens when a substantial "threat" to their having a continuing, integral role in instruction emerges. By "threat," we mean events—new political, procedural, or programmatic mandates—that have school-wide implications for everyone and that usually require schools to adjust or, more commonly, narrow—others would say "sharpen" and still others might employ "supplant"—their priorities. In such situations, those programs and practices on the periphery of "importance" tend to become ignored or discarded all together. As we said at the beginning of this book, this situation is the crux of the perennial problem for arts education: When push comes to shove, the arts usually get shoved.

Such was not the case in all of the A+ schools' experiences, and this chapter explores what it was about A+, the arts, and participants' actions that allowed most of the schools to handle a threat "from within" in the form of turnover of key staff and a threat "from without" in the guise of the demands of the state's accountability system. Leadership turnover, of course, is a perennial "reform stopper" and yet the A+ schools collectively demonstrated a remarkable imperviousness to administrative changes, as all of them maintained their participation in the Program. This flew in the face of the literature on the disruptive effects of such departures on reform efforts. A high-stakes testing atmosphere provided a more formidable risk to the schools' resolve to emphasize the arts. In this instance, the arts integration efforts of some schools continued to evolve while others stalled.

Given that the forces that might have weakened commitment to the arts emanated from two different sources, it should not be too surprising that data from the pilot period suggested that factors that helped schools minimize the damage were also of two different types. This chapter argues that specific characteristics of the A+ Program seemed to enable schools to persist with the reform despite personnel changes whereas how the schools themselves adapted and took ownership of the reform seemed more pertinent to enabling arts integration to thrive under the state-wide testing program. In both cases, however, certain developments appeared to put schools in the position of being able to buffer their arts commitments from forces that historically would have diminished them. In the first instance, the schools experienced a collective benefit from (1) their participation in the A+ network, which gave each school a more widely visible public identity as an arts school that new personnel would have been inclined to leave alone; (2) distributing leadership responsibilities across multiple roles so that maintaining some continuity with A+ was usually possible; and (3) enjoying a steady stream of A+-specific funding that, although reduced, obligated the schools to demonstrate at least a modicum of reform-related activity. The politically charged atmosphere of state-wide testing took more of a "divide and conquer" direction insofar as the A+ schools' shared endeavors did little to offer uniform fortification against local expectations for and interpretations of district-specific results. Instead, differences in the curriculum- and instruction-related roles that schools assigned to the arts seemed to determine whether music, drama, movement, and visual art would remain vital.

Sustaining Arts Integration in the Face of Leadership Change and Staff Turnover

The turnover of key administrators among the A+ schools was perhaps typical of what one might find in any randomly identified group of schools in North Carolina, or any state for that matter. That is to say that it was considerable. Table 5.1 summarizes the tenures of principals and superintendents across the 24 schools during the 4-year pilot period. Sixteen of the schools had at least one principal change; and 14 experienced turnover in the superintendent's office.

Both types of leadership changes held potentially significant implications for the schools. New leaders tend to want to "make their mark" on a school or district, and this often means shifting the focus of reform efforts. Principals obviously had much to say about school direction, especially given that the A+ Program was so determinedly school-based. Superintendents were more distant from daily building activities but were key actors in district decisions to continue its share of the Program's funding.

Table 5.1 Leadership Turnover in A+ Schools During the Pilot (*n* = 24)

Leadership Changes	Principal	Superintendent
No Change	8 (33%)	10 (42%)
One Change	12 (50%)	12 (50%)
Multiple Changes	4 (17%)	2 (8%)

Administrative changes were not inherently negative events for the reform. In some cases, the principal change had positive results, particularly in schools where the principal's vision of A+ did not always match that of the teachers—and when the principal left, the faculty became reinvigorated. For example, one principal imposed her personal vision of A+ on the faculty to the extent of stifling teacher dialogue about the Program's direction. Teachers felt compelled to follow the principal's lead and felt they had no voice in determining how to implement A+. A teacher at this school described the difference once the new principal arrived: "I think with that change in principalship, all of a sudden we started talking. As soon as [the former principal] was out, we knew it was OK."

In a few schools, the community had become so attached to A+ that members of the hiring committees and other parent groups would adamantly inform new administrators that A+ would continue.

All in all, the A+ implementation effort in these schools endured these transitions remarkably well. Principals and superintendents came and went with regularity. Yet all but one of the schools remained A+ schools—and as discussed earlier this one never actually started A+.

This commitment to the Program was also surprisingly steadfast because several of the schools unfortunately found themselves in an annual "mad scramble" to hire arts faculty. Schools in rural locales had a particularly difficult time recruiting, hiring, and retaining arts personnel. One principal described the transition his school was experiencing during the second semester of the second year of A+:

> As a matter of fact, since school opened both of our arts people from last year—drama and dance—resigned, so we have a new dance person and a new drama person, because around here, they're hard to find. They have no problem getting jobs closer to home . . . Both of them were good people. So this year we had to do it again. At Christmas time, our drama teacher, who we hired this year, resigned and she went back home to [name of city].

Thus, in the space of a year and a half, this A+ school lost three key arts staff. Later the visual arts teacher retired, and the drama teacher took a position with less of a commute.

Another A+ school in the same county experienced similar difficulties, as the two small schools often shared arts faculty. During the fourth year of A+, the school's principal described the county's ongoing dilemma with recruiting and retaining arts personnel:

> This year, we do not have a drama teacher. We just could not find anyone despite [the district arts coordinator's] hard effort. We share the dance teacher . . . She is here on Monday, Wednesday, and Friday.

We were supposed to have a semester with the art teacher and then a semester with the music teacher, but the music teacher was setting up a keyboarding lab over at [another school]; and because there were delays with the equipment, she just got that going.

The high rate of arts faculty turnover at these schools meant they had to practically start from scratch every year and sometimes every semester. Consequently, program continuity and coherence suffered, but not enough to cause the educators to throw up their hands in resignation.

Classroom teachers also had turnover, but this was of less significance to A+ because of the centrality of the arts teachers to the initiative. Turnover of classroom teachers, however, over time was an issue noted by the research team in year 2 of the pilot and led to new teacher professional development being offered later that year and in subsequent summer institutes. These efforts, of course, affected both new arts teachers and regular classroom teachers, and helped the schools maintain their momentum with A+.

Making Connections: Protecting Reform from Internal Staffing Changes

The above discussion clearly shows that staff members who were extremely essential to the goals of A+ were sometimes highly mobile. At some point, one would have had to predict that the pilot program would have experienced some attrition of sites. After all, the whole purpose of the reform dealt with subject matter and skills that had long existed at the periphery of the schools' operations. To be sure, leadership change and staff turnover caused arts activities to be put on hold in some schools and scaled back in others. Yet they all continued an affiliation with the reform and participation in reform-wide meetings and professional development. An explanation of why schools persisted with the A+ pilot is of interest, not only to arts-based reformers but also to all advocates of comprehensive school change. Three important characteristics of A+ as a reform served as "protective" factors: the network itself; multiple reform leadership roles in the buildings; and stable—if reduced—funding.

Participating in A+ carried with it membership in a network of schools. The network initially began as a small group of program planners with the Kenan Institute. Eventually, it grew to encompass the developers as well as all 24 pilot A+ schools, university faculty advisors, community partners, and additional schools interested in implementing the Program on their own. And it was through the network that regular professional development activities occurred and various meetings were held. The training often was open to all staff; the meetings targeted people in particular roles, e.g., the principal or the staff person designated as the project coordinator, or assigned members of a special committee, or teachers new to the school. This meant that while A+ was indeed school-based, the schools were rarely left alone to navigate their idiosyncratic reform paths. At least some staff members encountered A+ participants from other schools regularly, and nearly every staff member was likely to come into contact with other participants yearly at the summer institutes. In the course of these interactions, staff in every building received encouragement to pursue the arts and acquire new skills and knowledge with which to do this. Importantly, the occurrence of these events was not dependent on any one individual in a school.

As discussed above, following the second year of the pilot, the A+ network began offering an orientation for new teachers. Typically these teachers were hired after the summer institute was held and, thus, they arrived in the schools mostly unaware of A+ and its implications for them. Schools that had experienced particularly high rates of turnover were especially disadvantaged in this regard, as the new teachers often arrived with little training in arts integration.

A teacher at a school that experienced high rates of turnover described the difficulties of implementing A+ with many new staff members that had not participated in A+-related professional development:

> With our staff now, we have so many new teachers coming in . . . If they would have more training, workshops like I had, they would probably say, "yes, lets go for it." But at this point now, they're not familiar with it. It's been such a complete turnover with the staff.

Thus, the network offered a means of buffering the schools from having untrained cohorts of teachers weakening students' arts experiences and the schools' overall emphasis on the arts. New staff members were able to learn about A+ implementation and subsequently contributed to keeping the Program alive in some form in the classrooms.

The network served a similar reinforcing function for other groups. One such group was the A+ fellows. This subgroup of the larger A+ network was formed to provide the focus and direction needed for professional development efforts. As the creative grade-level and arts teachers in the schools played a larger role in planning activities for the annual summer institutes, they eventually formally comprised the majority of the A+ fellows. They had retreats three times a year to discuss, organize, and plan the professional development agenda. Not only did they serve as trainers at the Institutes, but also individual schools would call on them to work with their faculties.

The network, therefore, provided a systemic way of keeping school staff in touch with one another and sharing information about network events. It also sponsored regional conferences, "bright ideas" newsletters, and electronic discussion forums and websites. In this way, the network offered schools an ongoing, external source of emotional and professional support that was unaffected by the turnover turmoil going on at the building level.

Schools received an additional enduring boost from Kenan's initial decision to include all staff in the first summer institute. Never before had the whole staffs of any of the schools engaged in professional development for an extended period of time. The week spent at the institute far exceeded the usual 1 to 2 hours of whole-faculty staff development. For most schools, this Institute was instrumental in ensuring that everyone understood the commitments and responsibilities involved in a full implementation of the A+ Schools Program. The Institutes also had a strong curriculum mapping focus that brought all faculty together. Starting with a wholly trained faculty distinguished A+ from other reforms the schools had enacted that attempted to diffuse the reform from a small team of trained "insiders" to the rest of the building.

All of the network-sponsored activities—summer institutes/professional development conferences, on-line discussion forums, regional conferences—fostered opportunities for everyone to brainstorm ideas while receiving much-needed psychological support from colleagues. Schools leaned on each other and talked about core beliefs, frustrations, concerns, ideas, and strategies. Simply knowing that there were numerous schools in the state that were dealing with similar issues helped many of the schools, but it also built the capacity for schools to work together on issues that were too large for one school or individual to handle. Schools could collaborate on key issues, and find ways to reclaim some of the power that they felt they were losing to many of the challenges that they faced. They even pursued, and obtained, grants together. All of these activities cultivated a sense of belonging, displayed the enormous amount of support available to individual teachers and schools, and provided opportunities for schools to make informal connections outside of the network-sponsored activities.

The A+ network was particularly powerful and helpful for teachers as a psychological support since they dealt with challenges that were relatively outside of their control. For teachers who strongly believed in the A+ philosophies and theories, external politics and issues that challenged the successful implementation of the Program were disheartening. The A+ network often provided them the support and capacity to deal with the large challenges that they otherwise could not address as individual teachers or schools.

From the very beginning, program representatives regularly met with the principals of the pilot schools. Even though Kenan understood that A+ leadership would emerge from many different stakeholders, they also recognized early on the importance of offering support to official school leaders. These meetings modeled shared leadership, provided a forum for addressing the administrative issues that arose from implementing a school-wide, arts-based reform, and gave building administrators the opportunity to express their concerns. They also shared ideas about scheduling students for arts classes, finding time for collaborative planning, professional development and orientation for new teachers, and assessment. These conferences also introduced new principals to the A+ philosophy and culture. These meetings also came to have parallel sessions for the A+ coordinators—teachers who led the curricular efforts.

While the Kenan Institute and staff provided the initial direction for the A+ network, as the network grew, Kenan assumed a more facilitative role. The network's groups involved a host of teachers and, over time, the schools became less dependent on Kenan for leadership and guidance, and more dependent on themselves and each other. This leadership shift was intentional and placed many of the "A+ champions" from individual schools in leadership positions in both the network and their respective schools. During times of adversity, these people were often the leaders in the schools.

A teacher's response to a question about the leadership of A+ in her school illustrated the shared ownership: "The leadership from A+ is intrinsic . . . we do not have a leader." In other words, there was no single individual that people turned to for either inspiration or ideas; there were several such people distributed across a variety of positions and roles. In most schools, this cadre included an administrator, the A+ coordinator (often an arts teacher), any A+ fellow in the building (either arts or grade-level teachers), one or more of the arts teachers, and any members of network special groups.

These "A+ champions" provided program direction, and any new principal then had to negotiate with the existing A+ establishment about a school's direction. Sometimes the principal nudged, or more forcefully pushed, the Program in a different direction; but A+ was never completely abandoned. For example, in Albany Woods (see Chapter 4), the new principal was "very positive," "very supportive," and "willing" with respect to A+. Although the person was a literacy advocate and did not know much about A+, she "jumped in with both feet" under the encouragement of teacher leaders. The principal deliberately moved A+ in a different direction by making reading the focus of the school's efforts but valued and retained an arts emphasis in improving reading.

A+ leadership in a school, therefore, involved several people at least. Thus, all 24 of the implementing schools had multiple advocates for the arts who managed to keep the mantel of A+ alive. The point is that attaining the early stages of incorporating the arts into a school's identity in the A+ Program involved more than just a single idea champion. This more diffused advocacy for the arts enabled them to endure as important school values in the face of potentially debilitating personnel changes.

Aside from providing financial assistance to schools, one of the important leadership functions of the Kenan Institute was the brokering they did with the North Carolina Legislature. Through continued efforts, Kenan was able to get the Program added to the North Carolina General Assembly's budget as an approved reform effort, as well as secure a place for A+ as a recurring line item in the state's budget. This meant that A+ went from being a year-to-year appropriation to being part of the continuing budget. While this level of funding was less than originally desired, it nevertheless signaled to all of the schools that the Program was not going to be completely renegotiated legislatively each year.

The Kenan Institute provided financial support for schools throughout the pilot. However, the funding was often not enough to pay for the needed arts supplies or arts teaching staff. From the collaboration and commitment that the network fostered through its activities, schools obtained the skills to secure external funding to help their implementation efforts. The schools applied for numerous outside grants to keep A+ going. For example, several schools received small grants from local arts groups, and a group of schools secured Goals 2000 money to purchase art supplies and hire dance and drama teachers. (Other sites also pursued these funds successfully and used them for technology and other "basic" necessities.) Additionally, because by this time A+ was a state-approved reform (a remarkable achievement in itself), one school was able to secure a $50,000 Comprehensive School Reform grant after the pilot ended to continue their A+ efforts. The principal and teachers of this school contended that without the A+ network, they would not have been given the information about applying for the grant, nor would they have had the skills to collaborate to write their proposal.

Schools everywhere engage in this kind of "hand-to-mouth" search for special program funding. While such efforts often sow the seeds for new programs, these initiatives also often wither because they have no lasting roots in any stable funding source. The line-item status for A+ gave the schools a foundation from which to launch their other money-seeking activities, activities that might enable the Program to thrive but were not necessarily needed for the Program to survive.

This is not to say that schools had no funding worries. There was always the possibility lurking that a local school board might change its mind about upholding its matching amount. Indeed, several found it difficult to give special money to one school without doing the same for others. The happy consequence of such thinking might have been that other schools would also receive funds earmarked to support the arts, but this was not the case. Typically, the boards kept the level of their original commitment to the schools without the gradual increase over time that was originally part of the district's contract with A+ and the Kenan Institute. So, schools shuffled their discretionary funds and redefined certain positions to ensure that they could maintain their arts emphasis.

These three significant characteristics of the A+ reform—the network, multiple reform leadership roles, and the probability of at least a moderate level of continued funding—conspired to keep schools formally attached to the Program even when undergoing potentially destabilizing leadership change and staff turnover. That is, all of the schools kept their affiliations with A+ through the 4-year pilot, which was remarkable in and of itself given the short shelf life of many education reforms. However, the schools did not all establish the same level of arts integration and did not continue the same level of effort, and these differences proved vital when the schools encountered another powerful challenge to the arts—the state's testing program.

Maintaining Arts Integration in the Face of High-Stakes Accountability

In North Carolina, the primary challenge that most of the A+ schools faced during the evaluation period was the emergence of a new state accountability system known as the ABCs. The policy reflected a national trend toward standards-based accountability, with the centerpiece being a high-stakes standardized test. Under the system, schools received an "expected growth" score and designation based on it as either "low performing," "no recognition," "expected growth," or "exemplary growth." The state sent assistance teams to work with low performing schools; the highest performing schools got per-teacher financial rewards. Needless to say, such information was published widely in the state.

North Carolina garnered national praise for the program, and officials began to see the state's approach to accountability as the linchpin in its growing reputation as a state dedicated to school reform (Grissmer, Flanagan, Kawata, and Williamson, 2000). Still, the system also came under criticism. McMillan (1999) and Jones et al. (1999) reported that the ABCs negatively affected teacher morale and caused them to rely on didactic teaching methods. Thus, high-stakes testing appeared to stifle the creative passion of teachers as they felt the pressure to drill the basics into students' heads.

Not surprisingly, therefore, many A+ teachers considered the ABCs to be in competition with arts integration. Chief among their concerns was their feeling that the tests did not measure the kinds of success A+ was enabling them to have with students (e.g. greater interest, more creativity, etc.). The tests, they worried, would eventually drain attention away from these other important outcomes. They also spent considerable time figuring out what they could do to change the situation. The new impetus for change competed for the same time and energy that staff was already devoting to A+.

The network attempted to counter this discouragement—and to combat a perceived disjuncture between teachers' new ways of teaching with the old ways of testing—with a Goals 2000 grant to develop an A+ "enriched assessment" model. In fact, even in the first year of the pilot, teachers already recognized that improved means of assessing student learning was a primary need. The goal of the grant, therefore, was for teachers to develop alternative ways to accommodate higher-order thinking skills and multiple intelligences on assessment instruments.

Nevertheless, pressure to improve test scores, real or perceived, put a tremendous strain on educators. Emotionally, educators wanted others to view their schools positively. In most times, polls showed over and over again, the public believed that the schools were doing a good job—in the absence of any concrete information to the contrary. Test scores, valid or not, signaled whether this good will was justified. When schools were put into one of the two lower categories based on the ABCs, educators fretted tremendously about themselves and public opinion, believing that all of their arts efforts were unappreciated.

Faculty members in one school struggled to maintain their belief in A+. A teacher described how the ABCs contributed to conservatism and unwillingness to take risks in the school:

> The new ABCs program in the county, with the state, hasn't helped because it relies so much on your test scores . . . and the threats from the state that if you don't do so well on your tests, they're going to come in and take over. Nobody wants to put forth the effort to try to do something different because "why try something new and risk that?"

A+ teachers recognized early on that "we just need to be more inventive about how we assess." Nonetheless, they felt caught between their desire to use a particular philosophy of teaching and the "paper-and-pencil" assessment that exemplified the state's testing program. Teachers expressed almost a sense of hopelessness, as they perceived a contradiction between the way they taught and the manner in which students were tested. Thus, in another school, teachers became frustrated:

> They're telling teachers you have to be flexible, and you have to be able to teach to different learning styles, but they're only testing one learning style. I think it forced us to put emphasis on testing skills somewhat. Instead of learning in some integrated way, we had to teach them how to take a test, a standardized test.

The ABCs severely tested the schools' faith that adherence to the A+ teaching philosophy would not jeopardize test scores and would, in fact, enrich student learning. This was particularly the case once the test results were announced during the summer following the second year, and five of the A+ schools were declared "low performing." While most of these schools exhibited growth from previous test scores, they did not meet their benchmark scores and were thus labeled accordingly. Although none of the A+ schools designated low performing were assigned assistance teams, these schools were particularly devastated. A teacher at one of them explained how being labeled affected her teaching:

> Before I wanted to see [an assistance] team come in here and tell me how to do it and what to do—and on top of that—the threat of testing you all over again, there were some things in the A+ that I put aside, even in the regular curriculum—and concentrated on those things that I was going to be tested on.

Schools that performed well according to the ABCs also found they had to pay attention to the tests, as the stakes were just too high to ignore them. One principal explained that when she took the position at the A+ school, she told her faculty: "First of all, I will never become a principal that emphasizes standardized testing. If we do good instruction, the standardized test will take care of itself." While she continued to believe that was true, she went on to explain how the reality of the ABCs had forced her to rethink her position:

> I've changed my tune. We're talking test scores. We're analyzing test scores. We're looking at where the weaknesses are. We're looking at avenues to strengthen specific objectives. Is that bad? It's a different way of doing school. It's the antithesis of what I believe is good and right about teaching children. And it's a reality.

Although this particular school performed satisfactorily on the tests, staff still took time to emphasize test taking skills and strategies.

The principal at another school that had also had success with the ABCs experienced similar pressures to maintain its exemplary growth status:

> [There] is more tension this year than ever before. We need to consistently combat the fear among teachers that we are not going to maintain exemplary status. I know their stomachs churn and I need to keep giving them pep talks. They don't want to drop A+. It is who they are as teachers, and it is their philosophy . . . Kids love coming to school; they run in here. I don't want that to ever change. I don't want a testing program to dampen the true joy of learning that is in place in this building. [But] I had to fight to keep the spirit alive this fall.

All of the A+ schools eventually achieved at least the status of "expected growth" at some point during the pilot period, and some had made the leap from "low performing" and "no recognition" to "exemplary growth." While these schools felt vindicated, they also recognized that there were new pressures to maintain that status, as expected growth was based on prior growth. A teacher in a school that improved from low performing to exemplary growth in a single year understood that the expectations were now even higher:

> The trend will be for those schools to keep it. The thing is, you got lucky. You did something, but can you keep it up? That's what they're in it to look to see how long is it going to last for that many schools. Then they're coming up with the new test changes and the new curriculum changes, so there are going to be some schools that are going to have to regroup, and they're going to fall short again. It's going to be how long can that many schools stay at that level?

Needless to say, this situation was ripe for forcing the schools to nudge the arts away from the core of schooling, as had happened so often in the past. What actually happened was that, while all remained in the Program, some suspended much of their classroom arts integration and scaled back any school-wide events; some allowed individual teachers to continue arts integration but did little to further the cause; and some adapted their efforts to accommodate both testing and the arts. The varied responses of the schools to accountability pressures correlate to how deeply they had integrated the arts into their identity. The following three vignettes illustrate the variety of school responses.

A+ in Name Only at Jackson

Jackson Elementary is located in an extremely rural and poor part of the state. Under the principal who had completed the school's application for the A+ Program, the school had never seemed to fully embrace arts integration—at least according to the staff, particularly the part-time arts teachers who worked there. Although the principal participated in most of the network activities and the faculty attended the summer institutes, the school's attention centered on literacy. Thus, arts integration primarily evolved only within the arts department, with the specialist teachers trying to reinforce the state's Standard Course of Study in the various activities they designed for students.

The literacy priority became magnified under the glare of the state's testing program. The scores were not out of line with what research showed was likely with their student population. Yet, locally, the scores were well below those of a sister elementary. Although that school had a much larger number of higher income white students, comparisons were nevertheless inevitable and discouraging for the staff.

The principal believed that an all-out assault on reading was the only way the school's predominately minority student population would show noticeable progress in their achievement. He increased the amount of time devoted to the subject each day and marshaled nearly every adult in the building—including the arts teachers—to work with students. Arts classes eventually were suspended to allow the arts teachers to tutor students who had performed particularly poorly on the tests.

A+ on Hold at Hightown

Hightown Elementary had a diverse population of low-income students in a small town that had several other elementary schools. Its principal was a devoted advocate for the multiple intelligences, so much so that every faculty member received Howard Gardner's book on the topic. He was convinced that having the faculty teach to students' strengths would attract the students to school and eventually cause them to reach their full potential. The school celebrated students' artistic skills occasionally in school-wide events for parents and began to promote two-way arts integration, a term that meant that classroom teachers would enhance the Standard Course of Study with arts activities just as the arts teachers drew on content from the "major" subjects.

Historically the school had served its students well, with their achievement being higher than would have been predicted given their parents' income. This was a cause of some pride in the school until the advent of the ABCs. Its means of categorizing schools made it difficult for the school to achieve "expected growth," much less "exemplary growth." Statistically, students' scores originated at too high of a baseline. Thus, while the school's absolute scores were higher than the surrounding elementary schools, its ranking on growth was last.

This proved to be traumatic for the faculty and the principal. Staff wondered whether the time they were giving to the arts could be better spent. Collectively the educators went through a full year of soul searching, during which A+ moved to the back burner. At the end of the year, they spent two faculty meetings exploring their commitment to the arts and what they should do in the following year. Ultimately, they decided that many of their concerns about the arts really stemmed from the testing pressure they felt and that they had made great—if unmeasured—strides with students previously. They did not want to give this up and decided to renew their dedication to the arts, to the extent possible under the testing situation. It remained to be seen what kind of collective actions this shared agreement would foster. Indeed, the principal viewed the school as starting over with A+.

A+ as a Valued Instructional Tool at Creekside

Like the other two schools, Creekside Elementary also served a low-income student population, more diverse than Jackson but less so than Hightown. The principal was continuously searching the research landscape for ideas about how to better educate such students. She latched onto A+ as a potentially powerful vehicle for engaging students in the classroom and reinforcing what they were learning. The school also had a project coordinator who was well-versed in curriculum issues and, because of staffing patterns in the county, was able to work closely with teachers on instructional planning rather than having to teach a full complement of classes. Through the principal's insistence and the co-ordinator's guidance in small group meetings, staff throughout the school figured out ways to incorporate the arts into their classes.

The school's early test results were in line with what one would have expected given the income level of its students' parents. Because of the number of innovations for which the school had tried and received recognition, the principal felt that there was some smug satisfaction in the district about this "mediocre" performance, perhaps driven by jealousy of the publicity. The principal expressed a concern that at some point the district might force the school to give up some of the programs and practices that the faculty felt were benefiting students because the test scores could be used to call them "ineffective." Anecdotal data buttressed a belief that they should not scale back on the arts, but the staff could not deny that students were not performing as they should.

Rather than backing off of arts integration, the school decided that the students were not getting enough arts. That is, because of the size of the school, the arts teachers were spread thin. To counter this, the arts teachers were teamed with the teachers in intermediate grades to increase the amount of activities that could both reinforce class content and connect with students' learning styles. In this way, students—in the tested grades (3, 4, and 5)—would spend more time on reading and math and have increased opportunities for the arts. The obvious downside of the decision was that the primary students would have little arts instruction, except that which their regular teachers provided.

An Explanation for the Differences in Responses

North Carolina's new accountability system implicated many aspects of school operation, but most importantly the classroom. Unlike accreditation procedures that put considerable emphasis on resources and processes, the ABCs stressed achievement results. The onus was put quite squarely on teachers. Regardless of their beliefs about the value of standardized testing, they were responsible for their students' test results.

All three of the above schools faced similar testing pressures. Within their communities it was important for the faculty to be able to demonstrate that students were able to read and compute at acceptable levels. Not only were the accountability system's sanctions looming over them, but the publicity surrounding the system's ratings generated local pressure to perform as well. Under these pressures, the schools responded differently, by putting A+ on hold, maintaining a modicum of effort, or combining the arts with test score improvement strategies. We believe these differential responses reflect the extent to which the arts had already been integrated into a school's educational identity when they faced the external pressure of testing to focus on "basics."

The first two responses reflect specific instances of what always seems to happen to the arts in education. Advocates expressed remorse at scaling the arts back but shrugged at the inevitability of their action. The state was sending a signal that time spent on the arts drained time that should be spent on other subjects.

The Creekside Elementary response of teaming arts and classroom teachers to reinforce content in the intermediate grades was unquestionably a compromise. Given their druthers, the faculty would not have cut back on the arts for the younger students. However, they also wanted to retain the arts and did so under a shared expectation that the arts would enhance rather than detract from students' acquisition of other content.

The above vignettes are brief but do hint at an explanation for the differences in the responses. Staff in all three of the schools said that they valued the arts and thought that their students would benefit from arts integration. However, they had enacted their values differently. The first relegated their commitment to the arts (at the instigation of the principal) primarily to having more arts classes and occasional school-wide arts events. The second also engaged in school-wide events and was just beginning to move the arts to the classroom level. The third had already incorporated the arts into their instructional planning, and arts integration was evident in classrooms throughout the school.

In other words, educators across the three schools had the arts play different roles in the day-to-day operation of their schools prior to the ABCs. They sequestered the arts in the specialists' rooms in the first case, and only sporadically offered them in the regular classrooms in the second. Without firmly ensconcing the arts in lesson planning, grade-level curricula, and daily classroom activities, school staff could not put them in a position in either school to weather the sudden and powerful impact of pressure to raise test scores. On a small scale, these schools reflected the ebb and flow of attention to the arts that so often had occurred nationally in the past.

The third school avoided this situation and managed to embed the arts in the steps they took to address testing concerns. We argue that this is because the arts had already become a part of the culture of the school.

Teachers talked regularly about the arts with the project coordinator, and the principal constantly urged staff to integrate the arts. Both reinforced A+ as important to the school and stimulated the search for ways to demonstrate this importance. A+ had infused school-wide decision-making and the classroom. It was a regular part of the way people worked in the building. This deeper insinuation of the value of the arts into school life, then, made it more likely that the arts would be relied on as a solution to the testing problem they faced, rather than viewed as a competitor for time and energy to address the problem.

The pattern of responses described in the vignettes was repeated in other schools. Some saw the time and energy they were devoting to A+ as well as arts-related activities themselves as competing with the time and energy and types of activities that were needed to address the ABCs. In those settings, the arts lost out. Not completely—the schools continued some school-wide events such as student performances or "informances" in which students shared what they were learning in artistic ways. Yet, in the classroom, the arts became much less a daily occurrence.

Other schools did not see such competition. If anything, they saw the ABCs and A+ as mutually reinforcing an emphasis on students' academic growth. Certainly the two could have had different implications for the kinds of instruction that should go on the classroom, but these schools tended to try to figure out how both could benefit students. So, in the case of Creekside Elementary, the school increased its concentration on tested skills as well as the amount of arts activities in which tested students engaged.

Summary

In the pilot period, the A+ schools "bounced back" from two important and omnipresent barriers to continued reform: staff turnover and high-stakes testing. The explanation for this resilience with respect to internal turnover partially resided in the Program's building in three "protective" or "connective" factors that enabled A+ to become an "insinuated" rather than an "insular" reform. By virtue of supporting the state-wide network of schools, encouraging schools to distribute leadership responsibilities across several positions, and maintaining a continuous funding stream, the A+ Program decreased the ease with which new occupants of even key positions could dissolve their schools' participation. Together, these three characteristics of A+ as a reform seemed to enable all of the schools to maintain their affiliation with the Program, even when newly arriving staff and leadership were not particularly disposed to it.

The depth of a school's commitment to arts integration directly affected the fate of the arts in the school's response to the onset of the high-stakes testing program. Schools that had a somewhat superficial, although still enthusiastic, commitment to the arts had an extremely difficult time holding on to the steps they had made toward arts integration, much less continuing to develop their arts-based education efforts. Schools that had infused the arts into classroom planning acknowledged the necessity of ensuring acceptable student performance on the tests but also managed to at least maintain, if not further develop, arts integration. The experiences of A+ schools suggest, then, that part of the reason why schools seem so prone to abandoning the arts from time to time has to do with the extent to which they make the arts an indelible part of school operation.

Overall, then, this chapter offers some promising news for arts advocates. Strength in numbers (in terms of connecting to others involved in similar endeavors outside an individual school, giving several people within a building leadership opportunities, and continuing at least a modest flow of special resources for arts-related activities) and moving the arts from the periphery to the core of instruction tremendously increase the chances that the arts will endure when potentially debilitating events occur.

Chapter 6

School Identity and Arts Integration

The A+ schools showed a sturdy resilience to stick with their commitment to the arts. Bucking the past history of arts education, all of the schools that participated in the pilot program retained a formal attachment to the reform and a sizeable cadre of schools continued arts integration in the classroom in spite of challenges that could easily have bumped the arts off of the list of school priorities.

As discussed elsewhere, three characteristics of the A+ reform lent an air of permanence to the initiative and aided their overcoming personnel turnover. Participating in a network of schools, the emergence of multiple leaders within a school, and enjoying a somewhat predictable money flow all kept the schools at least nominally involved in the Program. Even for schools at the lowest level of involvement, most of the faculty still attended summer institute sessions, and individuals from the schools attended network meetings. Thus, information about the reform and knowledge about integrating the arts continued to flow to all of the schools.

However, the schools were less resilient in the face of the state's accountability system. Pressure to perform, from both external and internal sources, separated the more stalwart schools from the less committed. As we suggested in the previous chapter, those that had embedded the arts in their routines—particularly instructional planning and classroom activities—seemed to maintain and advance arts integration; those that had not gotten this far in their evolution as arts-based schools embarked on a hiatus from their school-level endeavors. The lessons to be learned from these different paths should be of keen interest to advocates for the arts in education because they hold promise for resolving the dilemma of how to keep the arts central to instruction, even when events seem to conspire against them.

We argue that the distinguishing feature of schools that held onto their arts commitment were those where people infused the arts into their regular ways of working and shared similar conceptions about what A+ should look and sound like in their buildings. In other words, the arts became an indelible part of the schools' culture and, thus, people invoked the arts often in their conversations and actions. The inability to alter belief systems in this way has long rung the death knell for reform after reform after reform.

This chapter, therefore, buttresses the argument that attention to school culture offers a promising avenue to thinking about how to give the arts a more prominent and permanent spot in schools. In the course of doing so, we will define more clearly what we mean by terms such as "a deep commitment to the arts," "a prominent spot in school life," and "a valued role for the arts." We use these concepts to flesh out three levels of school identity vis-à-vis arts integration—affiliative, symbolic, and substantive—and show how the level at which a school incorporated the arts into its identity affected the resilience of the arts-based reform there. We also attend to how the schools legitimized their ventures into the arts because such actions were necessary preludes to eventually imbuing daily school life with them. The chapter concludes with observations about the value of carving out a substantive role for the arts.

Identity Vignettes

But first, consider three schools that continued to participate in A+ activities and the diverse fate of the arts in them. The schools are Jackson, Rolling Meadow, and Hillside.

Jackson

The town's streets were lined with spectators as the children of Jackson elementary excitedly prepared for their end-of-year parade and celebration. Office workers left their temporarily closed buildings and poultry plant workers used an extended lunch break to join patrons of the few businesses along the main street of this rural community to clap and cheer as a float of first and second graders passed by. The children were dressed as Native Americans and sat around a large paper teepee. A local newspaper photographer snapped numerous pictures. Convertibles with local dignitaries, including previous principals of the school, mingled among the floats and marchers. The high-school band provided the music for dozens of other students to show off their costumes representing famous Americans they had studied in social studies. Even students from the town's other elementary school had been released to observe the festivities.

Students, parents, grandparents, and others returned to the school to enjoy a smorgasbord of hamburgers, hot dogs, and fried chicken. Children and teachers entertained the crowd with singing and dancing; and people visited booths with the works of local artists and looked at historical photos from the school's past arrayed on several tables.

It was the ending to a difficult year, a difficult 2 years really, as the staff had struggled to figure out how to integrate the arts into their classrooms amid continual and increasing pressure to perform better on the state's standardized tests. Teachers said that communication had always been an issue in the school and the lack of it became magnified as they had started with A+. Staff were not uniformly convinced of the wisdom of centering the arts in regular classes, held differing interpretations of what arts integration should look and sound like, and were frustrated by having another reform layered on top of several literacy- and math-related improvement efforts the school had already adopted. Mix in the less than satisfactory test results that historically plagued the mostly impoverished and minority students in the school and it was easy to see why misgiving was a subtext in the celebration.

Still, most had kept up a good front, holding on to the belief that singing, dancing, and drawing would engage students and somehow spur them to greater achievement. The end-of-year celebration was intended to give everyone a deserved pat on the back and to set the stage for a third year with an arts focus.

The subsequently received test results from the spring did not dampen memories of that day. They washed them completely away. The following fall found fresh white paint replacing walls once filled with student artwork and projects. Bulletin boards and other display areas were bare of student work as well. Walking the hallways, one was left to gaze upon state standards and grade-level curriculum objectives. Even the bright red A+ banner had been relegated to a closet—and with it was stored the spirit of arts integration, at least while the staff and students faced the overbearing countenance of state accountability.

"Since we got our low performing label from the state tests, it feels like somebody died in the building," remarked one teacher. Although in reality the scores had slightly increased, the gain was nowhere near enough to allow the school to escape the scarlet letter of being deemed "low performing." This presaged repeated visits from a state assistance team, whose role seemed more to criticize than to help. Almost unavoidably, teacher morale reached an all-time low according to those who had been around a while, and staff began to worry if maybe their jobs were now actually on the line.

What took place that year then was an all-out, nearly desperate attempt to raise test scores; and for most teachers that meant reverting to traditional instructional strategies and teaching to the test, completely devoid of the arts. In fact, around the middle of the year, the principal openly declared: "Right now it is truth and consequence time; A+ is still important, but it is difficult to do things that work with arts integration because we are scared of the status we're in. We reverted back to old ways, though there is still some hands-on in K–2, where they are not tested."

For their part, teachers also admitted that they did not emphasize nor do much arts integration as their primary push was to concentrate on the "basics." Even the arts teachers got in on the act and devoted half of their instructional time to tutoring students in reading, writing, and/or math rather than teaching them art or music. Because these teachers worked in multiple buildings, the amount of arts education dwindled considerably.

Tutoring in fact became more characteristic of the school's program than the arts. In addition to designating some of the arts time periods for it, tutoring also occurred after school—daily. Near the end of year, however, nearly everyone—adults and kids—was burned out from test prep and so extra help was reduced to three days a week. A teacher lamented: "A+ is really slipping away. People are scared and concerned and not focused on the Program at all. After we get through this hurdle, maybe we can try it again."

The hurdle was a tall one. Damaged morale within the building coupled with community blame to produce an intolerable working environment. Everywhere staff turned—newspapers, school board meetings, even idle conversations—the public seemed to view teachers and poor instruction as the cause of the unacceptable student performance. This development was somewhat ironic from the staff's viewpoint because parents were notorious for beginning to ease their children away from school work and on to farm duties as they entered their teenage years. If anything, teachers had always felt that parents' lack of responsibility for helping their children educationally at home was one of the primary obstacles to higher achievement. Now, however, it was educators and not the community that toiled in the glaring spotlight of public criticism.

Revealing the depths to which teachers' despair had reached, one commented: "Next year, I think we will just have more intense praying; if we don't pray, we won't be able to stay together." Indeed, if anything good came out of the year, it was an evolving closeness among the faculty—kind of the common goal or common foe theory in action. Communication that had long been a problem improved via commiseration and a budding desire to regain control of their lives.

The silver lining never materialized. A fear of straying too far from direct instruction, administrative changes, perennially strapped school budgets, and the like simply resigned the staff to being an A+ school in name only.

Rolling Meadow

The road to Rolling Meadow Elementary School led out of a nearby city and into the surrounding countryside. Big box retail stores and chain restaurants gave way to recently built neighborhoods with houses set closely side by side, which in turn yielded to more mature homes on more spacious lots. Eventually trees and livestock began to outnumber houses until the school itself appeared, surrounded by a satellite campus of the local community college, a rehabilitation center, and a decidedly up-scale development.

The school resided on land the district purchased in conjunction with the parks and recreation department. Thus, a softball field was at the back of the school and a soccer field at the front. Plenty of room was left for two well-appointed playgrounds. The school building—a sprawling, single-story structure—was a mere 5 years old and still had the look, feel, and smell of a new facility. Three long classroom wings sprouted off the distinctive main entrance area that housed the office, media center, cafeteria, and gymnasium. The total package gave off an aura of wealth and privilege.

This was only half accurate. The school started out that way but a merger of county and city schools altered enrollment patterns and the formerly third- through fifth-grade school with nearly all Caucasian students almost overnight became a K–5 building with a far larger number of minority children from within the city boundaries.

As part of the merger plan, each school in the new system chose an instructional focus. Faculty at Rolling Meadow voted to combine character education with the A+ Program. After all, administrators told them, the components of A+ were nothing new to the teachers. They were already integrating arts into their lessons, presenting material in multiple (and often hands-on) ways, and partnering with the community's arts council. A+, therefore, would provide an opportunity to expand arts offerings and obtain supplemental teaching materials—all without requiring major changes in practice.

The first year of A+ brought with it much more than a new program, however. The school day itself began and ended an hour later than previously, necessitating changes in before- and after-school duties, not to mention the schedule. The principal was promoted elsewhere in the system and so the school year started with a new administration. The addition of the three primary grades, in effect, doubled the number of adult and child bodies in the building. And there was the change in student diversity. Almost overnight, a medium-sized, suburban, community school became a large, less familiar, more urban one. Concomitantly, the school also experienced the cyclical swings in personnel, policy, and politics so typical of urban institutions. Turnover at all levels of the system made each subsequent year a revelation in terms of programmatic emphases and staffing. As one teacher related: "It's like being in a whole different school."

Those among Rolling Meadow's original faculty (both those from the original 3–5 building and the long-time K–2 feeder site) began to nostalgically associate A+ with the old days. One intermediate grade teacher explained: "We were doing more A+ kinds of things before A+!"

And the K–2 teachers immediately saw a natural fit with the Program, according to one of the teachers: "K–2 automatically makes us that way; it just does." A+ therefore became a symbol of stability in a sea of change.

While teachers embraced A+ emotionally and mentally agreed on the value of having instructional variety in the classroom, they had never really defined collectively what A+ meant. For example, one teacher commented that maybe the arts had too prominent a role in regular classrooms: "I am concerned that we're becoming too focused on the arts . . . and not the academics. And I know that the arts are supposed to support the academics but I have a real concern right now that that's not happening."

Another thought the issue was not emphasizing the arts more than academics but rather trying to appropriately blend the two: "A+ should be focusing on the integrated part, but also how the arts can help children excel." Other teachers indicated that the arts were best used as an instructional tool, akin to cooperative groups. A few in this group relegated the arts as one element in "a bag of tricks" to pull from to engage the lower achieving students, but most often teachers thought more broadly in terms of reaching the multiple intelligences of all their students. Not surprisingly then the teachers also expressed varying viewpoints about A+'s programmatic characteristics. For some, A+ was daily use of the arts in regular classrooms to enhance academic achievement; for others, A+ was "every child on stage" performances for parents and the community; and for still others A+ simply meant kids doing a lot of arts. Students agreed with the "a lot of arts" part. As one stated: "We have things that other schools don't have like dance and drama and stuff like that."

Despite the interpretative diversity in the building, it was apparent that all teachers had found aspects of A+ philosophy and method that they could utilize in their own classrooms. Nevertheless, adjustments in "doing A+" became necessary, each of which chipped away some at what a good number of teachers saw, from their varying vantage points, as how "we used to do it." For example, scheduling complexities associated with the school's having more adults and students seemed to rob the faculty of the spontaneity they once felt in going to each other for ideas to take advantage of "teachable moments." Collegial talk had to be planned for, in other words, rather than opportunistic. The concern was odd however in light of the fact that the schedule gave teams time to meet nearly every day should they need to do so. It was not like the teachers never ran into each other. Thus, the implicit point people were making in the complaints was not that the new schedule was wrong, but that they were generally uneasy about change.

Two additional sources of fuel fed the faculty's wariness about the school's future. One was the central office. The distance to "downtown" was more than geographic. Teachers feared that it was philosophical as well and that A+ might not be supported as strongly as in the past. The second was the state testing accountability. Test scores had always been good at Rolling Meadow. The teachers had high expectations and a track record that was difficult to beat. But they had a more diverse student body now and staff, in the upper grades especially, reported spending considerably more time and energy on test preparation.

Thus, as the dust settled at Rolling Meadow Elementary School, it was obvious that A+ had not been swept under the carpet but it did not always seem to be at the forefront of their efforts either. Getting to know new people (both young and older), meeting a wider variety of student needs, having a different schedule, feeling testing pressure, and worrying about politics all conspired to make the school's entry into A+ not the triumphant event the faculty had thought it would be. Teachers still held on to their commitment to the arts but enacting this commitment had become more difficult and frustrating.

Hillside

Hillside, a school in the Western foothills, served just over 500 K–5 students and was one of the earliest sites to become a part of A+. Its district had designated it as a "transfer" school, which meant that parents throughout the county could request to have their children assigned to Hillside as space permitted. While local lore had it that this allowed the school to get the "cream of the crop," the principal disputed this, pointing to the school's diverse population of approximately 40% African American and a little over 10% Hispanic children. Most of the latter were full-immersion, English as a Second Language (ESL) students, qualifying the school for school-wide use of its Title I money. Despite the fact that it had been a North Carolina School of Excellence for two years running, the principal expressed concern that there still was a gap between minority and majority students on the state accountability tests. The school used Title I to hire a tutor to work with low performers on testing remediation.

A notable feature of the school was that even in the face of county budget cuts, staff members wanted to maintain a sizeable cohort of classroom assistants, with one for each classroom in the primary grades and one or two for each grade thereafter. They therefore opted to use their Title I funds to pay for two teachers and five assistants. Nearly all staff in the building believed that having these extra adults in the classroom was a worthy expenditure, but the practice was not common across the other district schools.

The transfer status and the presence of the classroom assistants fed a perception among community members and educators unaffiliated with the school that Hillside was garnering an unfair share of resources and advantages. The school's participation in A+ exacerbated this unwarranted – according to faculty – view. To support the A+ goal of increasing arts teachers in each building, the Superintendent allowed Hillside to have a full-time drama teacher and refused to bow to other principals' demands that one of the necessary staffing cuts in the county be that drama position. The superintendent said that this was a commitment made to A+ and it would be honored, even though restricted funding precluded this benefit from being extended elsewhere. Having this drama teacher symbolized and solidified Hillside's "unique" standing in the district.

Hillside took pride in its building, program, and people, all the while feeling resentment from other educators who complained that the type of education being offered in the school was not replicable in their own. Parents, teachers, and students acknowledged that their building was a special place for them but stringently argued that this status stemmed from their intentional efforts to create an arts-infused school rather from special external dispensations.

And the school exhibited both a substantial arts presence and the supportive structures to sustain it. Staff members continually referred to the school as an A+ school in their conversations with visitors and placed A+ banners throughout the building. They backed up their verbal acclamations with their staffing arrangements. The drama teacher reflected the district's commitment, but within the school the administration and teacher leaders also created a "Connect Team" to enact the goal of "every art every week for every child." This ten-member group consisted of the arts and PE teachers, the media coordinator, guidance counselors, and a computer lab assistant. Together they tried to meet three times weekly and essentially took responsibility for the "visible" manifestations of the arts in the school schedule, such as hallway displays, extra-curricular trips and activities, and within school events. With their guidance, the school also had an art gallery of student work in the central foyer and soft classical music played continuously in this well-maintained focal point of the building.

Fourth- and fifth-grade students selected an additional arts class to attend once a week during a 45-minute block of time called the "Smart Block." The classes were identified by the type of "intelligence" they tapped—for example, "Body Smart" or "Drama Smart" and students could decide whether they wanted to do something they were already proficient in or something they tended to not to do so well. It was their choice.

All grade levels used a thematic approach to the curriculum, which they revised each year based on the teachers' reflections and data review from the past year's successes and failures. Their planning also indicated where in their lessons teachers would incorporate the various arts and how they envisioned using Connect Team members. A final component of their thematic approach was educators' identification of the multiple intelligences implicated in lessons and thereby assessments of which ones were being over- and/or under-utilized. Numerous teachers pointed to the units as a facilitative source of crucial instructional consistency within each grade and noted the added benefit of orienting new teachers to what the other professionals expected of them in the classroom. Ultimately these units became the means of transferring Hillside's arts commitment to subsequent generations of staff.

The grade-level teams met at least once a week, although they had common time to do so several days in that time period. A Connect Team member's schedule coincided with some of the teams' times and thus a Connect Team member met formally with each grade-level team at least once a month. Nevertheless, classroom teachers and Connect Team members alike admitted that arts teachers integrated regular subjects into the arts more than classroom teachers employed the arts in the bulk of their lessons. All of the curriculum and lesson planning enabled the Connect Team members to have a relatively in-depth understanding of the standards and content being taught throughout the year and so they felt comfortable with merging the arts with these topics in their classes. Classroom teachers were less confident, they said, guiding an arts portion of their lessons. For the most part, the teachers denied having any particular arts skills, plus they also had to be ever mindful of staying on track heading into state testing periods. A couple of Connect Team members, however, rose to their classroom colleagues' defense and claimed that while the depiction of the teachers' art use might seem spotty, most teachers were fully aware of the multiple intelligences and used them often in their lessons.

The less-than-reciprocated integration of grade-level subject matter and the arts did not dissuade staff from asserting that A+ was indeed a school-wide phenomenon. Both adults and students talked daily about the arts, and all of the students and most of the faculty actually engaged in some type of arts activity each day. Consequently, the staff reveled in their sense that the school was a special place to work.

Staff members were not without worry, however. They pondered the implications of state testing, staff turnover, and weakening central office support as much as did the other schools. What was different was their response. Instead of marshalling all of their resources and energy in a direct assault on test-identified weaknesses, the school sustained their arts focus and sought creative ways to strengthen students' test performance. For example, the administration parceled remediation to a tutoring initiative that left other teachers free to teach in the way they were accustomed and teachers formalized in writing their thematic units in part to help induct new teachers into the content and instructional activities that typified each grade level. Thus, instead of resignedly relinquishing pieces of A+ in order to meet other demands, the faculty came up with strategies that addressed their concerns *and* safeguarded the arts. Because of this, Hillside appears again in Chapter 7.

School Identities

We posited a number of possible explanations for the varying resilience of the arts in the three buildings. But from our vantage point we rendered much of the difference to organizational culture. That is, the schools varied in the extent to which arts experiences, arts integration in the classroom, and arts celebrations had been well-woven into "the way we do things around here."

Effective organizations have distinct cultures, so much so that the mere mention of the names of some of them immediately evokes clear images of the values they represent. These places continually enforce, reinforce, and thoughtfully revise widely shared definitions of purpose, exemplary practice, and visions for the future. This cycle of organization-wide reflection promotes intelligent growth, based on demonstrated strengths (Senge, 1990). Thus, the end point of attempts to change organizations is a noticeable, efficacious, and sustainable new way of doing work. "Noticeable" means that awareness of and agreement with innovative practices and policies is widely diffused throughout the enterprise; "efficacious" means that these new practices and policies enable the organization to achieve its purposes better than previous ways; and "sustainable" means that the innovations have become part of the regular patterns of operation. The devil, as the research shows, is in the detail of reshaping the culture of organizations.

So, too, with schools. Reform after reform espouses a set of appealing core beliefs about effective schooling to which all educators should adhere. Yet, the educational landscape remains bountifully blotted with the debris of mostly failed endeavors, a longstanding topic for numerous reform observers (e.g. Adkins, 1997; Cuban, 1990; Fullan, 1991; Sarason 1971, 1996). The best of reforms, it seems, leave behind mostly a mottled landscape of fresh practice, from which might spring a renewed effort at improvement in the future; the worst leave behind a tangle of frustration, disillusionment, and an avowed conviction to remain unmoved the next time the pendulum swings.

The lesson from the research on organizational change in general—and on school reform in particular—is that the most troublesome issue is not coming up with a good reason to change but rather devising an effective way of changing the culture of the place so that the new beliefs and practices infuse the day-to-day working lives of educators and students. Only through routinizing new ways of thinking and acting do new policies, programs, and practices receive a long enough trial to prove their worth. Deal and Peterson (1998), in fact, argue that shaping the culture is the central task for school leaders and the primary means for improving instructional effectiveness.

This lesson, we think, is especially pertinent for arts-based educational reforms and was demonstrated when one looks at the above three vignettes collectively. The first two schools verbalized a commitment to infusing the arts into their buildings, encouraged staff to pursue this goal and, from time to time, buttressed this encouragement with time to plan and other resources. However, arts-focused planning time and other resources shifted completely to other demands in the first school and endured a continual game of tug-of-war in the second. The third school, however, actually enacted its commitment deeply by taking numerous steps to make sure the arts became embedded consistently and thoroughly in the daily routines. Thus, regardless of "why" schools should do the arts, the perennial problem for arts advocates is figuring out how to get the arts to stick once they are introduced into a school. We think that deliberately weaving an arts identity into a school's organizational culture is probably the most promising way of doing this.

A school's identity, while not as encompassing a concept as its overall culture, concisely highlights its priorities and draws immediate attention to the most central of the values for which it stands. These are the ones that, when threatened, remain unyielding, the ones that schools tenaciously protect in the face of challenges. Jackson's defensive posture with respect to pressure to boost test scores clearly revealed the peripheral standing of the arts. Life in the bunker had no room for superfluous activity. Rolling Meadows evidenced competing values at its core rather than a communal sharpening of focus, which underscored the prominent role that distinct cadres of educators played in the building. Hillside, on the other hand, held the arts close and therefore sought creative solutions to budget cuts and other demands in order to preserve them. A school's creation of a place for the arts in its identity, therefore, is perhaps the best way to determine the likelihood of their survival in the curriculum in the future.

Three Developmental Levels of Arts Integration

During the first 4 years of the Program, schools employed various strategies to deliver arts instruction. Nearly all offered the arts daily, but the form varied by school, semester, or year—with only a few schools finding it possible to provide all four arts continuously. With limited resources (either financial or personnel or both), dance and drama were typically the two art forms either not taught or creatively offered in combination with music or PE. Some sites alternated between dance and drama or combined them into a single course, although the schools with middle and senior high grades did have a menu of arts courses that mostly covered all four of the art forms.

Besides the variety in staffing arrangements and curriculum organization, schools also had differing levels of arts integration in their regular, grade-level or subject matter courses. Partly this reflected the pragmatics of launching a large-scale program with limited resources, but partly it was also by design or adaptation. Schools ranged widely as to the degree that the arts courses reinforced the curriculum, varied in how thoroughly the arts were integrated by teachers who were not arts specialists, and generally revealed different orientations toward the arts that were used, thematic planning, curriculum integration, and parental and community involvement as well.

The schools, in other words, developed in different ways and at varying paces. The A+ Program recognized this likelihood and determinedly avoided prescribing any particular processes and activities that all schools should have used at a particular point in time. The events and communications associated with being part of the A+ network enabled the schools to hear about what others were doing and reinforced expectations such as the core commitments described earlier in this book. But the primary message was that schools needed to figure out how to best enact a commitment to arts integration within their idiosyncratic mix of circumstances.

A+ Identities

Most important, we think, is that in the process of implementing A+ in such a way so as to suit their situations, the schools defined their identities as A+ schools differently, thereby influencing how central the arts were to everyday school life. There were at least three such identities spread across the group of pilot schools:

- *Affiliative*—wherein a school adopted the formal designation of itself as an A+ building, attended the summer institute, several staff maintained contact with the Program, and the school occasionally highlighted the arts in building-wide activities.
- *Symbolic*—wherein most school staff acknowledged an appreciation of the arts, enthusiastically celebrated the arts in school-wide settings, and couched descriptions of their efforts in A+ and arts language.
- *Substantive*—wherein most school staff considered the arts in making important decisions about school operation and made repeated attempts to integrate the arts into major subject instruction and to integrate the major subjects into arts instruction.

These three ascribed places in schools' identities possibly represented movement, rather than exclusive categories, in the incorporation of the arts into schools' regular ways of working. First, all schools—by accepting their selection into the A+ Program and by participating in the initial network activities—acknowledged that they wanted to be seen as a school where the arts were more than frills. That is, staff members desired to be *affiliated* with an initiative that advocated the arts. Their motivations were varied. Some staff deeply believed in the educational value of arts-based learning, while others sought an attractive way of distinguishing their school from others in their districts. Regardless, they all accepted the increased responsibility for engaging in arts-related professional development and other network-sponsored events. Thus, even the affiliative aspect of participation required more than an "in-name-only" level of effort. However, as happened at Jackson, troubling situations tended to induce an organizational "hunkering down" that reduced participation in A+ events and removed the arts from the core curriculum.

Second, deeper than affinity, educators allowed the arts to take on more *symbolic* importance within the vast majority of the schools. They used artistic references and displays as signals about the kind of schools they wanted to be. Banners, hall displays, stationery, T-shirts and the like all announced to the community that they should expect to hear and see the arts in abundance within the school walls. Most staff members proudly noted the arts' presence; and few—in normal times—resented giving additional time to them, especially with respect to performances and "informances" (a type of presentation peculiar to A+ in which many students expressed what they were learning in school artistically but with much less practice than would have occurred with an actual performance). They also occasionally relinquished classroom time for arts-related activities and professional development. The school communities celebrated the arts and invoked them as a part of day-to-day conversations. And many of these schools viewed themselves as wholehearted believers in the arts. Yet, core content and the arts remained somewhat distant cousins, and students could still go through the day and very often encounter the arts only during their "specials." This caused teachers, like some of those at Rolling Meadow, to wonder just how committed the school and its leaders were to A+ and what would happen to the role of the arts in the face of mounting pressures to improve test scores and trim budgets.

Third, some schools' staff enabled the arts to permeate many aspects of school life. This happened at Hillside. Teachers began to dream up ways of using the arts in even the most ordinary of lessons. Groups of teachers worked together to coordinate what they were teaching and then they taught it to coincide with school-wide arts activities, and visa versa. Administrators adjusted school schedules to accommodate these activities as staff-wide professional development and planning. What was important was that these structural changes in connecting people to one another were devotedly used to further the cause of arts integration. The arts, in other words, began to play a *substantive* role in the life of some of the schools, becoming a part of their definition of quality teaching and learning, and the way that definition was enacted in the day-to-day work of administrators, students, and teachers.

Substantive identities varied from school to school. In some, teachers used the arts as a valued strategy for teaching, nearly synonymous with learning styles and multiple intelligences. In others, the arts were more an important subject for study, coequal to language arts and math. Regardless, the arts infused the thoughts and actions of most staff on a day-to-day basis. A teacher summarized this stage succinctly: "We just believe in our arts integration, and so we strive to do it."

Each level of identity had a different attachment of the arts to a school's core mission. In other words, the arts became more deeply ingrained in the minds, hearts, and actions of adults and students as one moved up the pyramid. The relationship was largely developmental, with a prior role providing a necessary foundation for the next stage. Schools, of course, did not always move forward linearly. Over time, in fact, several found that after facing a destabilizing change or external challenge that they were behind where they had been earlier.

We reiterate, then, that these differences underscore the cultural nature of school reforms and that staff's interpretations of the reform help explain its effects. The details of an arts program design, therefore, pales in importance if concomitant steps are not taken to entrench it organizationally. The lesson is that reform support for arts instruction and integration also has to include guidance for helping schools establish substantive identities and use these arts-related activities to "take charge of change" in the future (Noblit, Malloy, & Malloy, 2001).

Actions versus Commitment as Key to A+ Identities

The role that schools afforded the arts in their core identity was not simply a function of the extent to which schools implemented certain actions or aspects of the A+ Program. A school did not evolve into a substantive identity simply through adding arts teachers or holding more events. Rather, the affiliative, symbolic, and substantive categories represent the extent to which implementation reflected the depth of their commitment to the arts as a valued part of teaching and learning. So, it was not the actions but rather the staff's interpretation of those actions as an underlying commitment to the arts that separated one school from another.

As examples, we return to Jackson from the beginning of this chapter (at the level of affiliative identity) and Creekside Elementary, which appeared in Chapter 2 (at the level of substantive identity). Jackson implemented the same arrangement for its arts teachers (part-time visual arts and music teachers) as did its sister A+ school in the county— Newsome. This addition to the two schools' staff represented a significant increase in the historical availability of the arts in both buildings. However, at Newsome, the arts teachers worked closely with the regular teachers to identify ways of integrating the arts into major subject content and this relationship with the teachers continued throughout the pilot period, despite the presence of the state test. At Jackson, such integration never occurred and, as noted in the vignette at the beginning of the chapter, the arts teachers were assigned to be reading tutors for low performing students during the class periods they normally would have been holding arts classes as part of an all-out retrenchment to the "basics." Thus, the two schools adopted a programmatic aspect of A+ similarly but used this resource in sharply contrasting ways.

Creekside Elementary, like Jackson, also decided to use its arts teachers to reinforce students' academic skills. But rather than have the arts teachers tutor only the low performing students, the school teamed them with regular teachers in the intermediate grades (which were the tested grades in the state's accountability system). The principal and staff expected that increasing both the amount and variety of instruction on essential skills would benefit the students greatly. Thus, the value of the arts teachers in this school rested on how and what they taught rather than on their simply being additional available adults to work with students. Arts purists may question Creekside's concern with improving test scores, but the important point to be made here is that the arts were viewed as a desirable educational tool for helping meet the challenge of external accountability rather than being shoved aside in the face of intense pressure to improve test performance.

Thus, the depth to which educators embedded the arts in how the schools operated was not necessarily evident by simply looking at what formal components of the A+ Program the schools implemented. Depth emerged as participants used the arts in *everyday actions* and talked often with numerous people about their belief in the value of the arts and enacted those beliefs in classroom work. This meant that while particular planning meetings might have been specifically set aside for arts-related discussions, these conversations occurred at other times too informally. In fact, the notions of "everyday" and "informal" represent the best way to distinguish the substantive from the symbolic schools. Teachers in the former schools did not have to be "reminded" that the arts were a priority or "scheduled" to talk about them. The arts, in other words, had become habitual.

These habits were observable. For instance, the substantive identity schools demonstrated arts integration in a variety of classrooms on each grade level, in school-wide events, in coordination meetings, and in the schools' adaptations of the Standard Course of Study. The symbolic identity schools had more widely scattered pockets of classroom integration and less evidence of the arts being a part of formal decision-making. The affiliative identity schools tended to celebrate the arts enthusiastically in school-wide events, such as in student performances or artists-in-residence visitations, but generally left classroom integration to those with a particularly strong interest in the arts.

Based on this rubric, all of the 24 schools established an affiliation with the arts and continued to do so throughout the pilot period. Twenty of the schools devoted enough attention to the Program that the arts began to take on symbolic importance in the schools' operations. Ten of these then managed to deepen their commitment to the arts to the point that they significantly affected teaching and learning (substantive level). Figure 6.1 categorizes schools according to the role that they gave to the arts at the end of the pilot period.

Obviously the schools differed across categories, but even within categories in the pyramid schools did not look exactly the same. Albany Woods staff, for example, viewed the arts primarily as a tool for giving

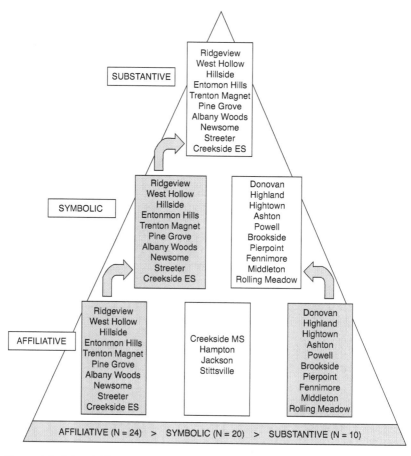

Figure 6.1 School Identities with Arts Integration

students alternative ways of acquiring, processing, and demonstrating content knowledge. Their commitment to the arts, however, was no less than in Treton Magnet where the school's formal purpose was to promote the development of students as artists, and the regular subjects served mostly to enable students to obtain the credits required for graduation. Likewise, A+ at Hillside opaquely resembled A+ at Creekside but what both had in common was a deeply abiding belief in the value of the role of arts in daily instruction.

This discussion might disappoint some readers because the chapter has not yet yielded any prescriptions for achieving substantive arts integration. This will remain the case. The spirit of A+ was that schools would work out a commitment to the arts in ways that best suited their individual circumstances. This "spirit," we think, proved justified, as all of the schools remained in the reform and almost half managed to embed the arts in sustainable ways that inured the arts from the forces that historically threatened their presence.

If there was a commonality across the substantive schools, it was the quality of "everyday-ness" that the arts enjoyed. "Everyday-ness" seemed both a cause and an effect. Early on, frequent interactions about the arts and their appropriate role in the building engendered shared definitions and expectations with respect to A+. Later, these same frequent conversations and activities served to reinforce, deepen, and broaden people's commitments to the arts.

The substantive identity schools, because they had integrated the arts into the day-to-day practice of teaching and learning, were more resilient in the face of major challenges to their reform efforts. Having an arts identity embedded in their culture, professional relationships, and patterns of work and language, substantive identity schools were able to respond creatively to both the specific needs of their local context and to external challenges such as state policy interventions. In creating responses to these challenges, substantive identity schools used their A+ identity to change— and to manage change. This means that these schools found that their A+ identity could be asserted as a solution to problems and not just defended in the face of them. The arts gave the staff ideas, practices, and connections that they used to push forward with their improvement efforts, and they coupled implementation and celebration to assert the value of the arts and their schools' A+ identities. The experiences of these schools made it clear that there was no one right way to "do A+" but the role of the arts became significantly more substantial the more that schools brought them into day-to-day activities and discussions.

Three Legitimizing Activities for Promoting the Arts in Education

We can be a little more direct with respect to how schools set the stage for being in the position of developing an arts identity in the first place. Some members of the schools that applied to be part of the pilot program had preexisting sentiments that favored the arts. But even where there were many such people in a school, the arts were not viewed universally as central to the task of improving students' academic performance. In part this was because the arts had a spotty history in North Carolina education. Although they were included in the state's BEP in the 1980s, legislative initiatives did not fund the sections of the BEP that involved the arts. Likewise, the arts were in the state's Standard Course of Study but were not included in the accountability system.

Thus, all of the A+ schools needed to get the arts back into public and political conversations about how to improve education. For the schools, this task of promoting the arts as legitimate instructional tools necessitated convincing people that the arts were essential to education, and that it would be worth the time and effort to implement various social and political arrangements that supported that belief, in addition to the instructional ones. One important strategy in legitimizing the arts was to show that they could complement rather than compete with what many viewed as the school's traditional academic mission. This preparatory work, then, served as a prelude to the energy-consuming effort needed to actually integrate the arts into the school and eventually into the school's culture. Such work generated an acknowledgment among staff that the arts could be valid instructional tools. Without this level of broadly accepted legitimacy, most classroom teachers would have been unlikely to go out on a limb by making the arts a fundamental part of their classroom practice.

Legitimizing activities tended to fall into three categories:

1. the provision of local funding to complement the money schools received from A+;
2. signs that some teachers took the arts seriously enough early on in the initiative to devote considerable time and energy to integrating the arts; and
3. noticeable efforts to promote the arts in the schools and in their communities.

Together these activities combated the notion that the arts were tangential to education in North Carolina and they engendered a degree of acceptance that the reform journeys the schools were on were worthwhile.

Local Funding Support

At the outset of the A+ initiative, schools had committed to increasing arts instruction. The ideal was for all schools to hire teachers in visual art, drama, music, and dance so that every child would have some form of arts instruction each day of the week. Although this ideal was not always achieved, every school managed to add arts teachers to their faculty. While funding from the Kenan Institute helped in this regard, the expectation was that over time the school's district would support the teachers with its own funds.

The reform literature is replete with stories of how new programs ended when the special funding that supported them dried up. The demise of these programs partially was testimony to the resource-starved nature of schools, but it was also indicative of the failure of the new program to gain in priority. Thus a critical indicator to school staff of the extent to which the arts were a local priority was the stability of the local contribution to the program. Even though local funds were relatively small, principals and staff often fought hard to retain this money because it sent an important message about the legitimacy of the arts in education. Staff and students would attend school board meetings to make the case for the arts.

At the end of the pilot period, all of the schools offered more arts to students than they had at the beginning of the reform. Few of the schools were able to achieve the goal of having weekly instruction in all four of the arts, but most of the schools did have three of the arts, as well as pockets (numerous in some cases) of frequent arts integration in the regular classrooms. The principals indicated that they and their faculties were convinced of the important contributions of the arts teachers and that they fully intended to continue to fight for those positions in the inevitable resource allocation battles that loomed ahead.

Early Implementers in the Classroom

While an unwillingness to change has many sources, the most positive interpretation of this phenomenon is that it is fed by a person or institution's failure to see how the change adds value to what they are already doing. In other words, the change does not gain sufficient professional legitimacy to warrant altering how one has always gone about one's work. For this reason, then, the degree to which regular classroom teachers in the schools began to infuse arts-based activities in their classrooms and the degree to which arts teachers adjusted their activities to support and accommodate grade-level content was indicative of their acceptance of A+ goals as worthy.

In a survey, administered after the third year of implementation, teachers in A+ schools were asked to identify which elements of the

Program they felt they had successfully incorporated into their regular classroom routines. Five such elements received the most mention:

- hands-on instruction;
- integration of art with core subject content;
- multiple intelligences;
- interdisciplinary thematic units; and
- collaborative planning among grade-level partners.

These results suggest that not only did teachers recognize the instructional value of the arts but that they had also accepted the necessity of designing and carrying out these elements in concert with colleagues. Because collaborative activities had traditionally been extremely difficult to schedule and maintain in these schools, indications that they had established a solid foothold in the organizational scheme of things was significant.

An additional sign of the extent to which the arts were becoming viewed as having a legitimate place in the schools was teachers' sense of which skills it was important for students to acquire. In the same survey, teachers were asked to rate the importance of a variety of student outcomes. These encompassed what might be best termed traditional academic skills (e.g. reading, mathematics, and writing) and workplace skills (e.g. communication, problem-solving, and teamwork). Teachers said that the latter were equally as important as the former and that the knowledge and skills they themselves had gained from participation in A+ were extremely helpful in enabling them to promote student growth in the workplace skills.

Thus, early and visible evidence that some teachers took the arts seriously had a cumulative effect on the rest of the school. Even teachers wary of the arts saw that integration was gaining a foothold in the school and that discussions of the arts were frequent and likely to continue.

Promoting the Arts

A third way that schools promoted an atmosphere of acceptance of the arts was through a willingness to promote the arts—both in the regular curriculum and the special activities in the schools and through soliciting the interest and support of others in their school communities.

Preexisting sentiments favoring the arts became reinforced and more diffused throughout schools especially through the extended planning period that the Kenan Institute required before pilot schools began program implementation. The initial 18-month planning process allowed many assumptions and biases to be identified, shared, and refined. The proposal process also allowed schools to articulate their beliefs and commitments to the centrality of the arts in education, even though in some school districts and for some school principals this is overlaid with an insistence that a school apply. Rather than imposing a top-down model, the planning process allowed A+ to be shaped from the school level, building on the beliefs and values of participants and thus enhancing the legitimacy of the Program from the outset.

Planning could go only so far in legitimating any initiative. Ultimately, it was essential that A+ demonstrated that the arts were central to education. The schools did this in a number of ways. First, as mentioned above, A+ developed a continuing public and private funding stream that enabled increased arts instruction at a level above that which the schools had initially. Second, providing professional development to all teachers each year signaled that A+ was permanently linked to the delivery of the Standard Course of Study and gave schools concrete strategies for making that link in the classroom. Third, the most powerful mechanisms for legitimating A+ for parents involved their children. Performances demonstrated to parents that the Program could develop the creative capacities of their children. Informances showed parents that the students were learning and able to express that learning in creative and artistic ways.

Finally, it is only recently that networks have been understood as vital in school reform (Lieberman & Grolnik, 1996; Wohlstetter & Smith, 2000). Networks work outside of formal organizations and exist only as long as they serve the needs of their participants (Schmidt, Scott, Lande, & Guasti, 1977). However, by spanning organizational boundaries and activities, networks can help keep alive programs that may have been in danger of being lost were an individual institution attempting the change independently. As noted earlier in the book, A+ evolved into an elaborate network that sustained the Program in spite of dramatic turnover in staff. The developing networks of schools, principals, teachers, and others also kept the arts emphasized in the schools and created a wide set of relationships linked to the arts in education. Moreover, the summer institutes and conferences created a host of informal networks among teachers within a school and among schools. A+ also promoted partnerships of various kinds. It asked schools to develop partnerships with businesses, arts and cultural agencies, and institutions of higher education. While partnerships with higher education were the most difficult, all of these partnerships had the arts as the basis of their existence. These various kinds of connections gave individual A+ teachers and schools the sense of participation in a larger movement, a commitment that reinforced their actions in times of challenge.

Conclusion

Against this backdrop of activities that elevated the arts to having a legitimate claim in daily instruction, the A+ schools were in a position to implement their versions of the Program and to deepen their commitment to the arts to the point that staff regarded them as customary elements in the classroom. As with individual identity, the roles that the arts played in the schools' identities were somewhat fluid. Some schools occasionally flirted with moving further along in the centrality of the arts, only to have some event thwart this. In fact, as we have shown, the most telling way of determining the depth of the role that the arts played in a school was what happened when the school faced some event potentially disruptive to its current direction.

Both administrator and staff turnover and the state's accountability program offered crucibles for testing pilot schools' commitments to the arts. Characteristics of the A+ Program such as a supportive network, extensive professional development, and stable funding helped all of the schools retain an affiliation with the Program. However, neither the affiliative nor the symbolic levels of identity were strong enough to keep the arts flourishing in the face of state-wide testing pressures. Only the schools that had reached the substantive level, integrating the arts into their educational identity, were able to do that.

The three types of roles for the arts served as signposts along the way to embedding the arts in schools' identities—with the culminating point being a school's willingness and ability to rebuff internal and external forces to dislodge the arts from occupying a spot among the school's treasured priorities. This returns the discussion to this chapter's starting point: the significance of infusing philosophical and structural changes in the ongoing culture of a school. When this happens, change has a much greater chance of receiving a full trial and eventually becoming an automatic part of the way people work. And the fate of the arts has a much happier ending when their protection becomes a stronger reflex than their ouster.

But it is important to point out that while many arts and education initiatives often see arts as instrumental in promoting learning in other subjects (Winner & Hetland, 2000), A+ eventually used the arts to reform schools. The Program started out to promote the arts and art education with the intention that this would also contribute to improved academic achievement. But, as the schools learned about and from the A+ Schools Program, those who were developing substantive identities with A+ began to see possibilities for their future that were not envisioned originally. This set of schools was able to use participation in the Program to improve how they thought about and practiced A+ instruction and how they asserted A+ as an organization to reduce uncertainty in their environments. Reform, in schools like these, is sustainable because the participants know how to change themselves in the face of possibilities and challenges. Thus, in the end, what the substantive identity schools shared was making the arts central to learning at both individual (student and teacher) and organizational levels.

Chapter 7

Sustaining Arts-based School Reform[1]

This chapter is the story of what happened in the A+ arts-infused school reform initiative after the pilot funding ended. We interviewed key leaders of all the schools to reassess their cultural identities.[2] We then paid visits to a subset of schools where a substantive identity remained, or in one case, emerged.[3] Thus, in this chapter we address the critical question of whether and how arts-based reform sustains itself.

We begin this chapter by updating the context in which arts-based reform continued to unfold in North Carolina—with declining support by the Kenan Institute, school staff turnover, and increasing accountability brought on by the state testing program. Yet, schools continued to incorporate the arts into their instructional programs. We offer four cases, describing what and how the arts were sustained, as well as an assessment of future prospects. We conclude with an explanation of how arts-based reform adds a different perspective to the issues of school reform sustainability.

The Context for Reform in the A+ Schools—The Pressures After the Pilot Phase

When the pilot period was complete, important changes took place within the A+ Program. While funding direct to the schools was always quite limited and often came too late to be used effectively, direct funding had been repeatedly reduced and ceased entirely as the pilot ended. Indeed, the original contract signed by the school districts to take over funding the local A+ efforts proved to be null and void. Some districts did allow the A+ schools to have more time with shared arts teachers than other schools. Yet the press to equalize resources across schools in districts meant that most A+ schools not only lost whatever A+ gave them directly but also any special considerations the districts had allowed over the pilot period. This press to equalize has little to do with A+ in particular. Metz (1986), for example, in her book, *Different by Design*, documents the power of this press even when a district is committed to magnet schools that have specialized programs and disparate needs. As she revealed, there is a politics in districts around treating schools equally and this works against efforts to make and keep schools that are somehow distinct. In this A+ was no exception. Yet the demise of extra resources was not the death knell to A+.

The schools were also asked to increasingly pick up the costs of professional development, especially paying for their teachers' expenses. The home base for A+ moved from the Kenan Institute for the Arts and into the University of North Carolina at Greensboro. It was expected from the beginning that A+ would be "spun out" of the Kenan Institute, but as the staff Institute learned more about school reform they were concerned that moving the Program out of the Institute would not lead to a sustainable reform effort. In part, the Kenan staff learned more about how different reform efforts "packaged" themselves in order to survive over the long haul. The fickle world of school reform taught the Kenan staff that most reforms waned in schools after about 3 years as priorities changed and as the annual costs of the reform mounted up. The Kenan staff saw A+ as a "process" rather than a product that could be sold to schools. Thus the most prevalent models of school reform sustainability seemed to be poor guides to them. Contracting with school districts to provide a package of services violated the existing relationships A+ had worked so hard to build. Network leaders did find the National Writing Project model interesting; they attended some meetings of the National Writing Project and found kindred souls. As a result, the Kenan staff seriously considered disseminating A+ through the National Writing Project. Yet they also came to realize that the distinctive contribution of the arts to school reform would be muted by such a collaboration. The lesson to be drawn was that A+ as an arts program needed to develop its own way to sustain the reform.

In the end, the "spinning out" of A+ was due to a change in priorities on the Board of the Kenan Institute. While foundations in other parts of the nation were intrigued with what a philanthropic organization had achieved with A+, the Kenan Board was changed to allow it to be more closely aligned with advancing the efforts of the North Carolina School of the Arts. Thus A+ left along with the staff leadership of the Institute. There was transition funding provided to allow A+ to become a self-sustaining organization at its university-based home. While it is clear that the A+ Schools Program will need to develop its own funding to survive, the A+ network exists as the basis of the effort and thus A+ has not had to turn itself into a school reform "package." Rather the network now (in 2007) funds itself using local school, state, and grant funds.

Turnover in principals and teachers continued to characterize the schools after the pilot period. Indeed, one of the laments of the principals was that they always have new teachers that need to be oriented and prepared to "do A+." Yet as happened in the pilot period, this turnover has not taken the toll it often does with school reforms.

Similarly, high-stakes testing has not waned. Indeed, with the No Child Left Behind federal legislation, the press of accountability policy has actually become heightened. Nevertheless, the A+ schools resoundingly declare one of the things that makes A+ sustainable is that "it works" both in terms of making schooling more interesting and in terms of raising test scores. We investigated achievement among the A+ schools, as measured by North Carolina's ABCs high-stakes testing program. We believe that high-stakes testing generates its own pattern of results and do not want to overplay the contribution of school reforms to such testing outcomes. Yet as we argued in Chapter 5, the A+ schools took these data to mean that their approach was productive. In recent focus groups discussions, principals and A+ coordinators repeatedly noted: "It works!" The reference here is more than test scores but clearly includes them as well. As with the pilot period, the patterns after the pilot period paralleled the pilot results: high gains were followed by less significant gains. Yet none of the A+ schools were low performing and almost all received some recognition as Schools of Progress, Schools of Distinction, or Schools of Excellence. In Table 7.1, we report the data for the year coinciding with the most recent assessment of A+ cultural identity. The table also shows a pattern worth noting. That is, relative success in the high-stakes testing is related to the degree to which A+ and the arts are integral to the school's identity. The only "no recognition" school is Creekside Middle School. This is the school we will discuss later in this chapter as a case of the "regeneration" of A+.

Table 7.1 A+ Schools: ABCs Results 2002–2003

	School Identity with A+ in Pilot		
	Substantive	Symbolic	Affiliative
Schools of Excellence	3	2	0
Schools of Distinction	5	3	1
Schools of Progress	0	3	2
No Recognition	0	0	1
Low Performing	0	0	0

Notes: ABCs definitions for 2002–2003: "School of Excellence" designation is 90%+ at/above grade level *and* expected/high growth achieved; "School of Distinction" designation is 80% of students at or above grade level and includes criteria of achieving at least expected growth; "School of Progress" designation given if the school has 60%–80% of students at or above grade level *and* achieves at least expected growth; "No Recognition" designation is 60% of students at or above grade level but school didn't achieve expected growth; "Low Performing" designation given if the school has less than 50% of students at or above grade level *and* fails to meet their expected growth and standards.

Given the above threats, how is the sustainability of A+, entrenched in its second decade of existence, to be understood? This chapter explores that question. Our argument lies in the special nature of A+ as an instance of school reform. This chapter examines recent case studies of four substantive identity A+ schools, several years after the pilot period, to determine what aspects of the initiative have given A+ its relatively unique staying power as a school reform venture.

Before considering the cases of schools, though, it is important to unpack sustainability as a concept. At first glance, it would seem to be self-evident. Sustaining something means you keep doing it. However, this assertion of constancy belies the real world of organizations, which exist in changing contexts and with changing personnel. This is one of the reasons that the sustainability of school reform is always at issue. It is much desired but much less often accomplished, and part of that is because we have not understood the complex work that sustaining school reform entails.

A Perspective on Sustaining School Reform—A Review of the Literature

In part, the interest in sustainable school reform is economic. How can states and the federal government justify spending money changing schools if the changes wither over time? Part of this question though involves an unfortunate assumption that school reform is appropriately a one-time expenditure of time and money. Fix the problem and it should no longer be a problem. Yet there is another possibility that this assumption obscures. After years of studying a wide variety of school reforms, we believe that for schools to sustain improvements the increased resources that were needed to establish the improvements also need to be sustained. Some A+ proponents may argue that A+ is a partial exception to this conclusion. Nevertheless, sustaining A+ does require sustained additional resources. The A+ network is an example of sustained additional resources in itself, even if it is not of similar type or scale to other school reform organizations.

But sustaining school reform is more than just an economic consideration. The American public wants schools to be better places for their children. What this means, however, has produced little agreement. Labaree (1997) has argued that schools serve three purposes and these actually exist in some tension with each other: democratic equality, social mobility, and social efficiency. Moreover, the political rhetoric about improving test scores has hidden this multiplicity as well as misrepresented the actual achievements of students. Berliner and Biddle (1997) and Bracey (1997) clearly demonstrated that achievement had been steadily increasing for U.S. students. They argued that much of the rhetoric of the accountability movement is actually disinformation aimed at creating political capital. There have been problems to be sure, but not the problems that are being articulated to the American public. This raises the concern that school reform itself is a solution without a problem that needs to be addressed. Playing this out further, there may be little reason to sustain such senseless activity. We, in fact, agree with Berliner and Biddle (1997) and Bracey (1997) and see the political machinations around school improvement and reform as simply that—using the public's concerns about their children as a way to shift power arrangements in our society.

The multiplicity of purposes that Labaree (1997) described suggests to us that what is actually needed is thorough and public discussion of what interests are being served in the politics that have come to characterize school reform. That said, there is also reason to be heartened by the efforts of hundreds of schools the research team has studied in various projects to make themselves better places for children. Thus, the state and national politics of school reform have seemed to miss the point. Sustaining school improvement efforts is important because it means that local schools can build on their own efforts. As sociologists, we are convinced that efforts at the level of schools and classrooms are the ones that count. While some might worry that this means that different schools would do things differently and thus not all children would equally benefit, there is ample evidence that schools are "institutionalized" organizations (Scott, 1995) and actually vary little from school to school. Further, when school participants are able to invest in what they value, it produces positive effects (Noblit & Dempsey, 1996). Hopefully, this book will help individual schools and districts better sustain their efforts to do what their constituencies value, even if there is reason to be somewhat cynical about the politics that surround educational reform.

This review highlights the fact that for all the concern over sustaining school reform, there are few empirical studies of sustainability. For the most part, the literature on reform has concentrated on implementation. (See Desimone, 2002 for a summary of this literature.) Moreover, these studies may be poor guides for understanding sustainability. Borman, Hewes, Overman, and Brown (2003) conducted a meta-analysis of studies of comprehensive school reform and found that the studies are concentrated on schools with an average of only 3-years' experience with the reform efforts. Moreover, strong effects are most evident after 5-years' experience with the reform efforts. They were careful to argue that the latter finding may be the result of only schools that experience success with the particular reform effort staying with it over more years (and this is not the case with A+), but the important issue is that not much is known about sustained reforms. They also reviewed previous studies and summaries of research and argued that the effects of a reform are dependent on successful implementation of the reform; that externally developed reforms that are rather delineated clearly tend to have better fidelity in implementation; that well-implemented reforms have strong professional development components and follow-up to address specific problems in implementation in classrooms; and that educators "must support, buy into, or even help co-construct the reform design" (p. 131). A+ seems to fit the latter characterizations rather well but did not structure itself as an externally defined reform or expect fidelity. A+ then may teach rather different lessons about school reform and its sustainability because of its approach.

The uniqueness of the A+ approach becomes more evident when examining the literature on reform and sustainability more closely. Moffett (2000), for example, argued that what sustains change in schools is already known. To manage change a district should develop a reform-support infrastructure; nurture professional communities; reduce turnover; and use facilitators to build capacity. The lessons about professional development included: provide abundant staff development, balance pressure with support, provide adult learning time, and reduce fragmentation and overload. Moffett concluded that "we know enough to act" (p. 38) but it is clear that the context is forced change. These lessons then were derived from a context where people must comply and thus sustainability involves keeping the pressure on complying. This is a limited definition of change. In this argument there is also an inadequate conceptualization of sustaining change. Here the notion seems to be that if one forces people to do something for long enough that they will modify their behavior. This behavior modification approach to sustainability, of course, is subject to all the limitations of behavior modification itself. Teachers' cynicism about reform is precisely related to this type of approach, especially when the particular reforms are set aside every so many years as administrators and political priorities change. Teachers and principals learn simply not to invest in reforms. Sustaining school reform then would seem to require a different approach—one that instead of "keeping the pressure on" involves harnessing the power educators have to do what they value.

The concept of sustainability is conceptually confounded as well. Some authors equate sustainability with institutionalization and/or structural change. Greenfield (1995), for example, argued in her study of 39 local school improvement efforts that change was more likely to be institutionalized under certain conditions. These included when: (1) there was sufficient leadership to define the change as permanent rather than an innovation; (2) the change focus is modest and focused on enhancement rather than substantive change; (3) whole staffs are expected to participate; and (4) provisions are made for institutionalization, especially funding continuity after the initial grant. Curry (1991) argued that it is institutionalization that accounts for sustainability: "It is with institutionalization, the final phase of the change process, that an innovation or program is said to be fully integrated into the structures of the organization . . . an innovation receives its staying power" (p. 1). However, this focus on institutional and structural change has a downside. Oldford (1998), for example, argued that "the greater the external resource support at the implementation stage, the less likely it is that institutionalization will occur when funding is terminated" (p. 9). Prestine (2000) in her qualitative study of four Essential Schools involved in a reform process since 1989 concluded: "Evidence seems to be accumulating that lofty visions, grandiose plans, and elaborate schemes . . . may have provided high melodrama and little else" (p. 143). Indeed, if a reform becomes institutionalized it is no longer remarkable in everyday practice, but this is also the case if a reform was simply rejected by the school. The same data can indicate either institutionalization or rejection of a reform. For her, the focus on institutionalization can also lead to goal displacement where the efforts are focused on making the reform permanent rather than making it work for students. Nevertheless, there seems to a consensus as represented by Fullan and Miles (1992) that "the failure to institutionalize an innovation and build it into the normal structures and practices of the organization underlies the disappearance of many reforms" (p. 748).

Elmore (1992, 1995) offered a perspective on structural change that is sobering. He noted that there is a significant gap between changes in organization and changes in educational practice and is skeptical that changes in one lead consistently to changes in the other (Elmore, 1992). Further, he argued that reformers like to focus on structural change for reasons of their own (Elmore, 1995). He offered three primary reasons for reformers to focus on structural change. First, he argued that reformers focus on structures to signal they are serious about change. Second, and ironically, structures are easier to change than, for example, the deepseated beliefs of teachers about how to teach. Third, reformers believe that structures are largely deterministic, both constraining and making possible certain types of teaching practices. Empirical studies, however, showed that "changing structure has a slippery and unreliable relationship" (p. 26) to changes in teaching and learning. He then suggested that reformers might better start with teachers and teaching beliefs and practices and then create the organizational structures that are appropriate. Of course, this process flies in the face of the current context of reform in which teachers themselves are demonized.

The concept of sustainability is also affected by the expansionist logic of externally driven school reform. This is seen, for example, in the concept of "scaling up" (Elmore, 1996) in which the concern is moving from a test of an externally designed reform in a small set of schools to a wider set. The expansionist logic assumes that when a reform package is field tested and refined in a few schools that this is a reasonable basis on which to "scale up" to a much larger set of schools. In a special issue of *Education and Urban Society* (1996), scaling up is closely examined. Yet the overall lesson is not heartening. For scaling up to successfully result in the institutionalization of externally driven reforms, new resources, system alignment across levels and between standards and assessments, support networks, focus on teaching and learning and a sound restructuring model are all necessary. As Stringfield and Datnow (1998, p. 274), conclude: "[W]ithout these important elements, scaling up reforms is unlikely to result in meaningful changes for students." Each of these elements is expensive in time and money, implying that successful, sustained school reform requires as a prerequisite the scaling up of permanent funding and other resources. This is, of course, contrary to the oft-heard claim of policy makers that "throwing money at schools will not solve the problem."

Corbett and Wilson (1998) approached the issue of scaling up from a different vantage point. Their concern was with what students experience in the classroom. Their research showed that students saw their learning as dependent on teachers' willingness to help, ability to be strict but nice, ability to explain clearly the content and assignments, and structuring learning as projects and experiments that allow students to work together. While these are elements of some reform packages, it is also clear that the press to expand reforms across a number of schools works against the deepening of a reform within the school. They argued:

> Our concern is that the pressure to reform in this country will gloss over these within-school differences in favor of demonstrating that promising practices can be "scaled up" to a large number of reforms. That is, there is a danger in reforming too quickly and too grand a scale leaving important classroom variations to remain, with the end result being lots of schools reflecting the all-too-familiar "pockets of success" implementation pattern.
>
> (Corbett & Wilson, 1998, p. 288)

Other researchers agree that teachers are the key factor in successful reform and in sustaining reform. Olsen and Kirtman (2002) argued that the teacher is the mediator of the reform, and without an understanding of teacher experiences, expertise, assumptions, career cycle, point of entry into the reform cycle, personal relationships, and personal interests, reform is unlikely to get beyond the pockets of success Corbett and Wilson discuss. Others argued that the ways to address these elements are to allow teachers considerable time to learn, experiment, and reflect on the reform (Adelman & Walking-Eagle, 1997). Moreover, time continues to be necessary after a reform is firmly implemented. Time is needed for "vigilance" (p. 104) and deepening the understanding of the reform. Time is necessary for learning about a reform but also for developing an interpretation of the reform. Hendricks-Lee, Soled, and Yinger (1995) found that the nature of interpretation of a reform was key in how the reform eventually played out. They argued reforms that were conceived as linear and tightly defined led to teachers being unable to envision what change implied and ultimately to rejecting such reforms. Yet a metaphoric definition of reform led to teachers being able to envision and communicate what change meant for themselves and for their teaching. It also led to teachers seeing themselves as learners and this has important effects: "[T]eachers who see themselves as learners create a supportive environment and are much better prepared for the massive challenges, the continual setbacks, and the incremental successes that enduring educational reform entails" (p. 289).

Clearly, there is a tension in the literature on sustaining reform between those who see sustainable reform as primarily an externally driven process that focuses on restructuring schools to change teacher practice and those who focus on teacher beliefs and practices as the prerequisite for more structural change. Yet, drawing a simplistic line between externally and internally designed reform or between process- or package-type reforms seems misguided (see Slavin, 2001). Shields and Knapp (1997) argued rather that there is a delicate balance, for example, between top-down and bottom-up forces in successful school reform. That is, sustaining school reform is a complex process and as noted above unlikely to deliver on grandiose claims.

Century and Levy (2002) bring some clarity to the confusion. First, they distinguished between maintenance and sustainability. Maintenance for them was focused on fidelity and making a reform "as designed, into a standing operating system" (p. 4). In their research, maintenance was confounded with the necessity to "continually adapt and improve them" (p. 4). Sustainability, Century and Levy argued, has three phases: establishment, maturation, and evolution. Sustainability is accomplished by first ensuring the reform is well-established. Next the reform must mature into habitual forms of action and ultimately the reform must evolve—both grow and improve. As a result, Century and Levy saw sustainability as: "The ability of a program to maintain its core beliefs and values and use them to guide program adaptations to changes and pressures over time" (p. x). Thus they revealed the tensions that surround the concept of sustainability, and also demonstrated that sustainability is both change and stasis. This corresponds rather closely to nature of substantive identity A+ schools discussed earlier.

A historical perspective may also help here. Kirst and Meister (1985) examined the history of secondary school reform and noted that reforms that last are of particular types. First, those that add new structures or personnel to existing structures tended to last longer. Second, innovations that fit within existing forms of organization were more likely to last over time. Third, reforms that are easier to monitor for compliance tended to be more sustainable. Yet reforms that call for new skills to be taught or for teachers to do more were less likely to last, as are reforms "imposed on teachers from a central authority and were destined for universal application with children" (p. 178). Cuban has argued that incremental reform is more likely to last than fundamental reform (1992a, 1992b). In this he argued that sustained school reforms "enhance, not disturb, the existing structures," "are easy to monitor," and "create constituencies that lobby for continuing support" (1992b, p. 171). In addition, the relative ambiguity of a reform may also contribute to its sustainability in that ambiguity of purpose allows institutions to adapt it to their own purposes and to respond to changing needs of constituencies. O'Neil (2000) agreed with Kirst and Meister above when arguing that "reforms that have the *least* potential for sticking are those that try to bring about changes in teaching, primarily because those innovations are often proposed by policymakers and officials who know little about classrooms as work places" (p. 8).

Such an historical perspective does not leave one sanguine about the prospects of the current wave of school reform writ large. The emphasis on structural change, as opposed to the addition of structures, the emphasis on narrowly defined goal of achievement, and the emphasis on imposition of universal practices all suggest that school reform as currently conceived is unsustainable. In this, A+ can prove instructive to policy makers, researchers, reformers, educators, and the general public. While it started with a specified set of "commitments," it moved to embrace adaptation rather quickly. Thus, it may be that Century and Levy's (2002) conceptualization was premised in reforms that have a fidelity requirement of a particular and enduring kind. A+ is a more grassroots reform than many (Gerstl-Pepin, 2001). It came into existence as a collaborative venture and is more facilitative than directive. It has more added structures such as the A+ network, the A+ fellows, summer institutes, and school-based coordinators. A+ focuses on teacher practices, a potential worry given the above, but these are largely designed by teachers. A+ represents a collaboration of constituencies that included arts agencies, philanthropic organizations, arts educators, and schools and school districts. It does little external monitoring in the service of allowing local adaptation, even though schools use A+ discursively to describe and value teaching practices. In short, A+ may allow us to understand sustainability of arts-based educational reform even as it exists as a critique of the national school reform agenda.

To examine sustainability in the context of the A+ reform, we revisited four schools that completed the pilot phase with a substantive identity. One of those—Creekside Elementary—became the case that introduced the book. In the remaining three schools we describe what has been sustained and how it has sustained. But in contacting all the schools, we also found one school had made a dramatic change from affiliated over most of the pilot period to a substantive identity afterward, according to observers. This "regeneration" school is Creekside Middle School. All these case studies were derived from data collected 8 years after A+ was first implemented in the schools and 4 years after systematic data collection for the evaluation ended.

Sustaining A+ in Schools: Pine Grove Middle Case Study

Pine Grove Middle is a small middle school (350 students) located in the Southern Piedmont region of the state. It is a grade 6–8 school, located in the center of a small, rural community of 1,000 inhabitants. The principal referred to the small town as a bedroom community to the larger county seat, located 10 miles to the North.

The Definition of Arts Integration at Pine Grove

The most notable feature of the instructional program at Pine Grove is the afternoon discovery course offerings—a diverse mix of hands-on and arts-based experiences. As the principal noted, "everyone in this school is united around a common goal—providing students with a variety of learning opportunities." This is reflected in the mission statement:

> We at Pine Grove Middle, are committed to providing an enriching, nurturing environment and a challenging curriculum while educating the whole child through continuous improvement, self-reflection, and the ability to adapt to change. We will prepare our children to become life-long learners who function successfully in an ever-changing society.

Note that in this approach the arts are not necessarily the primary vehicle for adding variety, but they are certainly an important one. Since Pine Grove became an A+ school they have diligently moved to enhance the proportion of arts-based course offerings during the afternoon discovery time slot. Each student is given the option of selecting three classes per 9-week marking period. Over the course of the school year students are able to select as many as 12 different courses. The catalogue of course offerings includes an impressive array of 142 courses organized by academic discipline (e.g. 18 math courses and 15 dance classes). Two required courses are mandated at the sixth- and seventh-grade levels (computer and health) and one in the eighth grade (computer). In addition, students are expected to take four courses from the core academic disciplines each year (math, science, language arts, and social studies) and one arts class. At a minimum, then, students will be exposed to one arts-related class a year.

But in reality, since 40% of the course offerings are arts-related (including some in the core disciplines), students typically enroll in four to six arts-related classes a year. Some sample descriptions of these arts-based offerings include:

> MULTICULTURAL DANCE CELEBRATION: Students will observe and evaluate peers with weekly in-class performances based on concepts learned. Students design their own dance through the use of improvisations.

> BECOMING COMPOSERS: Students will learn about musical periods in history and the composers. They will learn to compare "then to now." They will also write a song about themselves.

But A+ is more than just enhancing arts offerings. Another key aspect is looking for ways to encourage integration across subjects. Approximately one-quarter of all the discovery courses involve multiple disciplines of inquiry (as defined by catalogue cross-discipline entries). Sample descriptions include:

> THE NAVIGATOR: Students will review important geography skills as they use United States and World maps to identify specific locations. Activities focus on the kinds of maps, map scales, symbols, and geographic terms.

> MY ROOTS, MY LIFE AND MY DREAMS: Students will investigate their heritage, heighten their awareness of their present life, and contemplate the possibilities of their future. Each student will create a Lifebook, which will include a scientific study of the student's family, an artistic expression of life as he or she sees it now, and a poetic portrayal of the student's aspirations.

The afternoon discovery offerings also included developmental courses in reading and math (e.g. rudiment of math and reading, end-of-grade math and reading) targeted for students who are at risk of failing the state tests (end-of-grade tests, the elementary grade tests for the ABCs). While this could be viewed as a tracking device that denies equitable access to more enriching and diverse arts-based and hands-on courses, this was not the case for one student with whom we raised the issue:

> While the school picked some of my electives, I volunteered for others. [Did you find the extra reading classes helpful?] Definitely. It helped with organizing the main ideas of a story and I learned new reading strategies. For example, I now understand about things like metaphors and hyperbole.

The biggest boost for the arts at Pine Grove came with a federal magnet grant. This allowed them to renovate the school, adding a fully equipped dance studio, piano/keyboard lab, robotics and computer lab, TV/ video production studio, and an upgraded stage and auditorium area, in addition to the previously appointed art and band rooms. The grant was also used to hire full-time arts teachers. During the grant they added full-time drama, dance and technology teachers, and a half-time TV production teacher. This complemented their existing half-time art and music teachers. During the full grant funding period, these arts teachers taught their discovery classes in the afternoon. In the morning they were paired with core subject teachers to plan and implement curricula that infused the arts into the core subjects.

Funding from the large federal magnet grant has ended, but the diverse course offerings during the afternoon discovery periods remain in place. All the teachers, arts and core subject, share in teaching these classes. Without direct prompting, students waxed eloquent about the different kinds of opportunities afforded them in the discovery classes:

> This year was better than I expected, especially the afternoon electives. [Why?] Because it was fun. [What did you do that was different?] In my drama class I got to get up on the stage for the first time and perform in front of others. I also learned about stage direction, props, and costumes.
>
> I like electives. It gives me more opportunity to express my feelings and the arts. They give you elective sheets and you have electives to choose from [and] different subjects for different activities. I feel like a college student and like I can make decisions about life.

Several of the arts-based staff have been forced to part-time positions, but they still have a central presence in the school. They are in the building each afternoon (or for a 9-week intensive block of time), and several of them have been given opportunities to teach in the core subjects, allowing them to maintain their full-time status.

The school also continues to play an active role in the ongoing work of the A+ network. The school has five fellows who provide training and technical assistance to other A+ schools. Both the principal and the coordinator also regularly attend the semi-annual meetings directed by A+. Teachers also share a continued enthusiasm for the summer institutes where they have the opportunity to learn new teaching strategies, share with others what worked and did not work, and gain support for their efforts.

The school also continues to take advantage of its A+ designation. In the main entry hall there is a big banner that pronounces the "8 ways to be smart." While neither the formal school name, the home page of the school's website, the school's mission statement, nor the new principal's letter of greeting mentions it's A+ classification, most other documents (e.g. the school's course description guide) highlight that it is a "North Carolina A+ School." And when chatting with the principal who guided the school through the last 4 years of improvement, she was very intentional when saying "A+ is our school improvement model." She went on to describe how on the first day of school for the teaching staff last year she purposefully modeled a hands-on, arts-based jigsaw activity to remind everyone that the arts were still a central part of what the school is all about. The A+ project director suggested that their arts focus is what has made them a "model for the nation," citing two national initiatives where the school has received recent attention (an Annenburg video project on arts integration in middle schools and a series of case studies by the Arts Education Partnership in Washington, DC on high-poverty schools that are using the arts to improve performance).

There is still carryover from the arts teachers having worked with core subject teachers. This is enhanced by the fact that the staff is very stable, so there are few new staff without the arts infusion experience in the building. One of the arts teachers who worked with almost all of the classroom teachers during the morning when funding was available for her to do so, suggested that about one-quarter of her core subject colleagues were naturally infusing the arts in the their lessons and needed very little help in making that happen. About an equal number embraced her presence and worked collaboratively with her to develop lessons and units that enabled students to demonstrate content learning via the arts. The remaining half were more comfortable letting the arts teachers take the lead while they watched. After some time, half of those teachers eventually became comfortable offering some arts-infused lessons. So, in the end nearly three-quarters of the staff are actively and regularly using the arts in the core subjects and that percentage remains stable even without the regular presence of arts teachers. An example offered by the art teacher of an initially reluctant math teacher involved his recent inquiry about how he could get some Escher prints since he was doing a unit on tessellations. Prior to A+ this veteran high-school trained teacher would never have considered incorporating art into his lessons. Thus arts integration may still be working its way through the staff even without collaborative planning.

Students confirmed this assessment of arts-infused instruction when they indicated that in approximately three out of every four core classes they encountered some arts-based learning. Not unexpectedly, some students encountered more arts infusion than others. For example, one eighth-grade student reported no arts opportunities in two of her four core classes and only doing drawing in the other two, while another eighth grader routinely did a variety of arts in all four classes. Students also noted that the definition of doing arts varied from just drawing pictures of word problems in math to a more elaborate description of how the class "walked a number line so we could visualize it." But what best captured the experience at Pine Grove was the illustration by one of the magnet students who traveled an hour by bus to get to the school when his neighborhood school was across the street from his home. When asked what was different about Pine Grove and why he would endure long bus rides every day, he simply said: "In the other middle school they just read the story, while here we get to act it out."

There are things that have not been sustained as well including thematic units across grade levels, team planning for arts integration, and school-wide professional development involving the arts and arts integration. Without the grant funding, the school relies on A+ summer institutes for its professional development. The stable staff has meant that arts integration and an arts focus remains, but this is based in individual teachers continuing the practice.

How the Arts are Sustained at Pine Grove

There are a number of factors that help explain why the arts and their integration with other subjects remain a core part of Pine Grove Middle. Faculty, students, and administrators discussed seven such factors during our visit in May 2003. It goes without saying that there is a complex web of influences that help sustain the arts. A+ is not the sole contributor, but it had a hand in all of these.

First, there is no other arts outlet in the county—no theater, museum, or concert hall. So the school becomes the community place for the arts. The adults in the community recognize this both by sending their children long distances to the school, attending events, and voicing their beliefs about the special value in such a school to local board members. One teacher even suggested that it is the glue that continues to hold the rural, economically and commercially depressed area together. Another teacher volunteered that townspeople come to performances at the school and to open houses even when they have no relatives attending Pine Grove. They just come to enjoy the arts. The art teacher shared how an elderly woman with some valuable, private cultural artifacts asked the school to house them since that was the most public and secure place for them to be displayed.

Second, staff believed that their continued involvement in A+ meetings was vital to their continuation. The principal and coordinator attend meetings twice a year and the teachers tailor training for their specific needs at summer institutes held at the school.

Third, the school continues to aggressively seek grants to help the school support its discovery vision. For example, this past year they used a North

Carolina Arts Council grant to bring back the drama teacher for 9 weeks to do a big stage production. During that brief time in the building she managed to actively involve 60 students (about 20% of the student population) and she made sure the work was integrated with other subjects. There was also talk, on the day of our visit, that the school would soon be eligible again to apply for another federal magnet grant.

Fourth, the school has been creative about finding ways to employ their arts teachers, even if just part-time. Several teachers were adamant (although the principal did not see it as being so important) that the very dynamic drama instructor was a real driving force. This year she was employed only to do a single stage production but she hopes to return in a more regular role. The technology teacher is now hired as a teaching assistant, but she hopes to have new certification so she can be hired back as a core subject teacher.

Fifth, staff stressed the importance of having the arts teachers become part of the regular classroom teacher's experience. During the federal grant they did that by having the arts teachers rotate in the morning into the core subjects and help the classroom teachers infuse their content with arts activities. This is no longer possible, but several of those staff are still in the building during the entire school day. The school managed to accomplish that by encouraging the arts teachers to get multiple teaching certifications. So the dance teacher now teaches language arts in the morning while the art teacher just obtained certification to teach science. Even the core subject teachers have been willing to diversify their teaching responsibilities with one teacher willing to teach some music classes and another learned how to take over videography instruction. As the teacher who directed the now expired magnet program suggested, a cooperative enthusiasm pervades the place: "I have never been in a movement that is so sustainable. It has taken over the spirit of the school."

Sixth is the outside recognition the school gets for its efforts. This helps fuel the positive spirit in the building and keeps the staff motivated. Again, the school just finished shooting for a video being produced by the Annenberg Institute for School Reform on the role of the arts in school reform; the Arts Education Partnership in Washington, DC selected the school as one of several case study schools for an investigation of the role of the arts in improving achievement in high-poverty schools; the North Carolina Arts Alliance and Kennedy Center just gave them awards; and, of course, A+ researchers keep coming back to visit them.

Seventh, there are a number of experienced staff in the building who enthusiastically embrace arts infusion, including four National Board Certified Teachers and five A+ fellows. They represent a strong leadership and normative influence on the rest of the faculty. They, along with the building leadership, promote and support a strong camaraderie among the staff.

The Future Prospects for Arts Infusion at Pine Grove

There is ample evidence of strong leadership among the teaching staff and enthusiasm both among students and the community for arts-infused instruction to continue at Pine Grove. However, one large unknown is a change of building leadership. Several teachers believed the recently appointed (at least at the time of our visit in May 2003) new principal was open and did not want to change everything. But new leadership brings questions and unknowns. First, teachers were concerned because they had no input in the principal hiring decision. Does that mean their voice is being muted? Second, the new principal knows nothing about A+ and supporting it might depend on her personality. Will A+ be only one of many priorities or will it continue to be a defining part of who they are? Third, the new principal comes with a strong interest and background in technology. Will she see technology and the arts as working together, or will she see them as competitors? Fourth, this school also has a strong set of teacher leaders. Will they be allowed to continue acting as leaders in arts reform around the state (e.g. given released time to take on A+ fellow roles) or will they be required to only teach within their classroom? And, finally, as with all schools, there is a small pocket of resistors to arts integration. The previous building leader did not "leave the door open" for their opposition. Will the new principal do the same?

Yet Pine Grove Middle also has a stable, cooperative, and committed faculty who have sustained A+ even after the magnet grant ended. They are planning to apply for a new magnet grant with the idea that this will allow them to embrace their arts integration, hands-on discovery learning. Their curriculum, especially in the electives, allows for considerable creativity in course design and delivery. All these are resources upon which they can build.

Hillside Elementary Case Study

Hillside, a K–5 school in the foothills of the North Carolina's Western mountains, has just over 500 students, of which, 45% are eligible for free or reduced lunch. As an avowed A+ school, the school both enjoys and suffers from having a "special" status in its county, with students being allowed to transfer in from anywhere in the system, the administrators maintaining a sizeable cohort of classroom assistants, and the retention of a full-time drama teacher (a position not funded in other county schools).

The Definition of Arts Integration at Hillside

A visitor is immediately hit with the arts message. Signs and the secretary's greeting on the phone refer to the building as "Hillside A+ School." These are just the first indicators that an emphasis on the arts is institutionalized in the school. A host of structural and instruction-related arrangements reinforce it.

The heart of the school's approach to the arts is its "Connect Team." Through this team, the school maintains the goal of "every art every week for every child." This team, according to the music teacher, has ten members: two music teachers (one teaches 60% of the time and the other 40%), one drama teacher, one visual art teacher, two PE teachers (one is an assistant), one media coordinator, two guidance counselors, and one computer lab assistant. As many as possible of them meet three times a week and are in charge of scheduling for all activities at the school in addition to handling events related to their subjects and cultural and art events outside of the school.

The arts are apparent school-wide, most noticeably in special events and hallway displays. The events include one in the fall (that the A+ regional liaison attends and helps with), a first-grade play, and an arts extravaganza, among others. One of the first-grade teachers discussed the latter as a school-day festival that brings numerous artists into the building, such as spinners, pottery makers, percussionists, and dancers. Students attend "classes" with various artists. The school has an art gallery of student work in the central foyer that runs almost the length of the school. Soft classical music plays continuously in this well-maintained focal point. Murals dot the hallways. Some were created prior to A+ but the tradition of having a local artist involved in the process has continued, with one that displays animals and their habitats being finished in the last couple of years.

Fourth- and fifth-grade students can pick an additional arts class to attend (once a week on Tuesdays) during a 45-minute block of time called the "Smart Block." The block used to be 90 minutes but was reduced in the most recent year due to scheduling difficulties, and students now have one Smart Block class per semester rather than two. The classes are identified by the type of "intelligence" they tap. For example, one student explained that she had a "Body Smart" class in the prior semester and "Drama Smart" in the current semester. Some teachers and students said that generally students indicate their top three choices, and the administration chooses from there to equalize class size. However, some also made reference to a multiple intelligences test that students took to help guide them in choosing classes based on their strengths and weaknesses. In addition to talking about how they were smart, at least two students talked about an art or subject that they were not very good at but that they enjoyed learning about nevertheless during the block time.

Various staff at the school continue to attend the A+ summer institute and school-year A+ retreats. This attendance has ranged from 90% at local Institute events to 40% for far away ones (according to the principal). The principal also says that she and the coordinator and some new teachers go to the school-year activities. Second-grade teachers (all veterans) explained that they did not go to the overnight events any more. Several teachers felt that it hurt arts infusion to not have new teachers attend the Institute prior to starting the school year and worried about a slow demise of the "core group" of A+ teachers. No one wants to go overnight, they argued, but then pointed to how crucial the first week-long Institute was to getting the Program going throughout the school.

In the upcoming summer, the school is going to participate in a one-day, out-of-town session with a couple of other A+ schools; the principal predicts 60% will go. The principal encourages assistants to attend as well. For attending, teachers get a trade-off day. This means that during the school year, on a day that teachers are working but students are not present, the teacher can trade-off a day at the Institute for not having to come to school on that work day. The principal is planning to allow teachers to "bank" these trade-offs from one year to the next because snow days negated the work days this year.

Each grade-level has thematic units. The grades revise the curriculum map each year and identify the themes, the objectives from each subject that addresses those themes, the classroom arts activities related to the theme, enrichment activities related to the theme, and what the teachers would like the Connect Team person to do. There is a two-sided form on which teachers write this information and it includes a check-list to indicate which multiple intelligences the thematic unit "employs."

Several teachers pointed to these as crucial to allowing them to know about and discuss what each other is doing. One second-grade teacher made the comment that "I'll say something to my class and then a few minutes later I'll overhear one of the others saying the same thing to theirs." The two-sided sheet makes specific provisions for indicating arts activities and which intelligences are covered. Teachers pointed to these as the means by which teachers new to their grades are oriented to what they're expected to do in their classes. The teacher new to the second grade said: "I latched on to these. I can't imagine anyone not latching on if they were new." These same teachers noted that without the units and time to plan, there was no other training that would ensure that new teachers knew about A+ and what is expected in the classrooms.

Teachers at each grade level have a team planning time, including planning with the Connect Team. Grade-levels have common planning time (almost daily) and meet as a team at least once a week, although some grades had developed the habit of meeting more often. At least one Connect Team member's planning time coincides with one or two grade-level team's time. This makes it easy for a Connect Team member to meet with each grade-level team at least once a month and then share what that particular grade is doing with the rest of the Connect Team.

The school continues to meet with the regional A+ liaison. The principal says he comes to the school several times a year and does some professional development each time. One mentioned was a session on planning for A+ in the future. Through the work with this person, the Institute, and school-year retreats the school continues to engage in school-based professional development.

The general consensus of the interviewed staff was that the Connect teachers do more integration of subject content into the arts than do the classroom teachers of the arts into their subjects. The thematic unit forms, the once-a-month meetings, and the veteran Connect Team teachers' knowledge of the curricula "history" in each grade allow the Connect teachers to plan ways of reinforcing what is being taught in the regular classrooms. Several examples emerged in interviews. One student described doing monologues in drama that were based on characters in a book being read in class; a fourth-grade teacher stated that the art teacher introduced watercolors to students by having them paint lighthouses when North Carolina lighthouses were discussed in class; and a first-grade teacher said that when insects were being taught in class, the drama class did a "cute" play about insects.

Responding to a question about how many teachers in the building integrate the arts into their classrooms, the principal said "one or two teachers do this a little bit" while the others do it often, contradicting what some teachers had said. Examples of regular classroom integration of the arts were observed during a site visit. In one classroom observation, the fourth-grade teacher had students working in stations for social studies (one was reading and answering questions on the computer; one was writing signatures with actual goose feathers as if they were signers of the Declaration of Independence; and two were reading about and coloring the state seal and flag). In another, the first-grade teacher also set up stations: at one, students read "in whispers" a book the teacher had just read to them; at another, students drew on an overhead sheet a representation of what their caterpillars looked like in their container (each has his or her own caterpillar to watch over the next three weeks); and at the last, students put paint splotches on one half of a butterfly that the teacher had cut out for each child and then folded the butterfly over to create the "symmetry" that all butterflies have. The teacher had shown pictures of butterflies in a math symmetry lesson prior to sending them to the station. Finally, in one of many subtle ways in which the arts permeated the building, a first-grade teacher had classical music playing softly throughout the lesson and the level of talk in the classroom was such that this could always be heard.

However, in student interviews, when asked about the use of the arts in regular classes, only one out of five came up with an example—using movement in science. Likewise, grade-level teachers were not very forthcoming with a wealth of examples of arts integration. A follow-up query about this topic with one group of teachers yielded comments from two of them who mostly did visual art—allowing students to do illustrations and color—and an admission from a third who was new to the grade: "I'm just trying to get the curriculum down this year so I haven't been doing as much; I will next year."

So, the depiction of arts integration in a school known for its arts commitment was somewhat thin and misleading. Two Connect Team members mentioned that despite the generally accepted notion that the Connect Team is more thorough in its integration efforts, part of the issue is one of labeling. They explained that the regular classroom teachers are fully aware of the multiple intelligences, believe that lessons should take them into account, and, thus, often teach the same skills and material in several different ways in a lesson. As mentioned earlier, students and faculty used the phrase "smart talk" to refer to various intelligences. Students, and teachers, might not necessarily think of their attempts to "tap" the intelligences in a lesson as "the arts" but the activities themselves—moving, illustrating, writing, singing—were actually artistic in nature.

For example, one fourth grader observed in the aforementioned social studies class stated that he did not do art at any time of the day other than in art class. When asked whether he was sure about that, the student thought for a moment, remembered that he had seen the interviewer in social studies, and then recalled that they were working on coloring the state seal and state flag and using a quill pen that the teacher made to sign the Declaration of Independence in a manner that reflected their commitment to the act. The student simply had not labeled what they were doing in social studies as an "art" activity; they were doing social studies.

The first- and fourth-grade teachers explained how they incorporated arts in the classroom as a component of reaching out to students' different intelligences. The first-grade teachers stated that they all integrated drama when acting out spelling words. One first-grade teacher stated that they used "Body Smart" strategies, such as clapping, stomping, and punching the air. Another teacher stated that she integrated music by having the class do songs that went along with phonemics, letters, and math. One fourth-grade teacher who taught science stated that during her lessons on sounds, someone came in and played the guitar. She also used bells to show pitch and loudness.

The interesting point here is that the above examples came up in a discussion of the role of the multiple intelligences in the classroom, although they clearly were appropriate in the previous discussion on arts integration. This suggests that the cumulative impact of A+ and an understanding of the theory of multiple intelligences was perhaps that the arts had become a way of teaching—and learning—rather than either a separate subject or an instructional tool, such as math manipulatives.

How the Arts are Sustained at Hillside

Hillside has clearly institutionalized an arts emphasis school-wide. That is to say that the arts have been incorporated into parents', educators', and students' images of what the schools' priorities are, that there is a core of committed arts and A+ advocates in the building, and that there are organizational arrangements (arts events, planning time, thematic units, Connect and grade-level teams, professional development, and meetings with the A+ regional liaison) that keep the arts visible in peoples' conversations and actions. The images, advocates, and arrangements all mutually reinforce the elevated status of the arts.

The school enjoys several additional circumstances that serve it well in sustaining this institutionalized role of the arts. First, the same superintendent has been in place for the duration of A+ and refuses to even discuss cutting the drama position at Hillside, despite sizeable budget cuts throughout the system. He visits each school two times a year and always praises Hillside (according to the principal) and says that if he had a school-age child, he would be glad to have the student attend Hillside.

Second, there are veteran Connect teachers. The drama teacher is "new" (having been there 3 years) so the team knows everyone and what they do and how the arts teachers have "connected" with their lessons in the past. These teachers handle the many visitors to the school and often entertain them.

Third, Hillside has a School of Excellence designation. The principal and the coordinator made reference to this as signifying the value of the school's arts-integrated approach to educating children.

Fourth, the arts have had positive effects on students. Teachers, at least the second-grade ones, had trouble pinning down how students benefited other than to say "they enjoy it." But, nevertheless, they saw value in the arts and thus had no questions that the school should continue in the direction it was going. One fourth-grade teacher indicated that students learn more about how they are smart. Another stated that students are more enthusiastic and everybody is spotlighted as having a strength. A first-grade teacher stated that using the arts allows subjects to stick in their minds and students think they are playing, as teachers are coming through the back door with the material students are supposed to learn. Two teachers indicated that incorporating the arts ensures that students do not get bored.

Despite the tendency for people in the building to play down arts integration in the classroom, there was perhaps a greater use of them in daily routines than came readily to mind to people in interviews. At Hillside, A+ and the multiple intelligences intertwined, to the point that their usage had perhaps become habitual and therefore less noticeable and remarkable. This presented a sharp contrast to the vibrant display of the arts throughout the building.

The Future for Arts at Hillside Elementary

Hillside staff revel in their sense of being in a special place for people to work and learn. Nevertheless, a sense of uncertainty clouds their view of the future. Several issues feed this uncertainty. First, they are uncertain because of teacher turnover. As mentioned, the second-grade teachers worried that newer teachers were not "trained" in A+ and that the "core" of A+ teachers was slowly dwindling away. The drama teacher added another angle to the role of turnover. As a new teacher, and one who was expected to "connect" with classroom subject matter, the teacher said that the fact that the thematic units were in place and revised before the school year started, meant that she had no input into these plans. Thus, the only integration that she could influence was how she carried out the teachers' wishes; she wasn't able to help inject drama ideas formally into the classroom part of the units. So, the imparting of ideas went one-way, from old to new, in this instance. On the other hand, the A+ coordinator felt that some new teachers were definitely a boon to the school and the arts and were highly likely to not only carry on with arts integration but also enhance it. Regardless, all staff agreed that having a considerable core of teachers dedicated to the arts and the multiple intelligences was critical to giving substance to all of the many visual and aural symbols of the arts that dotted the building.

Second, administrator turnover is a concern. The "new" principal has been in the building for 4 years, 2 as an assistant and 2 as the principal. Her commitment is as strong (she was an arts teacher herself at one time), second-grade teachers say, but her style is different. They described the former principal as having a "vision" for the school while the new principal is more "laid back." Overall they conveyed a sense of A+ "weakening" in the building. Everyone in the building was aware of what would happen if the current superintendent left: the drama position would go.

Third, testing is a cause for uncertainty. While the principal and the A+ coordinator took heart that the School of Excellence designation validated what the school was doing, other teachers made reference to the continuing pressure on their time to cover the objectives that were tested. Even in second grade, although there were no standardized tests, the teachers still have to do individual assessments of students that sometimes take an hour per student. A first-grade teacher said that this had taken 100 hours in the first grade (about 25 per teacher)! Thus, several teachers made reference to not having the time to do "as much with the arts" as they would like to.

Fourth, there is a reliance on the Connect Team. In conjunction with the discussion of teacher turnover, the teachers were asked to speculate what would happen if turnover hit the Connect Team. Of course, the drama teacher has changed but there was a general shaking of heads at the thought of the A+ coordinator leaving. Teachers regard the team as being the true champions of the arts in the building.

The staff concerns reflect the tenuous nature of change in a building. Even a widely-acknowledged transformation of a building over time faces continual challenges to its being sustained. Certainly there is a widely diffused core of leaders in the building that will play an important part in helping the arts to still be celebrated in events, the hallways, and classrooms; and using multiple ways of teaching skills and concepts bountifully dot daily classroom routines. But, still the teachers conveyed considerable worries about the future. This may have been reflective of the overall climate in public education today and it may have been borne of having taught in an "ideal" setting for a while and simply being concerned that it could not go on forever.

And, indeed, losing a superintendent or a principal or an A+ coordinator might dramatically alter the vibrant, visible representations of the arts through no longer having the arts resources the school currently has or a charismatic champion who ensures that art room creations tangibly reflect the curriculum. However, as long as teachers remain committed to the idea that students learn in different ways, then every lesson will still at some point allow students to move like electrons spinning around an atom, to act out a character from a book, to write from the point of view of an historical figure, to sing math facts, and to illustrate their thoughts visually. As a way of teaching, therefore, the arts would likely be inured from the potentially devastating triad of turnover, testing, and budget cuts.

Ridgeview Elementary School Case Study

Ridgeview Elementary School is high in the Appalachian Mountains. It is a K–5 school in a small town that is essentially a crossroads. There is a small college noted for its dramatic arts program, a few restaurants and motels that survive basically on the ski season, tourists, and wealthy retirees to the mountains. The children at Ridgeview School are "locals," that is their families are from longstanding mountain clans. Many of the parents work at minimum wage jobs and/or are seasonally employed for the ski season or other tourist-related seasonal jobs. Ridgeview Elementary has approximately 200 students, of which, 32% are eligible for free or reduced-price lunch. The school is small and is well-maintained, but in an almost 70-year-old building.

The Definition of the Arts at Ridgeview Elementary School

We had not been to the school for three years when we returned to study the sustainability of A+. Entering the school, we were struck by student artwork and products emanating from arts integrated lessons and thematic units. As it turns out, we were not expected at the school. The new principal's wife had had a baby a couple of days prior and he was at home with them. Moreover, he had neglected to inform the faculty that we were coming. The acting principal was in fact a school administrator in training who was doing her practicum at the school. As a result, we were able to see Ridgeview Elementary when it was not prepared to be seen as an A+ school. The artwork on the walls and the lessons being taught were simply the way the school was that day.

We toured the school and classrooms seeing repeated examples of arts integrated lessons. A kindergarten teacher demonstrated some of the arts integrated activities the class had used. Departing from a discussion of African animals, the teacher picked up an autoharp she had bought with a grant that was to link storytelling with literacy. They played "name that tune" and the students were engrossed in what was obviously a favorite game. The teacher then noted that they had created a song about how to add "ing" endings to words, mixing music with literacy learning. Then she moved on to an example of kinesthetic learning associating movement and rhythm with learning the months of the year. This class was of course not the normal lesson of the day, but it did show that arts were commonplace in this classroom. The students knew the activities and their routines well and were able to move into them with little or no transition. Other kindergarten classes were drawing and coloring animals as part of learning about the names and characteristics of the animals, or making paper giraffes. All of these activities were organized as part of a thematic unit on Africa for grades K–1 in this multi-graded school.

Each class was pursuing the thematic unit teachers had created for the year. The skills being developed across all the subjects were guided by an essential question for each of the subjects that linked to the overall essential question. For example, classes for grades 2–3 were studying "earth from the inside out" and grades 4–5 were studying "the shapes of our past." Each of these thematic units was guided by an "essential question" (e.g. for grades 4–5: "How does the past affect our present and future?"). For grades 2–3, the mathematics essential question was: "How do fractions appear in and outside of earth?" For technology, the question was: "How can we use technology to enhance the study of earth's structure?" For art and music, respectively, the essential questions were: "How can students show elements of three-dimensional art through clay sculpture?" and "How is music structured?" These questions and those for science and social studies as well were all linked in the exploring of the ideas of structures in nature. Teachers over their years of experience with A+ had learned that a new thematic unit each year did not allow teachers to develop them further and to improve their teaching and integration of the arts. Since the school was multi-graded, the teachers had decided to pursue two thematic units for each set of grade levels, each on alternative years. Thus in K–1, the two themes were centered around Africa and Australia and this allowed students to get to both themes before they moved on to the grades 2–3 class. The overall curriculum management was overseen by a teacher who served as the curriculum coordinator and who helped schedule the school so that curriculum planning was possible for all the grade levels and with the arts and other "special" teachers.

Our classroom observations saw a range of activities from content-based discussions to integrated lessons to arts classes themselves that pursued artistic productions consistent with the grade-level themes. It was clear that the arts were central in all the classes and across the school. The arts emphasis and multi-grade structure of the school also had led to not using textbooks for classes. This focus on teacher-made materials both celebrated the creativity of the teachers and their professionalism as well. The teachers were and are responsible for the curricula and instruction in Ridgeview Elementary School, and they have a long-standing commitment to a "hands-on" and arts-based approach. There is variety in the school in the use of arts, of course. As the principal intern explained: "Some teachers use more A+ curriculum than others. New teachers are still trying to feel their way with it."

The state-wide "high-stakes" testing was to begin in a couple of days after our visit and the presence of the arts in instruction was all the more impressive because of it. We even saw an example of arts-based math "drill" for the upcoming test. In the grades 4–5 math class, the teacher wanted to focus on recognition skills of various math forms, including such things as a point, a line, geometric shapes, etc. The art teacher brought in clay and the two teachers worked with the students to create the various forms on their desks and had the students engage in discussions about how to distinguish the shapes from each other. The discussions were lively and both achieved the intention of helping students learn the shapes and appropriate names as well as having aesthetic discussions about when was a clay figure a good example of that shape and why it was a good form or not.

The partnership with the local college continues with students working in many of the classrooms (either as volunteers or as part of a service learning course requirement) and doing their teacher preparation practice at the school. Parent and community support has been continually strong even in a community where innovation is not always accepted well. However, the arts draw in the parents and community, which demonstrates to the wider public what the students are studying across the curriculum. The multi-grading structure has continued even though it existed prior to A+. This has also led to the "year A, year B" structure of thematic units that enable students to stay two years with the same teachers but not repeat content.

In short, Ridgeview Elementary School has sustained A+ in its classrooms and as a commitment of the school. The parents we interviewed were in agreement: "We like it!"

How A+ Was Sustained at Ridgeview

In our observations and interviews, it was evident that the staff at Ridgeview Elementary School were sustaining the A+ approach at rather high levels. The staff identified how this was being accomplished. As the teachers reminded us, A+ was "not as new an idea for this faculty as for faculty at other schools. Before, we had not been using textbooks. The philosophy of hands-on was there and the teacher commitment was there." The staff at Ridgeview Elementary are seen as especially creative teachers: "This faculty is wonderful. They just run with an idea. They plan and brainstorm and alter it."

The teachers recounted that at the first A+ summer institutes: "We worked on philosophy, the approach of A+, what it was, how we could implement it and where we could do so." They noted that because the whole faculty, including the arts teachers, was there it was possible to plan for arts integration. They continue to attend the A+ summer institutes to get ideas and to enable curriculum planning across the school. As one teacher said: "Every A+ summer institute has been excellent. You always come away with new ideas. It's great to have the time to do this." She continued: "A+ gives you this 'ah ha!' idea and you can then put your stamp on it."

Ridgeview Elementary School has sustained A+ both because it fits who the faculty are, had champions in the school for the Program—most notably the second principal, and because it has worked for them. As one teacher stated: "Teachers here support it because they've been here to see the results." The school has received many accolades for their efforts in the community and state-wide. They have been highly successful with the state's high-stakes testing program, repeatedly meeting and exceeding the state's achievement goals to be named a "School of Excellence" and a "School of Distinction" based on their exceptionally high achievement growth. Yet success also has consequences. The A+ Program and the achievement outcomes of the school have led many parents of special needs children to transfer their children to the school. The teachers take this as testimony to their capabilities but also recognize that they are relieving the other schools in the county of the need to do better with these students. Success has also meant jealousy between the schools about the media coverage Ridgeview Elementary had been getting with the arts and other activities. The school now seeks less media coverage so as not to compete with the other elementary schools in the county. A more positive consequence has been that the county's two middle schools are now trying to become A+ or least arts-enhanced schools. This means that Ridgeview Elementary's students will have a consistent program of studies through at least the middle-school years.

The 2-year cycle of thematic units allows the teachers to develop these units over time and to refine and enhance them. The thematic units and the curricula being organized around essential questions that link all the subjects together, including the arts, has been essential to enabling arts integration. The school's commitment to use teacher-made materials, and not textbooks, also enables integration as the teachers create the curricula and instruction, within the state's Standard Course of Study upon which the testing program is based. Finally, the school has taken the "enriched assessment" process that A+ developed during the pilot and has continued to refine how they do assessment, linking both authentic assessment strategies and standardized assessments with some success.

Sustaining A+ has also meant dealing with a host of issues as well. First and foremost on teachers' minds at Ridgeview Elementary is their new principal. He, like all new principals, has new ideas as well as a commitment to carry A+ forward. Yet as a new principal he has much to learn. The teachers note that he is pushing more emphasis on technology which they have now integrated into their curricula. Yet they are clear that he wants to support A+ and is asking for "some refocusing and revisiting." With the change in principals, however, there has been less emphasis on "informances" to show the integrated curricula to parents and the community and fewer staff development opportunities.

As the new principal learns A+, the teachers are clear that they are "carrying A+." The experienced teachers also recount that it is the new teachers that need to be brought into A+ and cannot be until the summer institute after their first year at the school. Here the need for support has been filled in by the curriculum coordinator in this interim period, working with teachers who have not had professional development as well as helping the experienced teachers plan the curricula. Due to inadequate resources arts instruction has become more limited. Dance and drama have been covered only for part of the year, and the art and music teachers are shared between two schools. The school is trying to decide how to best work with this. Finally, a perennial issue in all A+ schools is evident at Ridgeview Elementary as well. Planning time with the arts teachers to enable integrated instruction has been less available and this inhibits curricular development and instruction.

The Future at Ridgeview

The future at Ridgeview Elementary is in part about getting their new principal oriented to A+ and regaining some of the school's momentum. Teachers are already discussing a new school-wide theme to link all the grade levels: "Make the world a better place." They will plan this at the A+ summer institute when all the teachers can work together. They will also work on the schedule for next year, helping the principal see how to organize more planning time with the arts teachers. One idea about how to deal with insufficient resources for dance and drama that the teachers are discussing is using the dance teacher monies to fund "mini-studies" on different specialties, such as quilt making or mountain dancing. This also enables the school to take advantage of local community arts resources. Finally, since the assessment strategies related to the state's assessment program have been difficult for the local parents to understand, the teachers plan to make them more transparent.

The staff are committed to A+ and to what they have done with it. It is a mark of distinction for themselves as professionals, and creative professionals at that. As one teacher explained:

> We saw that this works. It's a lot of effort. This teaching is not [for] teachers who don't want to put in the effort, who can't think outside the box, who have to have everything in black and white. You have to be in that gray area . . . to be a successful teacher [with A+].

The challenge for Ridgeview will be to continue finding teachers comfortable working in a gray area.

Creekside Middle School: A Regeneration Case Study

Creekside Middle School was one of only two sixth–eighth-grade schools in the pilot. Situated next door to Creekside Elementary School, the pair of schools held much promise for offering uninterrupted arts-enhanced instruction for students from kindergarten all the way through eighth grade. The neighborhood context described in Chapter 2 for Creekside Elementary is the same for the middle school as well. It is located in a low-wealth area of a small city in the piedmont of North Carolina. Unlike its elementary counterpart, Creekside Middle never suffered from a "low performing" designation, but its results on the ABCs tests during the pilot period were mixed, varying from "no recognition" to "exemplary" and back to "low recognition."

Over the course of the pilot period, the A+ Program at the school went through a period of decline due to a number of factors. The system was redistricted which, according to the school's former principal, decreased its diversity and took away the active, supportive segment of their parent population. Though the school retained a strong contingent of arts faculty throughout the period, a number of classroom teachers who had been strong supporters of A+ also left Creekside Middle as new schools were built in the county. The school enjoyed a successful partnership with an A+ elementary school in a nearby town with the help of some Goals 2000 monies, but partnering with Creekside Elementary never panned out because of philosophical differences in how to approach the Program. The school also struggled with feeling disillusioned by the network. Since most of the schools in the Program were elementary schools, much of the staff development focus and many of the implementation strategies didn't quite fit their middle school. There was not a good model to follow, nor were there many other similar middle schools to collaborate with to figure it out. Finally, the decline of the Program can also be attributed in part to the former principal. He was the principal during the first 5 years of the Program and, according to one teacher, "was resistant to pushing teachers to do things they didn't want to do." He did not make all of the teachers go to the training, though he did financially support those who wanted to go. By his own account, he no longer had the high level of energy he believed to be necessary for the job.

Yet, through all this, pieces of the Program survived. The A+ name gave the school focus and helped it market itself to the community. There was never a move to disaffiliate from the Program, even when there were only pockets of successful integration. The school held on to its core of arts teachers who were acknowledged as "always being there" when a classroom teacher wanted help with an idea. The model they developed involved using sixth grade as an exploratory year during which time students were required to take a little bit of all of the school's offerings: dance, drama, visual arts, and a selection of music including piano, chorus, orchestra, or band. Seventh and eighth graders took at least two arts classes (which met two or three times per week) each semester. Additional "focused" arts classes offered in-depth study and provided incentives for students to perform well in their academic classes.

Currently, Creekside Middle serves 415 students, most of whom are African American and 82% of whom are on free or reduced lunch. One-quarter of the students have been designated "exceptional," requiring additional services. The A+ Program and the arts are experiencing a period of resurgence, which again, can be attributed to a number of factors.

What Has Been Regenerated at Creekside Middle School

Communication and collaboration between and among classroom teachers and the arts staff have increased significantly. Whereas sporadic communication used to occur via email, teachers now place a priority on connecting with each other. As one stated:

> We make time for it. It's difficult to have time but most of the quality teachers do it and look for ways to connect to kids. Sometimes it's a core teacher going to an arts teacher. Other times, it's the arts teacher knowing what the core teachers are doing.

In general, the atmosphere of the school is more open now than it used to be:

We've moved to a more open, transparent communication process. We don't always get to be pretty or clean but we get to be honest. Even disagreeing is more important because it's for the students' good. We're encouraged to be positive, and thus positive about disagreement.

The A+ coordinator explains how this happens:

We get substitute teachers so the teachers can meet with the arts team. They sit together with the curriculum map and plan how they will integrate the arts. It's for us to plan into their curriculum but what happens is . . . it's like cross-pollination, they and we become each other's resources. We [the arts team] become incidental, which is how you want it to be. You don't want to be the star of the show all the time.

One result of all of this collaboration is the increased variety of integrated instruction and greater amount of work done in the school that is connected to the arts. Teachers supplement face-to-face contact with a listserv that allows them to share what they are doing so the special teachers can incorporate the content into their classes. Some of the projects from this year that involved the arts included an eighth-grade unit on Native Americans that combined art and science and was also tied into the Harvest Bowl. (This unit was filmed for a documentary on arts integration in the schools.) An eighth-grade Harlem Renaissance unit combined language arts, social studies, music, drama, dance, and visual arts. Seventh graders studied Africa and were treated to visiting African dancers. An additional seventh-grade unit asked: "Can a frog dance?" This unit combined science and dance, using the dissection of frogs to discuss the muscles that dancers use when dancing. Sixth graders incorporated learning how to dance the Flamenco with their studies. As a result of its efforts toward arts-integrated instruction, Creekside Middle School was one of three schools to receive the "Creative Ticket Award" this year from Washington, DC for activities related to arts integration.

One teacher shares her impressions:

For me, it has surged. I've done several units . . . Harlem Renaissance, with 80 student dancers, poetry readings, dramatic interpretations, etc. It was phenomenal. I've done an integrated unit on the book *The Weirdo* which is based in North Carolina with themes that come out of social studies. We worked in visual arts, we took the novel and did place settings based on the characters of the book. There were distinctive parameters for that project where different pieces of the place setting represented a piece of a character's identity. We called it "Who is Coming to Dinner?" It was one of the neatest things I have ever been involved in. The kids analyzed the book much more deeply than they ever could have otherwise.

As this quote indicates, in addition to integration, the arts seem to have brought about a certain sense of excitement for the teachers. The "special" teachers (including special education, PE, arts, technology, etc.) in particular expressed the sense of excitement they get from their teaching. In addition, teachers talked about the excitement for learning that they see in their students.

The teachers and administrators talked about the success of their students in ways other than high test scores and good grades. Most of the faculty members we talked to mentioned the success of their students. They commented on the importance of success in areas other than the traditional subject matter:

It is the one thing that hooks kids into being here, to wanting to come to school, to feeling like they are a part of the school. Students might not excel academically, but if they can sing, dance, act, then we can still get to them. In any other school, the kids wouldn't get to see this type of stuff. They wouldn't see it as an option for them.

The principal expressed a similar sentiment:

What I have been impressed with in coming here is that the state has been focused on teaching for the test and the students here are offered a very good education. They have progressed. They haven't reached state standards but they have a more well-rounded education, not just language and math, but also art is important, dance is important.

The quality and stability of Creekside Middle School's teaching staff have also been regenerated. Even though the school serves a large "at risk" population, in the last few years it has been able to attract and retain high-quality teachers. The principal states: "We have the highest percentage of teachers with National Board Certification in [the] county. One teacher here helps across the nation with National Board Certification. The commitment to teaching excellence is there." And a teacher relates: "We've had a doctoral student here studying about how to keep top teachers at hard-to-staff schools. She's found that we're very unusual and that's reaffirming." The principal credits this success to the A+ Program and to good faculty morale. He has the feeling that, in terms of hiring, people really do want to come to Creekside Middle School.

How Creekside Middle School Has Regenerated Itself

It appears that the most crucial element at Creekside Middle School has been leadership. The arrival of a new principal has brought new life to the school, though the role of a core group of dedicated teachers in sustaining the Program should not be underestimated. Several participants claimed that the success and regeneration of the A+ Program was due to a committed core group of staff members, including the dance teacher, the art teacher, the media specialist, and the gym teacher. The principal noted: "There is a core staff in place committed to the A+ philosophy. The arts teachers are keys to the success, as are certain core teachers who have bought into it." The dance teacher was the 1997–1998 Arts Teacher of the Year and is the recent National Dance Teacher of the Year. This dance teacher is also the school's A+ coordinator. She describes her role as follows: "I'm the A+ cheerleader, and I have been from the outset . . . I am a spokesperson to the community. I recently went to Raleigh and spoke to the legislators. I am the keeper of the flame." A language arts teacher notes:

> The media coordinator works tirelessly for you. She goes to the hilt for a unit if you are interested in expanding it beyond what you could do by yourself. She actually helped to fund a field trip for us to the wetlands here and gathered a number of resources.

In addition, leadership has come from a recent influx of quality teachers committed to A+. As one teacher relates: "We've had an infusion of National Board Certified Teachers. When they get something, they take it and run with it! The teachers have taken some responsibility for doing A+ and not just leaving it to the arts teachers." Not only does the school have the highest percentage of National Board Certified Teachers in the district, one teacher is even an NBCT trainer. Several of the teachers commented on the commitment of the staff to A+ and on the quality of the faculty. For example:

> We are blessed to have very strong teachers, some of whom are National Board Certified. The arts are respected. We have a full piano lab, a chorale group, a wonderful band teacher. Also, a true belief by the teachers in A+, a caring attitude, and a fundamental belief that this is good for the children.

Last but not least, the leadership of the school's new principal has made a tremendous difference in the school. When he became principal 2 years ago, the A+ Program was still supported by some teachers but was no longer a school-wide program in any real sense. With the help of the school leadership team, he helped bring the Program back and several teachers point to his support as a major cause of the regeneration. One teacher relays: "In my class, it can look chaotic. You have to have an administrator that accepts things other than kids sitting in rows. They know there is learning going on. There is a trust." Another notes: "[He] lets you do things outside of the box and be creative. He is a great administrator and all the teachers think so." His support of the Program is only part of the story. He probed the teachers, trying to understand the Program and asking them if they really wanted it. One teacher goes so far as to say that he asked "significant questions [such as] 'is this the place you want to be?'. It brought out our attachment to that identity. It wasn't just the arts people." Upon determining that there was support for the Program, he made arrangements for all of the staff to go to training and helped A+ gain a new school-wide footing.

A discussion of leadership would not be complete without mentioning the role of the district. Originally, A+ paid for drama and dance teachers for the school. These positions are now paid for by the school system. The principal credits the district as being very supportive of the arts. While other areas (such as foreign languages) have been cut, the arts continue to be supported. In his words: "Art is not seen as just an add-on. It is seen as integral."

Participation in the A+ summer institutes has also been instrumental in the regeneration of the Program at Creekside Middle School. The principal relates:

> [The institutes are] very valuable. Off campus is a good situation. The teachers actually carry out planned activities. The planned units are actually carried out. They have the time to focus on making a plan, but the challenge is to carry it out.

He sees the ongoing professional development of the A+ Schools Program as an important difference between A+ and other reforms that usually spend little money on training. A teacher comments specifically on what the institutes have done for him:

> We use it to do different shapes and learn about angles and degrees. We also tie it into anatomy and physiology, like the proprioceptors in the body. I didn't realize about how to incorporate this stuff before the A+ conferences. I realized that I could do these things in PE.

A final cause of regeneration is the power of affiliation. It is important to remember that even though Creekside Middle School had not sub-stantively reformed around the A+ Program during the pilot period, the school had come to consider itself an A+ school. As mentioned above, an

A+ identity had been formed that rose to the challenge when threatened. This threat came in the form of the creation of an arts-based magnet school in the district. The principal describes the influence:

> A magnet school program started in the county. They tried to recruit our arts teachers, to get three of our arts teachers to move to the arts school. They [the teachers] decided to stay and make this an arts school. This galvanized the faculty, not just the arts teachers but got the other teachers to want it as well. Also, the superintendent tried to get all the creative students to go to the arts school. It's been an evolution because people who hadn't done it before decided they were going to. It's been ingenuity and creativity on their part.

In previous reports, an affiliative stance toward reform has been interpreted as less meaningful than a symbolic or substantive stance. The story of Creekside Middle illustrates the possibilities presented by even a basic level of commitment and its potential for transforming an arts identity to a new level.

Challenges and the Future at Creekside Middle

While Creekside Middle School has rekindled its relationship with the A+ Program and with the arts, it remains to be seen just how far they will go. Some of the challenges that the school faces as it moves forward include getting new teachers to adapt to the school's A+ model, time to foster collaboration, and funding.

Acclimating new staff to the amount of cooperation and integration that A+ commands is an ongoing challenge. However, with such a strong core group of teachers, and now administrators, committed to A+, this should assist new teachers to adapt.

Though a lot of collaboration seems to occur, teachers and the principal alike express how difficult it is for teachers to find time to collaborate. This problem has been exacerbated by the school calendar. Creekside Middle School has both a year-round and a traditional academic year program at the school. However, the problem may be alleviated as they move to one calendar next year with a 1-week fall break and 2-week spring break.

Training new staff will undoubtedly become even more difficult as funding for A+ summer institutes comes into question. A short-term solution is to hold the Institute locally next summer instead of traveling. The school is committed, however, to ongoing participation in the A+ summer institutes and the principal is already looking at alternative sources of funding for both professional development and integrated projects. The curriculum coordinator states: "Despite the budget cuts, I am optimistic. Art is usually the first thing to go but it increases test scores and intelligence. I would like to see it keep growing. This school is a success story."

Creekside Middle School's story of rebirth as an A+ school represents a different perspective on principal leadership that needs discussion. During the pilot, Creekside Middle had at best an "affiliated" identity with A+ and the arts. Staff participated only sporadically in A+ professional development and network activities. The then principal was at best laissez-faire in encouraging participation and when pressed in interviews pointed to one or two teachers that were his evidence of A+ in practice. To be fair, Creekside Middle may well have been suffering from the defeatism that characterizes many urban schools filled with children from low-income families with troubled lives. As the pilot ended, the school district began to move to open enrollment and the principal realized that to survive the school needed a distinct identity to attract students. All of a sudden A+ was promoted by the principal as the way to save the school. Yet the principal was unable to rally the teachers, and left. The new principal saw potential in A+ and immediately began to explore the teachers' commitment to A+. He found the staff willing but unprepared to pull it off. This principal regenerated A+ by getting active in the A+ network and finding funds to get his teachers the professional development they needed. The competition with an arts magnet in the city has pushed them to new heights. Instead of despairing, the teachers now accept that their mission as an "equity plus" school is to use the arts and arts integration to effectively educate children who often come from poverty. They also began to attract other students and new teachers. The distinctive identity as an A+ school and the sense of capability that came with it has proven the value of the arts to this school. Comparing this regeneration principal with those in the pilot schools, we see that principals are important in getting arts-based school reform off the ground.

A+, however, is sustained by its effects on teachers and the community. Over the long haul, then, the role of the principal is altered from leader to potential "spoiler." This is also the reason all the schools are concerned about teacher turnover. Sustainability is tightly linked to maintaining the culture of A+ in teacher beliefs and practices. The community's commitment is created by how A+ affects students and their view of school. When the students are engaged, enjoying school, and doing well academically, the parents and community are a positive force in sustainability. All of this is built on top of a culture created among the teachers. In these schools, the arts were able to build teacher cultures that contribute to distinctive, and substantive, school identities.

Conclusion

School reform is not easily sustained. Yet A+ is a reform that has been a remarkable long-term success. Moreover, it represents an unusual case if we are to believe the literature on school reform. The literature, of course, is not monolithic. Authors emphasize different elements and have different beliefs. Most of the contemporary literature is shaped by the dominant approaches. These approaches are largely focused on requiring schools to change. Enforced reform then is grounded in a distrust of schools and educators to do what is needed. Thus the literature favors reforms that are "packaged" and then use fidelity to the package as a marker of successful implementation, which in turn can then be correlated with achievement gains. The A+ schools had statistically significant gains in achievement during the pilot phase, but the accountability system in North Carolina raised the bar so that this standard was deemed insufficient. The A+ schools did well on this heightened standard and continue to do well. Importantly, how A+ and the arts were implicated in a school's identity was related to how well they did on the accountability standard.

This result then raises the question regarding what the literature is missing in its understanding of sustainability of school reform. Our argument is multi-faceted. First, the literature largely ignores more grassroots reform and thus represents only a partial picture of school reform. The lessons it offers must be specified: they pertain only to enforced reforms that have compliance as their fundamental base.

Second, enforced school reform has a particular image of what constitutes reform and thus sustaining reform. As Century and Levy (2002) point out, the usual definition of school reform is that of maintenance of fidelity with a reform package. No business could survive with such a definition. Businesses use their view of themselves as a guide to how to change, discover new markets, products, and constituencies. Century and Levy ask for a higher standard but one likely to better serve both reform efforts and schools. Sustainability is using core beliefs to manage change. What we have seen in this chapter is that schools with substantive identities with A+ and the arts meet this standard. What is important about this for school reform in general is that fidelity to an external idea is less important than centrality of core values to how the school thinks about itself.

Adkins and Gunzenhauser (2005) describe perhaps an extreme case of this in an A+ school, West Hollow (see Chapter 4). Here a school dramatically transformed the A+ approach to fit the community's desire to keep its students within the community. They were concerned that conventional definitions of school success sent children away to school and work. They used A+ to develop ideas about how crafts (from music to woodworking) could be the basis of a local economy. The school then used this idea to seek other funding to expand on this. West Hollow formed a consortium with other high schools and successfully competed for an Annenberg grant for place-based education. If one was asked about the fidelity of this to A+, one might resort to a focus on the arts and thinking creatively about education. While the A+ schools in this chapter shared other common elements including integrated instruction, participation in the A+ network and professional development, and the distinctive identity as an A+ school, this is far from the usual notions of fidelity in school reform.

Third, sustaining school reform is not as much about the reform as it is about encouraging people to participate. In the cases above, the mechanisms for sustaining A+ are all reducible to engagement with the A+ approach and in adapting it to fit the specific context. School reform cannot be sustained without such participation.

This returns us to our opening remarks in this chapter. There we noted that sustainability is rooted in ideas of economy and mechanistic assumptions about school change. Yet the lesson of this chapter is that schools are not machines. Adding a part to a school does not "fix" the school for all time. Even leaving the analogy of machine maintenance aside, sustaining a change in schools requires not a one-time expenditure but a permanent influx of resources. As all these high-sustainability schools show, they understand future growth to be conditional on ongoing professional development to maintain the school's identity with A+ and the arts. Culture can carry a school for a while but all cultures require certain socialization experiences and rites of passage. Elders must be created and youth inculcated with ways of believing and ways of acting. The A+ schools seem to understand this much better than do school reformers.

Sustaining arts-based school reform thus represents a different perspective than that represented in much of the literature on school reform. Indeed, it is worth returning to the historical studies of school reform to understand the salience of the lessons here. Recall that historians argue that reforms that are about changes in teaching are less likely to be sustained. A+ then seems to be a contrary example to this generalization. However, remember that this generalization was conditional in two ways. The historical argument was that reforms that stay have constituencies emerge around them. Also, the reason teaching changes were less likely to stick was because they were proposed by policy makers and officials who were not versed in how classrooms and teaching work. A+, then, is a compelling example of the historians' assertion. These schools are still doing arts-based school reform after more than a decade in part because the innovation was begun close to schools and adaptation was encouraged. But most importantly, A+ has been sustained because it became deeply engrained in teacher culture in these schools. This is why collaborative planning and A+ professional development are key ways to keep A+ alive both as ways of believing and ways of doing. Moreover, A+ continues to be sustained because it was in part the creation of constituencies from the beginning. It brought together educators, arts agencies, and philanthropic organizations, and as importantly created a constituency of the teachers who have participated.

Yet a question remains: *Why has A+ gone so deeply into the culture of teaching?* One might point to the many attributes we have discussed so far: extensive and ongoing professional development; a more grassroots approach; an emphasis on adaptation to local context; leadership of the principal; teacher champions; and the network organization. All of these are implicated in important ways. Yet throughout this book we have talked around the key to A+. The reason A+ reached so deeply into the culture of schools is because it speaks to the bottom line of teachers. For A+ teachers, the arts invite all students to learn and this makes teaching worthwhile. We will examine the unique contribution of the arts next.

Chapter 8

Sustaining Change[1]
The Difference the Arts Make in Schools

As school reform researchers, we of course first looked at sustainability in terms of sets of beliefs, practices, and processes as we discussed in the last chapter. Yet it was apparent to us that the arts themselves were key to sustainability as well. In this chapter we explore more closely what the arts have contributed to the sustainability of the A+ schools. As the preceding chapters have shown, the A+ Schools Program was successful in creating a network of schools, which emphasized the arts and arts integration but let schools adapt these emphases to the local context. Moreover, the A+ Schools Program was able to sustain these efforts over 12 years (as we write this chapter) and expanded the number of schools within North Carolina and expanded efforts to other states, including Oklahoma and Arkansas.

In the last chapter, we noted how unusual this pattern of sustainability is in school reform efforts. Most school reform efforts have expanded through a process of "packaging" the reform that was believed to be necessary to preserve the elements seen as essential to the success of the particular reform package. This package is then marketed to schools and districts to be bought through a combination of federal and state grant funds (Comprehensive School Reform Act and Title I funds, for example) and local tax dollars. For a large number of reforms (see Pink & Noblit, 2005) implementing the packages with fidelity is seen as key. Yet as we noted, A+ was more like the National Writing Project with less interest in packaging the reform and focusing on fidelity. This was a reform created by cultural arts proponents, arts educators, and schools with some interest in the arts. A key ingredient was having the schools create something themselves with the ideas and professional development of the A+ Schools Program, using the arts as both a vehicle and an outcome. While there were some guiding ideas, they were not used to enforce how a school should go about A+ and over time these ideas gave way to networks that deliberated how and what ought to be going on in A+ schools. Professional development and a focus on North Carolina's Standard Course of Study as the content to be integrated with the arts were the primary mechanisms for enabling ideas to be put into practice. If fidelity has been the key to most school reforms, for A+ the key was creativity. Like in the arts themselves, creativity in the A+ Program was not free form but rather developed in the context of a community of artists or artist-educators. The A+ Schools Program worked to facilitate this context. The networks created and professional development gave this community context both embodiment and venues for participation.

In Chapter 3, we noted that the A+ Schools Program took a somewhat novel approach to the arts. Usually there are two approaches to the arts, arts for arts' sake and arts as instrumental to other ends. A+ in large part refused to choose one of these and, in the language of postmodernism, took a both/and approach. Individual schools were to develop their own approaches and typically these were various combinations of both more arts and more arts integration, usually led by a group of arts teachers and regular classroom teachers. The A+ schools altered their local definitions over time but both/and continues to characterize the schools' approaches to the arts. Further, in schools that have an affiliated identity with A+, we have learned that more arts are easier to implement than integrated arts. While many value arts for arts' sake (the marker of higher social status), arts for arts' sake involves less disruption and thus less widespread commitment and capability than integrating the arts across the curriculum. Understanding all this, however, leaves the larger question of what it is that the arts do for schools. Thus far we have not addressed this directly. We have offered an explanation of the processes that have sustained A+ over many years, in face of challenges of turnover, high-stakes testing, and decreasing funding. In this chapter, we will explore the contribution of the arts to sustaining the reform in participating schools, but as importantly, to the lives of teachers, parents, and children within the A+ schools.

The primary approach to understanding the role of the arts in sustaining the A+ Schools Program was to stay as close as possible to the experiences of the schools. As noted earlier, this meant that during the pilot period data collection, we spent an average of 180 person days per year in the schools, or put another way, we spent a whole school year in the A+ schools for each of the 4 pilot years. After the pilot period we did case studies in specific schools in year 5 and year 7. A number of A+ meetings were attended by us each year after the pilot, and focus group interviews were conducted with key stakeholders in years 7 and 8, and in year 7, 34 of the A+ schools were surveyed via phone interviews and we conducted case studies of five schools. In all this data collection activity, the goal was to learn what was happening "on the ground" and what contributions the arts were making to the sustainability of the reform in schools.

While the arts and education literature is wide ranging, the particular focus on the arts contribution to a sustained school reform initiative has not been addressed in the literature. Much of this literature is focused on cognition and on instruction and, while this helped inform our work; it was only a small part of the larger concern. Moreover, the direct studies of arts and educational reform are rather limited. A notable exception is the work of Remer (1990) who has documented the lessons from the Arts in General Education initiative in the 1970s. This arts-based school reform initiative ended when the philanthropist who funded it died. Another sponsor was never able to be negotiated. She notes as a result while there are still some schools embodying reform, "there is little evidence of the original, comprehensive district-based programs in the six cities [in which it was piloted]" (p. 4). Thus while Remer is helpful in understanding the development and implementation of arts-based school reform, she cannot speak to sustainability. Rabkin and Redmond (2004) review a set of arts integration in education initiatives, including A+, but do not speak directly to sustainability. Indeed, they make the case that sustainability is decidedly difficult:

> We have seen schools "tipped back" by forces beyond their walls—district policies, budget cuts, new mandates, accountability provisions, or work rules. We've also seen them tipped back by forces from within—new principals and retirement of key leaders. The challenges faced by American education are enormous, and the conflicting political demands on educators are extreme.
> (Rabkin & Redmond, 2004, p. 145)

When discussing the key elements of arts integration programs they discuss the role of the arts largely in terms of resources, teaching artists, and arts specialists, but the actual role of the arts in sustaining school reform seems to have not been addressed by the programs they were reviewing. Thus it was clear that there was much to be done in conceptualizing the role of arts in school reform, and the A+ Schools Program can provide a beginning point in this deliberation.

From our experience with A+, we argue that the potential significance of the arts in school improvement and change has not received the attention that is needed. It is under-theorized and rarely investigated in itself. Indeed, some of the literature (Geahigan, 1992; Goodlad, 1992) that directly deals with the topic focuses on the opposite of our concern. This literature argues that educational reform movements and eras constrain the possibilities for the arts. We want to examine the topic from the opposite direction. Instead of limits and constraints, the goal is to unpack the possibilities the arts bring to sustained school reform and improvement. Without direct guidance in the form of previous studies that examine how the arts contribute to sustained school reform, the best course is to extract possibilities that we can consider in light of A+ experience. Implementing a reform is heavily an instrumental and strategic affair, and so is much of sustaining reform. Our argument though is that sustainability must be more than strategic action. As is clear, substantive identity schools went well beyond the instrumental and strategic to make key changes in school culture. Sustainability is about becoming part of the grain of school life and part of what is valued about that school.

We will examine the particular contribution of the arts to the sustainability of A+ in several ways in this chapter. In the next section, we will review the role of the arts in our analyses so far in this book. While we have discussed the arts reform effort in considerable detail, we have not focused as specifically on the arts themselves. This is important because many people concluded that what made A+ sustainable was the fact that it was about the arts, and less so because it followed or did not follow patterns of other school reform efforts. Following the determination of what difference the arts make in school reform, we will present the perspectives of those involved with the reform about the role of the arts in sustaining A+. We will delve into these perspectives in two ways. First, we will recount a story that was told to us repeatedly by teachers, principals, and Program staff after the pilot period had ended. This story offers one way to tap the perspectives of educators. It is a form of folklore that has come to have special meaning in the history of A+. Second, we will present what the educators told us about the role of the arts in sustaining A+ when we asked them directly. These two data sources are somewhat different but complement each other in important ways.

The Role of the Arts in the Reform Effort

Let us first review what we have said so far that speaks to the contribution of the arts to sustaining A+. In the preceding chapters, we have not tried to parse out the unique effects of the arts in large part because the arts and the reform effort were joined at the hip, so to speak. The arts were part of so much of the Program that we can only analytically pull them out of the wider matrix of Program elements and effects. In doing this analysis, we will highlight five contributions of the arts to sustaining the reform effort.

In A+, *the arts were part of bringing new people, roles, and resources into play*. In the initial planning, community arts agencies, arts funders, cultural arts advocates, and arts educators brought their views of what schools and instruction should be like, resulting in what we have earlier termed a creative approach to school reform. The emphases on arts integration as well as more arts were the direct result of their participation and this had other consequences as well. For example, it was the arts that drove the reform to focus on curriculum and instruction as deeply as it did and to create integrated lessons and thematic units as the signal pedagogy for these schools. The professional development provided by A+ changed over time. Initially, the professional development was driven by artists, but as teachers began to be proficient in creating arts-integrated instruction, the professional development was transitioned to the teachers from the A+ schools. The creation of the A+ fellows was in part a recognition that there was a new role definition in play in the schools. There were still arts teachers and regular classroom teachers but now there was a third role—teachers who could infuse the arts effectively into instruction. The arts also became the reason to closely examine and learn the full curriculum that the teachers were charged with teaching. This in turn led to the A+ schools retaining a fuller curriculum than other school as high-stakes testing was ratcheted up. There were also more arts teachers in each school, expanding curriculum offerings and freeing up time for regular teachers to do more collaborative planning. Artists have been funded by arts agencies to work in schools for many years but a common complaint has been that the contributions of the artist are hard to articulate with the rest of the curriculum. A+'s focus on the arts and arts integration and the extensive professional development all led to better use of the artists in schools and better connected their work to the instructional program. Finally, the arts teachers took on new roles in the schools as well. As the schools devised organizational strategies to manage both planning the new instruction and the scheduling to allow teacher collaboration, arts teachers moved into leadership roles that often were new to the schools and certainly were new to arts teachers who in the past were not seen as central to the instructional program. One of the unique contributions of the arts to sustaining this reform effort is that it led to new people being involved in the reform, new roles being established, and older roles being newly defined. One of the results of this was that time, a scarce resource in schools, could be assigned to sustaining the reform in the everyday life of the school.

In A+ schools, *the arts led to a new focus on the curriculum.* Early in the professional development, the A+ Schools Program became aware that the teachers' knowledge of the whole curriculum was decidedly limited. In the name of arts integration, A+ began the process of having teachers consider the full curriculum. The curriculum then became more than the content to be taught. It became the vehicle for collaboration. Teacher talk was now about what to teach and how best to teach it. The arts were implicated in both of these topics as the schools began to focus on two-way integration—teaching the required knowledge and skills of the arts in other subjects and teaching the required knowledge and skills of the other subjects in the arts. This led to the arts teachers being perceived as more fundamental to the efforts of the other teachers as well as the "regular classroom" teachers seeing themselves as arts teachers as well. This curricular focus, the mechanisms developed to manage arts offerings and arts integration, and the new role of arts teachers all are ways the arts contributed to sustaining the reform effort.

In A+ schools, *the arts made the schools and classrooms materially different*. The arts' focus on production (Eisner, 1998b) naturally led to more materials being sought by the schools. Schools developed partnerships with businesses and arts agencies to procure these materials. These partnerships had other effects, such as making the school more visible in the community. The new materials also were transformed into arts. While schools often display student work on their walls, the A+ schools had more art to be displayed. Some schools created galleries or obtained space in other galleries for the work. Informances and performances became much more common in these schools as a way to show parents and others what the arts and arts integration were contributing to the schools. In this way, A+ schools were materially enriched as a result of the arts.

For the A+ Schools Program as a whole, *the arts contributed to a network form of organization*. From the initial planning on, A+ worked via networks rather than a hierarchy. Because arts education has a long history of spanning the boundaries of schools via local arts agencies and artists, A+ from the beginning saw itself as building on the established networks. This happened at the state and national level as well as at the school level. As time passed, the internal network organization also developed networks of principals, of A+ coordinators, of A+ fellows, of subsets of schools, and so on. These networks meant that schools did not have to go it alone. They could talk with others to help better understand what was going on. The networks were key to inventiveness across the reform effort. At the level of the state-wide reform effort, the networks of foundations, key influentials, and others meant that A+ was able to anticipate and respond to a rapidly shifting political and educational landscape. Accountability was clearly the most challenging shift in the environment external to A+, but there were also the efforts to reduce state expenditures that were also part of the larger political shift. Between schools, the networks enabled pursuit of grants for collaborative projects as well as considerable sharing of knowledge and experience. The A+ fellows became a brain trust for A+ that spanned the schools. At the local school level, the new curriculum and schedule management structures put teachers together—both giving teachers unparalleled power and enabling collaborative planning. This network organization was supported by a view drawn from the arts that one supports and facilitates the works of others, rather than dictating to them. Thus the arts set the stage for this creative approach to school reform.

Finally, *the arts allowed a distinctive identity or identities for the A+ schools*. As we have analyzed in some detail in Chapter 6, the arts provided the schools the opportunity to develop new identities. These identities in turn enabled the schools to remain distinctive when some of the districts decided to implement plans that allowed families to choose what schools they wanted their children to attend. These identities also gave meaning to actions within the schools and in some schools became so central to the school culture that the identity was deployed and employed to deal with external threats. At the level of the A+ Schools Program, we can see this as well. The development of the enriched assessment idea showed how the identity enabled the A+ schools to avoid being swallowed up by the press of accountability policy. The arts enabled schools to have a new idea about what they were about, and this proved to have traction in school systems and communities, and especially for parents. While the arts had distinct effects on each level of the network organization, sustaining A+ ultimately required educators to see it as so valuable that they would carry the Program on even in face of uncertainty about the wider environment and with the understanding that they would have to give meaning to the reform instead of simply implementing the ideas of others.

In each of the above, the contribution of the arts is embedded in the complex attributes of the A+ reform effort. Yet the arts were not just part of the reform—they became part of classroom life and this offers another view of the role of the arts in sustaining the A+ Schools Program.

Arts in the Classroom

The research team saw countless hours of arts and integrated arts instruction over the course of the 8 years we were in A+ schools. In some ways, we probably became somewhat inured to the magic of the arts. Yet students early in the Program clearly saw it as novel: "This year we did social studies *with* drama. Last year we did social studies *then* drama."

Over the years students became used to the presence of the arts and, like us, were less likely to make such dramatic comparative observations. Nonetheless, we observed repeatedly that integrated arts classes had some characteristics that distinguished them from other classes even in the same school. These included multiple ways of knowing, hands-on instruction, and connections to larger learnings.

Multiple Ways of Knowing

In all the schools there was the emphasis on knowing in more than one way. While we have argued elsewhere that "multiple intelligences" (Gardner, 1983, 1991, 1993, 1999) was more a metaphor for what the arts could permit than an actual instructional device, it was clear that in arts integrated classes students were asked both to know and to do. We do not want to engage in hyperbole here. It is true that some teachers and schools were more systematic in planning lessons that engaged "multiple intelligences" and this was evident in their formal lesson plans that required them to identify what intelligences were to be engaged. Other schools and classrooms were less systematic about this but equally enthusiastic about finding a way to use the arts in instruction. In such classes, the arts were used to allow more active involvement in the lesson or as, in some ways, a reward for being cooperative during more direct instruction. This latter point is not to be taken as cynical. Much of school instruction, especially that driven toward accountability testing, is geared for rote learning. While this may increase test scores, it also requires children to be passive. This passivity can be enforced through either increasing the severity of punishments for activity outside that required for the lesson or by rewarding students with more interesting and active learning if they will cooperate in the more rote aspects of the lessons. There is an irony here, of course, about the arts becoming entangled with student discipline but such entangling is not all that unusual in schools. Participation in sports is dependent on adequate student performances in class as well.

Hands-on Instruction

Students also were regularly engaged in making things. School walls were covered in artwork in the A+ schools. Yet compared to other schools we have visited that emphasize the arts there was a notable difference in this visual art. In most schools, artwork emerges from two types of endeavor. First, it is the result of arts classes and the products invariably show the student's capabilities and progress in learning visual art. Second, it is from the other classrooms often as part of a teacher trying to allow the kids to do something they enjoy amid the arid environment of a curriculum driven by testing. In the A+ schools, the artwork on the walls was varied, from drawing to quilts, but also signaled a different approach. The artwork displayed other content knowledge. That is, the artwork displayed what the children were studying in so-called "core" subjects and showed artistic representations derived from integrated lessons and units. Displays of pottery or presentations of music would often be accompanied by an explanation of how the art involved was related to the other contents being studied. Informances, which we have discussed before, represent the dramatic and/or performance version of this logic. As noted, schools found in the first years of the A+ Program that holding student performances was a wonderful way to get the parents to the school and to have children learn the skills of drama that are also useful in life: role-taking, voice projection, purposive movement, timing, teamwork, etc. Yet preparing for repeated performances each year took a considerable amount of time, competed with classroom instruction, and burdened the performance arts teachers (usually music, drama, and dance) disproportionately. The invention of informances was to reduce the demands that performances put upon the school but to retain performance as a key art form and to have it focused on demonstrating what the children were learning.

As noted earlier, many of the schools saw A+ also as an extension of their emphasis on hands-on learning. For some schools, this meant that the arts were reduced in some senses to an instructional device, more instrumental in logic. For other schools, hands-on was more clearly connected to the production emphases of the arts. West Hollow, for example, favored hands-on instruction but this was also in the context of defining the arts as crafts that might lead students to stay in the community and develop businesses creating mountain crafts. In this scenario, wood shop was highly valued both for its hands-on orientation and for its potential to create future local artisans. When an emphasis on hands-on instruction was married to a definition of the arts as production, students were more likely to experience the arts as a creative act and not solely an instrumental one.

Connections to Larger Learnings

Students were also able to see their instruction as part of something larger. For them, it was a school-wide program. They, of course, witnessed the A+ schools banner in the halls and other artifacts. Moreover, they would explain to outsiders that their school was distinctive in the role the arts played in it. While the explanation varied by school, the children communicated that they knew something different was going on at their school and that they were proud to be part of something larger. Some students, of course, knew about the wider reform effort, but this knowledge seemed of less importance than the general idea that the use of the arts made their school something distinctive. In studies of school reform, culture is often seen as that which retards change (Sarason, 1990). Yet in the A+ schools the change in the schools ran deep into instruction and their experiences in classrooms. Here was a cultural change that they could see, articulate, and connect to other things happening at the school and sometimes across a number of schools.

As we visited schools for the last time to understand the sustainability of the A+ reform, we began to see just how deeply A+ could affect the experiences of students. The integrated lessons linked different disciplines together and students were able to see the connections between the disciplines in ways students in non-A+ schools could not. In one elementary school, we saw a thematic unit on geology taking form. The students were studying volcanoes and had taken over the classroom floor to construct a model volcano. It was large enough to walk inside to see the vents and magma and so on. The students were consulting the plans to make sure that they had correctly painted the interior. We started to flip though the plans and saw that the teachers had integrated math (exploring both various triangles and the proportionality of the sides in each type of triangle) into the designing of the scale-model volcano. The students were about to begin writing papers on what they had learned and in the folders the students had assembled for the materials to be used in the writing we found the expected geology content and more math than was revealed in the design plans. We also found accounts of eruptions and surveys of the new landmasses formed by eruptions amid poetry and photo essays on volcanoes. One of the teachers said that the students would be asked to write the paper from a perspective they chose, and one young man said he was going to write about volcanoes from the perspective of being magma contained and then released. He said his paper would have drawings of the inside of the volcano at different stages so that the reader could see as well as read what was happened with the magma. Art, science, math, social studies, and language arts were all being integrated.

A+ classrooms also were able to link the arts-integrated instruction to the state's testing programs. We visited Ridgeview Elementary School a few days before end-of-grade high-stakes testing. The principal was attending to the birth of his second child and had forgotten to inform the staff that we were coming. What we saw was clearly unrehearsed. Notably integrated instruction was everywhere in the regular and arts classrooms. As we moved from classroom to classroom, we repeatedly saw integrated lessons even as they prepared for the looming testing.

In an upper grades math class, it was drill for math skills time—to prepare the students for what the test tested. Yet this was unlike any drill we had ever seen. Since the class was after lunch and the children had little physical activity during the day, the teacher started off what she called the "brain gym." Putting Aretha Franklin's "Think" on the CD player and donning a microphone headset, the teacher opened the class with an aerobics dance session that lasted about 5 minutes and in which she participated as much as the children. The arts teacher joined her as they moved into the "math drill." Balls of colored clay were given to each student at their desks, and they were asked to make a set of geometric shapes that were expected to be part of the end-of-grade test. The shapes were organized into seven groups that the students were to move through creating and demonstrating to each other and the teachers. The shapes they were asked to form moved from simple (e.g. point, ray, line) to more complex (e.g. different types of triangles, polygons, etc.) and to those that required more critical thinking (e.g. reflection, revolution, translation). While it was heartening to the teacher and us that the students seem to know the content, what amazed us was the nature of the students' discussions. In assessing each other's clay representations, the students talked about the aesthetics of forms. They argued about when a form was an adequate example of the geometric design they were focusing on and, when not, what would need to be changed to make it adequate. This was unlike any drill session we had ever seen. Integrated instruction here was being mirrored in how the students talked about the forms in both their mathematical properties and aesthetic qualities. The students, the teacher admitted, were showing off for us, and admittedly geometry is more amenable to aesthetics than some other forms of math. Nonetheless, this example brought home to us what A+ meant in the classroom. We only wish more students could experience test preparation in such a fashion.

In sum, A+ had an approach to learning that was quite expansive. Multiple ways of knowing, hands-on instruction, and connections to larger learnings also characterized the professional development offered to educators. The arts were used to reconsider how to teach, to transform the objectives and suggested strategies in the Standard Course of Study into thematic units and integrated lessons. At the summer institutes and on-site workshops the arts were used to allow teachers to experience what the students might experience. The enriched assessment process that was developed also enabled the schools, as with Ridgeview above, to link the arts-based instruction to even standardized content knowledge. As a result, A+ was quite unlike any school reform the research team had ever seen, and this was because it was about the arts.

These data are drawn, of course, from our observations, interviews, and interpretations. They represent our perspective as qualitative researchers who have spent a lot of time in the A+ schools. Yet we would be the first to acknowledge that there are many perspectives on what is it about the arts that helped A+ work to be sustained over the years. The most important perspectives are those who have sustained A+ in the schools. One way to tap the perspectives of the educators in A+ schools is to examine the stories they tell. We heard many stories about students who used to be uninterested in school but, since A+, came even when sick, about parents who so enjoyed the A+ school that they began to come to the school regularly, just to be part of the action, and so on. But one story began as the pilot period was ending, and we heard it time and time again. The story was about one of the A+ principals, but in its telling it served as an analogy for the meaning of the arts as embodied in A+.

The Transformation of a Principal

There are many stories of the arts in the lives of those involved in A+ schools. A number of school principals in the pilot schools had in fact been arts educators and thus had personal experiences and commitments that they brought to the Program. However, A+ participants repeatedly referred to one story when talking about the arts to the research team. Mr. Horara (a pseudonym) was the subject of this story. Part of this story will be familiar because he was principal of Entomon Hills Elementary. Mr. Horara had shepherded his school through a difficult period, and was key in A+ becoming the substantive identity of Entomon Hills Elementary School.

To reiterate, originally Entomon Hills had been a "classical" magnet. It had been thought by the large urban school district that this type of magnet would attract those who wanted a more traditional curriculum and strong emphases on order and discipline. Yet this had not proven to be the case. The school, located in a largely African American, working-class neighborhood, was largely unable to attract new students from outside the traditional attendance zone. As a result, the school had to reconsider the type of magnet it was. As Mr. Horara led the school through this difficult process, he and some of his arts teachers became aware of the planning for the A+ Schools Program. They learned what they could about the reform and in the end shifted Entomon Hills into an arts and sciences magnet. To ensure commitment to this reform effort, the teachers had to reapply for their positions by demonstrating they were able to integrate the arts among other things. In the end, the teaching staff was reconstituted and a new magnet program was developed. All this was simultaneous with applying to be one of the A+ pilot schools. Entomon Hills was selected to be one of the pilot schools and opened that fall as a new magnet and as one of the original A+ schools. In the subsequent years, Entomon Hills was one of the schools with a substantive identity around A+ and the arts. Teachers at Entomon Hills were seen as truly inventive with A+ and soon were included in the network of A+ fellows that guided and provided the professional development offered teachers. Mr. Horara retired at the end of the A+ pilot period, which is part of the story. This loss was devastating to the school, but Entomon Hills recovered in part because the new principal recognized what A+ brought to the school, and is now recognized as one of the leading principals in the A+ network. The school is regarded as a success story by A+ participants. Some of the Entomon Hills teachers from Mr. Horara's era now lead major efforts on part of the A+ Schools Program. Yet all this is but context to the story people recount about Mr. Horara.

As is clear from the above, Mr. Horara was a highly capable principal—able to make difficult decisions, dismiss unsatisfactory teachers, and rally his staff and school community for new and untried ideas. Moreover, he kept his school at the forefront of the A+ Schools Program for many years, and successfully survived high-stakes accountability. He could both maintain and change a school. The story told about him varies a little by who is telling it but it usually includes the following.

Mr. Horara began to see what was happening to the children at his school. He noted the change in their attitudes toward school and learning, and ultimately in their achievement. He watched how the arts contributed to this and became, if anything, even more committed to the arts at Entomon Hills over time. His arts teachers were seen as some of the best in the A+ Program and his regular classroom teachers were seen as very committed and adept in arts integration. Entomon Hills was about the sciences as well but in Mr. Horara's school it was clear that the arts were central.

There was another change in Mr. Horara that the story recounts that begins the analogy of the meaning of the arts. Mr. Horara decided that his own life needed the arts as well. It started small. He enrolled in a pottery class and found it quite rewarding. He began to see what it was that the kids were experiencing and this was demonstrated in how he began to talk about the arts in his role as school principal. Then he took another step, he enrolled in a sculpture class, and then another and then another. In less than a year, he had set up a studio at home and was enthralled with what being an artist meant to his life. He continued to develop his capability and people began to note his skill. He started to give gifts of his work and as we interviewed people they would comment quite positively on his sculptures and on his transformation from an educator interested in what the arts could bring to children into an artist in his own right.

As the A+ pilot period was coming to an end, Mr. Horara reached the minimum retirement age for educators in North Carolina. His professional career was soaring. He was a noted school leader, had turned a school "around" in the jargon of educational administration, and had demonstrated the power of the arts so persuasively that the middle school into which Entomon Hills fed its students had decided to become an A+ school. In his career, everything was as good as it could get. He had a school of which others were envious. He could have moved into school district administration, receiving more pay for work that would be less demanding on his energies and time. Yet Mr. Horara decided to retire and become a full-time sculptor. He had learned that the arts had much to give, even with their demands on talent and time. He had convinced countless others of the value of the arts to people and now wished to live an artistic life fully.

The story usually ends with when the teller last saw him and how happy he is. His continued and more ambitious artwork is recounted and the meaning of the overall story is asserted: the arts offer something that is irresistible when once experienced. It is argued that Mr. Horara should be seen as proof of why A+ is such a successful program. It enables children and educators to see human endeavor differently and to see their own capabilities differently. The story concludes with the admonition: should not everyone have such an experience?

As we noted, the story varies a little by who tells it and the context in which it is invoked. Yet the story is still told, years after Mr. Horara retired. The transformation is what people are highlighting. The arts can remake one's life, redefine one's sense of oneself, enable a career in art production, and make one happy as well. A+ participants tell other stories as well, of course. They tell of the child who so wants to go the school after the arts have become central to the curriculum that the parents can threaten the child that she can't go to school unless she behaves—a dire threat indeed! They also tell of the time that a new principal arrived to assume the leadership of an A+ school to only be met by the group of parents who just wanted to be sure the new principal understood that this was an A+ school. And so on. Such stories can have many meanings but they helped us understand that, whatever A+ meant as an instance of school reform, it was its message about the arts that had to be told. Moreover, it taught us that school reform is ultimately adjudicated by the perspectives of the educators who implement and sustain it. Much of the meaning of Mr. Horara's story can be seen in what the teachers say directly about the role of the arts in sustaining A+.

What's Art Got to Do with It? A+ Educators, Arts, and Sustainability

In this section we highlight the themes that capture the essence of the differences the arts make for schools in the A+ Program that contribute to the sustainability of A+. Those closest to the A+ Program (teachers, administrators, and Program staff) reported four themes:

- The arts make learning fun.
- The arts reach more students because success is defined in different ways.
- The arts make learning more meaningful by adding important connections.
- The arts tap a core need for identity, creativity, and growth.

To illustrate these themes we make use of reflections during a day spent with some 80 A+ school principals and coordinators in the fall of 2003. (The coordinators are teachers in the A+ schools who spend time coordinating curriculum, professional development, materials dissemination, and teaming schedules in their schools.) With the principals and coordinators we used a process called "nomadic graffiti" (a technique A+ uses routinely to capture people's thinking on different topics). We put questions about the role of the arts in sustaining A+ on newsprint along the walls. People circulated and wrote what they thought in response to the questions. Finally, the key staff from the Kenan Institute for the Arts also offered their views in a focus group interview. The focus of our conversation was what difference it made that this was an arts reform, and not some other kind of reform, for the sustainability of the A+ Schools Program. There was no hesitation in either process—people were eager to share their views.

Learning as Fun

The current environment in education includes a strong push at the state level for standards and frameworks. These more carefully define the important attributes of what children need to know and be able to do, often constraining what happens in the classroom. Also, with the federal No Child Left Behind legislation, the stakes on the accountability front have increased dramatically. This means that most classrooms have become much more task oriented. That often translates into a situation where the word "fun" is often stripped from the classroom vocabulary. To be sure, all the A+ schools have felt the same standards and accountability pressures, but with a strong arts focus there is still ample room for fun. The educators explained:

> When asked "What did you learn in school today?" The response is no longer "Nothing." The children *talk* about what they learn. Actually the children think they just had "fun" and learning was incidental. (Coordinator)

> It's always a positive and joyous learning environment—centered on the success [of the students]. The parents and the community get tired of dealing with bad grades, low test scores, or the need to "push" students. [Students] soak up these opportunities to shine, to learn, and celebrate learning. (Principal)

> It gives a wonderful feeling as soon as you walk in the front door. The children are happy, teachers are happy—there is something for all children to feel good about. (Coordinator)

This latter comment makes an important point about the increased fun quotient in the A+ schools. The focus was on education being enjoyable for the children, but with the arts there is more enjoyment for everyone involved. Everyone noted that it is not just the students that are having more fun, but also the teachers:

> Teachers can bring their personal artistic talents into their instruction. Teaching becomes more *fun*! (Principal)

> The arts make learning *fun*. They help us as teachers have *fun* as well and we are able as teachers to *love* what we *do*. (Coordinator)

> It is exciting, teaching is never boring—always able to update and modify what and how you are teaching. (Principal)

Both teachers and students finding life in classrooms more fun is probably sufficient for the school to want to stay with the A+ reform. It was an ancillary bonus though that the educators were aware that parents were also able to see the excitement in their children. They explained:

> Parents like happy kids; A+ is a happy way of doing education. It is for life not just for a test. (Coordinator)
>
> Parents see their children "eagerly" wanting to come to school. (Principal)
>
> They see their kids beaming with excitement about . . . all things . . . when kids love school and talk about learning with excitement, then the parents and community *take notice*! ☺ (Coordinator)

Educators and students are used to seeing school as work. Teachers are used to assigning schoolwork and homework, and students are used to complying with the demands "do your work." Work signifies a seriousness to schooling that other terms may miss. Fun is one such term. In schools, fun is often opposed to work. Teachers often use it as an incentive or as a reward for the work, but it is not the work itself. There is an interesting juxtaposition in the arts where production, that is work, is seen as a dominant logic (Eisner, 1998b) but in being coupled with creativity produces enjoyment (Egan, 1992). One of the reasons A+ is remarkably sustainable as a school reform is because the work is a form of creative production. For students, learning is no longer as rote as it is in other schools because it is coupled with a more creative form of production than filling out worksheets; school work becomes fun. Teacher work also becomes more creative as well. Designing arts integrative lessons requires a teacher to consider lesson planning not only as a way to cover required content but also as an act of creation. The lessons more fully draw the teachers into the art of teaching itself. Moreover, assessment can be reframed as well as artistic production. This is creative fun as well as the day-to-day job of teaching in an A+ school. Working hard at something you enjoy and seeing this stimulate students to do likewise makes A+ a compelling commitment. When parents recognize this as well, the A+ Schools Program is easier to sustain than other reforms we have witnessed.

Reaching More Students

One of the most vexing problems of American education is finding ways to ensure the success of students who traditionally have not fared well in the past. Nearly everyone we talked to made the point that the arts, and its focus on tapping a range of different intelligences, is a key tool in this battle to find ways to make all students successful. They argued, very convincingly, that A+ is sustained because the arts give students a different way to show themselves, their peers, their teachers, and their parents that they understand important concepts and content that eluded them in the more traditional learning environments:

> The arts provide avenues of learning that are not available in "traditional" classrooms, which allow students to find a successful/familiar way to transfer knowledge. (Coordinator)
>
> Multiple intelligences creates a richness of entry points. There are many ways move on this and teachers are becoming more fluent in the recognitions of the assets of different children. (Kenan staff)
>
> All students are able to become involved. It is a natural way to learn. And authentic! (Principal)
>
> Students have the chance to experience knowledge and success in many different ways. (Coordinator)

One administrator, in a play on words from the new federal legislation, shared how the arts provided a way for all students to learn: "The 'arts' are good for all children and leaves no child behind in its presentation." A key message in recognizing the value of the arts for struggling learners was that it offered success in situations where success had rarely been encountered in the past, as this coordinator noted: "The arts often engage children who do not feel successful in other areas. What a delight to turn the light on for that child!"

Not only do the arts help reach a wider range of students, but as the educators emphasized, it is done in a way that parents can see and appreciate. It is important that parents see the arts as more than just fun to be supportive of a school reform. School personnel argue parents are recognizing that the arts are part of how the school meets the needs of their children:

> Parents want to know that their child's individual needs are met . . . Arts allow the child to learn and express himself [or herself] in a unique way. (Principal)
>
> Parents want to know that their children are succeeding but they also want to know that the "whole" child is being recognized—A+ children have a chance to excel somewhere. (Coordinator)

A+ billed itself as "schools that work for everyone" but this does not distinguish it from a wide variety of reforms. Most school reforms are about serving all students better. The fact that this is hard to accomplish in any school does not demean such intentions. The usual approach to serving all students better is remedial instruction, better student services, more careful assessment and placement, and thus differentiated instruction. A+ is distinguishable in many ways from other whole-school reforms not in the intention to reach more students but in the distinctive features, arts, arts-integrated instruction, and multiple intelligences, that are argued to make this possible. Part of sustaining A+, then, is in the role these features play in making this argument.

Learning as More Meaningful Through Connections

The last theme pointed out that the arts are seen as a significant avenue for helping a wider range of students become successful. The obvious question is how. The comments from this theme help answer this question. What the arts do, according to those who work with students, is add a richer and deeper meaning to the learning process, and this makes A+ an approach that educators want to sustain. The arts provide a way for students, teachers, and parents to "connect the dots" across a set of diffuse and seemingly random activities, producing a clearer picture of knowledge and its connection to life:

> Art makes connections for students—They see, feel, do things that make sense in their lives; they are experiencing themselves. (Coordinator)

> Concepts are presented in a way that children will remember what they learned. They tie learning to an activity that they do not forget. (Principal)

> Although *all* subjects have a state curriculum to follow, it's the *integration*, the connecting that helps students and faculty to sustain interest in learning/growing. (Coordinator)

> Hands-on experiences make the abstract tangible . . . more of a see it, taste it, feel it approach. (Principal)

A+ educators conceived of "connections" very broadly. Some stayed very close to the curricula. For them, connections meant linkages among disciplines and one result was more holistic understandings and critical thinking:

> The arts are the *glue* that helps tie the subject areas together. We use the arts to help our students see the *"Big Picture"*—how do we make connections—and through the connections we help them become critical thinkers. (Coordinator)

> The arts make the connections between disciplines; they create holistic learning. (Coordinator)

Others wanted to elaborate connections to be about more than just what school teaches. They argued that arts integration meant students having conceptual models about connection and having content connect to the larger world, including a broadened definition of how students should spend their social time:

> The arts help students realize that learning, like life, is connected. They help students in our fragmented world make bridges. (Coordinator)

> The arts [make] connections outside the school—children point out arts events, asking to attend performances, etc.; increased involvement in after-school and private arts organizations (i.e. piano, dance . . .). (Coordinator)

As with our discussion of "fun" above, the connections provided by the arts extended beyond students. These connections were broadly conceived as well. They were about relations between teachers and with students. It was also that through connections, teachers can make more meaning of their work:

> A+ and the integration of the arts and curriculum make learning meaningful and it makes teaching meaningful. Teachers are just like students. We are passionate about learning and we teach best when our heart and soul are in the teaching. Meaningful teaching equals meaningful learners. (Coordinator)

> The arts made it impossible to work in isolation . . . It is the nature of arts integration that there is more dependence on the arts teachers . . . Collaboration becomes the lifeblood of the school. (Kenan staff)

> The arts offer great opportunities to focus on a particular strength that a student may have. Teachers and specialists collaborate and integrate to make a whole learning experience. (Coordinator)

But equally important, the arts helped parents connect to what their children were doing and learning in school in ways that an A or an F on a report card simply cannot capture: The parents learn that A+ is more than just being about enjoyment for the children:

> As they sit in an audience and watch with awe what their thirteen-year-old boy is doing in a choreographic offering on war and peace, or stroll through a gallery with artworks reflecting inclusion and thoughts on alienation, or hear music played for a slide show on mechanized security, and other sharings—they come to realize that the arts and the A+ philosophy has offered their child *power* and a *voice*. (Coordinator)

Parents see a sense of pride in the accomplishment of their child. (Principal)

While parents may find it difficult to help with homework, when the arts are evoked parents have more opportunity to bring their skills to bear on the project. In sum, the arts make the schools more inviting places. (Kenan staff)

Finally, connections were also being made among the schools. This cannot be overemphasized since teaching has often been characterized as a lonely profession, with the work of instruction being done behind closed doors with little sharing, even across the hall, let alone from building to building. The collective focus on the arts brought educators from around the state together to make their work much more public:

A+ provides a network of principals and coordinators and teachers who support each other through collaboration at regional and state-wide meetings—to share arts/artists and ways to keep art really alive and a part of the curriculum. Collaboration is key. Art has therefore become part of what we do—who we are. (Coordinator)

In the above quotes, connections are seen between disciplines, between school and life, and between people. As school reform researchers, though, we see connections as having other dimensions as well. Sustaining a reform is more than a belief that it works. It requires a set of processes that enable people to make meaning of the reform together. This is one reason many reforms require teams from schools to come to professional development. A+, in emphasizing that the whole school participates in professional development, pushes this to a new level. Connections are about the resources people have to make sense of their lives. A+ is sustainable as a school reform because it developed the mechanisms, such as networks, collaborative curriculum planning, professional development, etc., that enabled teachers and principals to use A+ to make meaning of schooling in new ways. In the above, we see that teachers took these lessons into the classroom and found that they worked for students as well. A reform that reaches this deeply into the life of a school is likely to be sustained.

Creating Identity, Fostering Creativity, and Encouraging Growth

Any organization operates more smoothly when everyone is focused on the same issues and moving in the same direction. That focus provides a synergy that encourages people to be creative and look for growth opportunities. This was argued by many to be key to the sustainability of A+. The arts, according to many of the educators we listened to, provided that focus for the A+ schools and the students in them:

> It provides a "center" or "pulse" for our school. (Coordinator)

> It provides a common ground where creativity engrains the curriculum. (Coordinator)

> The arts give middle school students a place to fit in—one student told me "I don't read well, but I am a great dancer." (Principal)

> The arts help bring positive attention to the school. They allow students' personalities to be expressed—self-expression—and give the school a "personality." (Coordinator)

The principals were especially sensitive to this theme since their responsibility is for the school as a whole. They used words to describe this such as "identity and common purpose," "much more teamwork," "more thinking and doing out of the box," and "deeper instruction." They even went further to suggest that such actions contributed to "improvement in school climate—learning and teaching is more fun," which also "provided a delivery focus that is natural for children, fits how they relate to the world, promotes a neurological impress[ion] that brings learning back to them over time."

This focus had the added feature of being inclusive, allowing everyone in the building to be part of it, instead of having something that was imposed from the state or some national "model" of what a school should look like:

> The arts are a reflection of their [the community's] own cultural values. Each school capitalizes on the talents immediately available to them. (Principal)

> Everyone can find "their" place to belong. (Principal)

This sense of identity for the school helped spark a creative side that was not evident before A+. In response to our questions about what made A+ sustainable, many argued that A+ created a spark and excitement that encouraged staff to continue growing:

> Arts allow you to wake something up where it wasn't before. (Kenan staff)

> The arts added a creative element to our school that did not exist prior to A+. It set us apart and added depth to our teaching that cannot be measured, nurtured our kids and made them better. It wouldn't have been the same result without the arts. (Coordinator)

> It's [the school] constantly growing! It's amazing how open our staff is and each year we continue to grow. With new folks coming

aboard—they feel the energy of the rest of the school and jump right in. (Coordinator)

The arts provide a huge dose of creativity. They contain optimism about the real possibility of doing things differently because artists do things differently. (Kenan staff)

This sense of excitement and possibility is another reason A+ has been sustainable as a school reform. While many school reforms wane with staff turnover, there is the belief that A+, and the creativity it involves, is sufficient to counteract this. An ownership in learning among A+ schools, fostered by this spark of creativity, is illustrated by the difference between change as mandated from the outside (how it is often done at the state and federal level) as opposed to arts and arts integration driving individual school choices from the inside (how it was done in the A+ Program):

I look at the Department of Public Instruction and legislatures, who created mandate after mandate. My experience is when grownups mandate things all you get is compliance. There is no generative power, only compliance. You can't add your own piece to that process. But what you really want is if a school thinks it can commit to something more than is required of them that this is not considered stepping out of line. (Kenan staff)

Finally, the staying power of that growth potential is best captured in a comment about how an arts focus helped rally the entire network of schools, even in the face of strong adversity:

While the original agreement with school districts was that they would assume funding A+ at the end of the pilot period, they did not. Yet the network developed a way to deal with the loss. They decided to work out collaborative arrangements and make the institutes more school-based and lower cost. Further, the potential loss of arts teachers [because of funding cuts] meant the network decided to make the institutes themselves even more about the arts so that the classroom teachers could further develop their knowledge so they could do arts integration more on their on. As one person said of the network: "It does take on a life of its own." (Kenan staff)

Conclusion

In the preceding, it should be evident that coordinators, principals, Kenan staff, and our research team see the contribution of the arts to the A+ Schools Program somewhat differently. Coordinators are teachers, and tend to focus on students, while principals tend to focus more on teachers and parents. The Kenan staff, not surprisingly, are somewhat more focused on the Program across schools. The research team had somewhat more of a focus on the schools as organizations, A+ as a reform initiative, and on the various roles being played by various elements of the effort. Nonetheless, it is also clear that the arts are key to making this school reform different from others. As the coordinators and principals repeatedly commented: "It works!"

Whatever the original reasons for the reform effort, the effect on students has become the driving force in sustaining the reform. The emphases on multiple intelligences, hands-on-instruction, and connections to larger learnings observed by the research team would likely have long-waned if students had not found A+ as engaging and fun. This result of the arts, noted by Egan (1992), also made A+ inviting to teachers. Teachers found that the hours spent planning integrated instruction were worthwhile because it made learning fun, because it "worked" in ways that resulted in significant learning, and because it put teachers in creative control of both curriculum and instruction. A+ engaged teachers as professionals who care about their students and what the students are learning. All the schools had at least one (and many had two or three) principal change over the 8 years we were gathering data in the schools. While principal turnover often leads to demise of a reform, it has not with A+. In the above, we see that the arts explain this in fundamental ways. The principals see students enjoying learning, teachers enjoying teaching, and parents pleased by both. They also see changes in school climate as well as in student achievement. The arts have also made their schools distinctive and "marketable" as open enrollment has become more common across North Carolina. The arts thus have a big pay off for administrators, even if they inherited the reform rather than initiated it.

The engagement and learning the arts engendered also affected the Program overall. In the initial professional development, the educators were somewhat uneasy about engaging in the arts. This uneasiness gave way to excitement as they got used to this and more importantly as they saw what the arts were doing for the students, themselves, and the schools. These lessons taught the educators that the arts could be a productive way to approach learning *and* school improvement.

In all this we can see a fuller meaning of Mr. Horara's story. It signifies not only the power of the arts in an individual life, but also how a school administrator was disconnected from the direct effects of the arts in the A+ Schools Program. Mr. Horara became an artist so that he could participate in what the students and teachers found so valuable. He is enjoying now what before he facilitated, witnessed, and even professionally benefited from—the power of the arts to change the salience of education for teachers and students.

Finally, the A+ experience also speaks to the literature on sustaining school reform as well. The arts enabled hands-on production in classrooms as well as the production of distinctive identities and meanings of education in the A+ schools. The arts became the basis both for imaginative learning and teaching but also allowed schools to imagine education differently. When this image came into reality, it has proven difficult to imagine giving it up. The arts created a host of new connections between the arts and other subjects; students and teachers; teachers and other teachers in the same schools and across the network; teachers and principals; principals and other A+ principals; teachers/principals and the Kenan Institute and other arts organizations; and so on. These connections served to sustain the identities of the A+ schools in the face of the challenges they have faced, and to imagine an A+ outside the Kenan Institute. The arts also have culminated in connections within and between the schools, within the A+ fellows and across the network. Each school has a somewhat different A+ and thus plays different parts in the network community. This in many ways is the cumulative result of how the arts have sustained the A+ Schools Program over the dozen years since it first selected the pilot schools. The literature on school reform misses so much of this in its emphasis on fidelity over time. Sustainable school reform requires engaging educators, students, and their families in something that calls to their imagination. Indeed, we would argue that the emphasis on fidelity is actually in the way of sustaining school reform. Staying with a reform requires that the reform be generative, not definitive. We can now argue that in allowing the reform to be adapted and turning the reform's direction largely over to the schools and networks, A+ in essence created the conditions for generativity. As noted in the chapter on identity (Chapter 6), not all schools developed the same level of generativity with the arts and A+. However, we know of no other reform in which a large set of original schools have a similar level of sustainability. On this, A+ is remarkable.

The arts have made all the difference in sustaining the A+ Schools Program and in sustaining the individual schools. The arts have made the A+ Schools Program the "mold breaking" example of school reform that it has proven to be.

We also want to add an additional interpretation. People find it difficult to see their own assumptions and thus it often takes an outsider to be able to articulate what is assumed by members of a group. There is an assumption in the above that the participants share but are not explicit about. It seems to us that the A+ schools came to see the arts as a value, indeed a moral, stance. They chose and continued with A+ through high-stakes testing, leadership change, and the uncertainty that A+ itself engendered in asking people to take responsibility for the reform itself because they believed the arts made their schools better places for children, for teachers, and for the community. That is, A+ schools were making a moral claim as well as any other claims about arts for arts' sake and/or the arts as instrumental in teaching other content or even in changing schools. The power of moral belief exceeds that of any instrumentality. Doing what you believe is right, true, or beautiful is much more compelling that doing just what works. The A+ schools in many ways reformed their practices to productive ends. Yet these schools also experienced a fundamental shift in values, with the belief that their arts-enhanced school was morally better than it had been before. It had a basis for a school identity beyond what other reforms can claim to foster with their emphasis on more content and better test scores. A+ schools could create and recreate themselves because they were clear about what they valued. School reform studies and evaluation are rarely designed to investigate moral belief, but we think it is time to do so. The result will likely change how we think about school reform in dramatic ways, and what power we subscribe to the arts in education as well (Noblit & Bettez, 2004).

Chapter 9

Creative and Lasting School Reform

Lessons from the Arts

In December 2006, we and other A+ researchers and evaluators were declared "rock stars." Aside from what we have said about our attraction to the music of our youth, this is not something we would have predicted would result from being researchers of arts-based school reform. This declaration came from Eric Booth who was serving as the conference facilitator for what was dubbed informally at least as *the* national research conference on A+. The conference was funded by the NEA, which had become fascinated by the research and evaluation studies that led to this book. The A+ Schools Program held this national conference to examine what was know from the research and evaluation studies of A+ in North Carolina, Oklahoma, and Arkansas. We were there, as were many of our original research team and the researchers for Oklahoma and Arkansas. It was a heady few days where we presented what we had learned and interacted with interested educators, A+ school personnel we had not seen for a couple of years, national and international experts, and policy makers and others. Rock stars or not, we learned that there were some amazing similarities across the states, even given the adaptability built into A+.

Mike Gunzenhauser was on the evaluation teams of both the North Carolina and Oklahoma A+ efforts, and through the latter was knowledgeable of the Arkansas initiative as well. He also reviewed what had been learned through the three evaluation efforts. In his presentation (Gunzenhauser, 2006), he concluded that two themes ran across all three evaluations. The first theme was engagement. He noted that engagement in A+ was an ongoing affair, not the one-time vote by teachers that is so common with reform efforts. He argued engaging in A+ "is a commitment to self, to colleagues and to students" (p. 2). Since A+ was not a reform package but more of a process, he argued that this engagement entails "working towards coherence" and "creating new models" (p. 2) as schools adapted A+ to their contexts. The second theme was accountability. Here he noted the enriched assessment process that linked "external documentation" with "student learning" (p. 3), where most schools had succumbed to the former only because of the press of high-stakes testing. He went on to elaborate that this meant that A+ added to external accountability a form of internal accountability where a school decides "what's important for students to know, makes a plan for assessing it, and works school-wide with scope, sequence and collaboration to make it happen" (p. 4). He argues having a strong sense of internal accountability puts external accountability in perspective. Gunzenhauser went on to argue that A+ enabled a stronger sense of responsibility widely shared across the educational institution. Clearly, we see these themes in what we have written here. Yet we also want to emphasize that there is something about the arts that makes a difference in what A+ was able to accomplish.

There is much that the arts can teach us about school reform, and the A+ Schools Program provides a powerful example on which to base these lessons. Yet, as noted in the conclusion to Chapter 6, there are reasons to be cautious about schools just trying to do A+, or some version thereof, on their own. A+ overcame serious threats to sustainability but did so in a very particular way. Reformers did their political homework and created a wide range of constituencies from the planning phase on. A+ had an influential sponsor devoted to developing the support needed and assiduously avoided directing what the schools should do. The meetings, the professional development, the enriched assessment project, and the network were structured carefully to suggest ideas and then left it in educators' hands to determine what should happen in each building. The focus was on the "process" more than the product.

This approach was extremely frustrating in the early years to the A+ schools as they were well used to being told what to implement. Being drawn into reform decisions was new to them. A+ however was all about connecting people, providing a wide range of ideas, developing organizational capacity, trusting teachers to design appropriate curricula and instructional processes, attending to students, and ultimately valuing the arts.

All this, and the other topics discussed in this book, therefore point to the fact that A+ is not a reform that a school can just adopt like a new curriculum or program. That would violate all that A+ stands for. In both the arts and school reform, A+ has embraced creativity as well as instrumentality. It has emphasized both bottom-up and top-down reform. It is more a dance than a program in many ways. None of this, however, should deter us from learning from A+, as long as we remember that it is what one does with these ideas that is key to the potential of the ideas for schools and for art education. In this final chapter the focus will be on the lessons that can be taken away from A+ and its experiences with the arts and school reform.

The Accomplishments of A+: A Summary

In this book, the culmination of two studies of the A+ Schools Program in North Carolina, we have been exploring the role of school identity in building and sustaining arts-based comprehensive education reform. Like other comprehensive education reforms, A+ begins with a vision of improved teaching and learning—in this case integrating the arts through-out the curriculum to create enhanced learning opportunities by tapping the multiple intelligences of students. That central vision drives the changes in policy and practice necessary to make it a reality in the classroom. We have shown how the ways in which schools integrated the arts into their identity—their organization, their culture, and their definition of quality teaching and learning—have been key to the resilience of the reform.

School reforms have a notoriously short life cycle, quickly being under-mined by challenges such as staff and leadership turnover, a lack of time for training and implementation, and competing policy mandates. The arts have had a particularly tenuous position in public education, often being the first to be sacrificed in political and budgetary battles. Thus, the resilience of A+, an arts-based comprehensive education reform, is striking and suggests that something about the Program enabled at least some of the schools to embed the arts in their identity, the central values for which a school stands and on which it will defend in the face of external challenges. During the pilot period, three "protective factors" gave schools the time and resources to truly integrate the reform: (1) a rich network of professional development opportunities and support; (2) the development of multiple leadership roles within each school; and (3) relatively stable funding. With these in place, we witnessed how schools developed identi-ties around the arts. There were three identities: (1) affiliative identity, in which A+ was mostly a matter of formal designation and participation in network events, to (2) symbolic identity, in which schools began to celebrate the arts in their activities and use Program language to describe their efforts, to (3) substantive identity, in which arts integration was a major driver of decisions about school operations and day-to-day class-room practice.

We also analyzed case studies of schools that succeeded in reaching a substantive level of A+ identity and analyzed how they used that identity to manage change during the pilot period. We then discerned a set of common factors among those substantive identity schools, including: (1) the development of new internal and external connections; (2) an increased capacity for organizational learning; and (3) a focus on how the Program benefits students. Again, these factors were fully imbued with the arts. The arts were the "substance" in each of these factors in two ways. First, the arts and A+ enabled each of these factors. Connections, school-based training and evaluation, and accountability (of multiple forms) were all sponsored by A+ and the arts were why these happened. Second, each of the above factors enabled the role of the arts to be enhanced in the A+ schools.

After the pilot period, A+ continued to evolve toward a self-sustaining organization. Yet it resisted the prevalent model of "packaging" reform so that it could be marketed as a product to be purchased. For A+, the process has been more important than the product. It was the process that led schools to creatively adapt A+ to their contexts and to develop the organizational capacity to mange change. As the case studies in Chapter 7 revealed, the schools have continued to adapt A+ to their changing circumstances, including the loss of the small direct funding.

With some transition funding from the Kenan Institute and increasingly funded by the schools themselves, the A+ schools have been able to continue to rely on A+ summer conferences and other meetings and workshops to glean new ideas and develop curriculum and instruction plans that integrate the North Carolina Standard Course of Study. The A+ network remains a central support feature and now is planning for the future of A+. The new schools (17 in North Carolina) have provided their own funding for participation in the summer conferences and other activities. The A+ fellows continue to serve as a "brain trust" and as the professional developers for the Program. Outside funding from government and private sources has allowed A+ to develop new initiatives and programs in other states. As we showed earlier, schools we studied as part of the sustainability study funded by the Ford Foundation had not sustained some parts of A+ including the level of collaborative planning, a sufficient number of arts teachers, and sufficient professional development—especially for new teachers. Nevertheless, the schools we studied have been able to retain their substantive identities around the arts. A+ makes them resilient in the face of the challenges of leadership, staff transition, and increased accountability pressures. The case of Creekside Middle School also shows that even after the pilot period professional development, consultation, and support of the A+ network provide necessary resources for a school to change its identity vis-à-vis the arts. Finally, the sustainability of A+ is ultimately driven by what it does for children and for teachers, principals, parents, and schools as a whole. The schools were fully able to maintain continued growth in student learning as measured by North Carolina's end-of grade and end-of-course high-stakes tests and satisfy the accountability system. Yet this was not what teachers, principals, and parents talked about. They wanted to talk about what it did to the life of the school. Children were enjoying the increased participation in the arts and in the arts-integrated instruction. It engaged students in their learning in notable ways. Parents recounted this as well. Teaching was also more fun for teachers as the Program engaged them intellectually in planning curricula and teaching as well as creating engaging classrooms for the students and themselves. Principals observed the effects on the school as a whole, and better relations with parents and the wider community, and noted "A+ works" for students and in so many other ways.

In our experience studying school reforms, this is a remarkable accomplishment that has many implications. Below we will examine how arts made a difference in more detail. This will lead to what we argue are the promises of A+ and promising signs A+ has for a range of audiences: educators, arts reformers, and policy makers, and arts researchers and evaluators. We approach this closure with some trepidation. A+ is still going strong, and we continue to have some role with it. We learn something with every encounter with the Program. Moreover, there is so much more that can be said about the A+ Schools Program. We have reported here only a small amount of the data we have on A+. The research team has published a number of papers and the evaluation reports are extensive. Nevertheless, there is so much more to be analyzed and to be said that we find it hard not to move on to the next analysis rather than to close out this book. We owe it to those interested in arts-based school reform and school reform in general to say what we think this research means, at least in some limited ways.

The Arts and School Reform

School reform is a particular form of cultural production. As we argued earlier, school reform is largely conceived in the context of making people do something they are not already doing. Such coercion may prompt compliance but compliance by definition is based on the continuance of coercion. The behavioral theory used in much school reform simply assumes that if forced to do things over a period of time people will come to accept this as what they should be doing. Historians of school reform argue that this model does not lead to lasting reform, but then these same historians suggest that reforms related to changes in teaching are not likely to be sustained anyway. Their argument, again, is that since reform is created by policy makers who know little about the contexts of teaching, such changes are unlikely to be found workable. A+ was able to sustain changes in teaching approach largely because of the focus on teachers' planning instruction. Teachers also came to be the "brain trust" of professional development and ultimately of the future of the Program.

A+ also developed a set of constituencies to the reform effort that is exceptional in recent efforts at school reform. In the last chapter, it was also evident that the arts were key to this process. The argument is layered but the bottom line, if there is one, is that the arts were engaging to the students and made learning more enjoyable. It also seemed to work across the broad spectrum of students, serving to advance equity in the views of the teachers. The arts also reinvigorated teaching itself. By using the arts, teachers were reminded that they have the power and knowledge to make classrooms better places for children and learning. Arts integration meant teachers needed to collaborate around creative ideas. The creativity of teachers was tapped in both the arts and teaching. A+ also helped the school be better organized around the curricula, both in terms of scheduling and mapping. This in turn led the schools to see how to align instruction better with even high-stakes testing, negating a potential threat to emphasizing the arts.

A strong teacher culture around the arts and A+ developed. In the substantive identity schools, A+ meant that there was a set of beliefs and practices that enabled the schools to take charge of change instead of being subjected to change. The change in culture and organization meant the school principals also found the arts to make their jobs easier in communicating what was distinctive about their school, and by also having teachers and students more engaged and excited about what they are doing.

Finally, parents found that the arts also made school more inviting for their children. The A+ schools also found that the arts were a reason for them to be connected with community agencies in ways that were not true before, even though the original thoughts about the centrality of partnerships to the reform effort now seem overly ambitious. Nevertheless, the development of the A+ network became the partnership of note. It became a way to sustain a culture around arts integration that linked the multiple levels of leadership that A+ sponsored in each school across the 24 schools. The Kenan Institute deserves much credit for these efforts and for managing the politics of reform in the state. In this context, schools learned how to think about reform not as compliance but as about adapting ideas to local contexts in service of creating a new identity for the school. The result of all this was a dramatic increase in organizational capacity both within the schools and between the schools and their various constituencies.

The arts were central to all of this for at least five reasons. First, the arts challenged the existing logics of schooling, which among other things valued the "core subjects" more than the arts. A+ led the schools embracing the arts as part of school identity. This gave arts teachers and teachers of other "special" subjects (i.e. physical education, special education, vocational education, etc.) new leadership roles in the schools. Teachers of other subjects saw this and worked to get back into this new center of power. Yet even in challenging the existing logic of schooling, A+ also meant the schools had a better grasp of the whole curriculum, including that of the "core subjects." Through thematic units and integrated instruction, the entire curriculum was enhanced and instruction was made more interesting and enjoyable for students and teachers alike.

Second, the arts invited people to think differently and creatively. Parents, students, and teachers found a new meaning to schooling when the arts became more centered in the organization. Parents saw their children as excited and began to see the possibilities that school could be different than they had previously experienced it. Students found they were invited to learn and to demonstrate their learning in ways that schools did not usually value. Being creative in these ventures made learning fun. Teachers were also pushed outside their normal patterns. While many of the schools initially had one or two teachers who could see their work as akin to A+, the summer institutes, on-site A+ workshops, regional meetings, new teacher orientation programs, and the enriched assessment project all contributed to developing wider cadres of teachers "doing A+." While some schools achieved "pockets of success" in certain grade levels or at times of the year, the substantive identity schools found A+ to be sufficient to guide their thinking in a wide range of educational issues and sufficient to rally parents and the community. On the state level, the work of the Kenan Institute was central to keeping A+ visible as the state moved to embrace accountability. Kenan also was the keystone of the arch of arts and philanthropic organizations that supported A+. The schools had never seen school reform like this and found that thinking creatively was central to dealing with policy changes.

Third, the arts basis in production also changed how schools thought about schoolwork. Before student work was carefully circumscribed to demonstrate what had been taught. Yet as A+ developed, teachers and students began to see schoolwork as artistic production. Sometimes this took the form of performances and informances, but more often this took the form of students creating artwork that existed as its own product as well as a demonstration of learning. Learning became less passive and artistic production became a new logic for demonstrating and assessing learning. This also fits many schools' interests in "hands-on" instruction. In many ways, it was the production logic of the arts that changed the students' experience of schooling and made it more "fun."

Fourth, the schools came to realize that the arts also enabled a set of skills that are essential to the new economy but which normal schoolwork did little to develop. There was a report on workplace preparation widely shared across the A+ network (Secretary's Commission on Achieving Necessary Skills, 1991). The report, *What Work Requires of School*, resonated with the A+ fellows and schools. The report advocated the development of a set of competencies including managing resources, teamwork, working with others to acquire and use information, understanding complex interrelationships, and working with a variety of technologies. The dialogue revealed that the A+ fellows saw what A+ was doing as completely consistent with these skills, which they referred to as "soft" skills.

In the new global economy, there has been much consideration to the new forms of knowledge that will be needed. The distinction is made between "mode 1" and "mode 2" forms of knowledge (Gibbons et al., 1994). Mode 1 knowledge is based in a manufacturing economy and requires developing distinct specializations that were linked to the production processes of stable industry. In our view, the recent accountability policies complete the factory model of schooling just when the factory is disappearing from the economy in the United States. Mode 2 knowledge (strategic, interdisciplinary, and application driven) will replace mode 1 knowledge as the new global economy continues to develop. The "soft" skills referred to above are key to this economy. Mode 2 knowledge has been termed "connective specialization" by Young (1998). The new economy will require an ability to bridge disciplinary specialization. This requires the ability to integrate various ways of knowing and work with interdisciplinary teams to create new products and processes. As Schramm (2002) has argued, arts integration facilitates this new form of knowledge and the skills it requires. The open question is why policy makers are acting in ways that undercut the nation's preparation for this economy. In this the arts are both creative and instrumental resources, and many involved in A+ see this as one of its unique contributions.

Finally, it cannot be overemphasized that A+ and the arts made school fundamentally more enjoyable places to be and learn. The A+ schools were able to satisfy high-stakes testing, maintain the full curriculum, even fuller than other schools in the face of testing, and to be creative in what and how teachers taught and students learnt. As noted in the last chapter, this made the schools inviting and exciting to the students, teachers, parents, and principals. The point here is not that we should embrace schools being "fun" as the goal but we should embrace the arts as both promoting learning and making learning more enjoyable. Teachers felt a new form of control over their craft as they were the authors of what and how the Standard Course of Study wanted them to teach. They taught the full curriculum when schools across the state were narrowing what was taught to what was tested, and taught the arts as well. For us, the value added by A+ and the arts was impressive. It changed what students thought about school as well as what they thought about and how they thought about it.

A+ provides an unusual account of school reform. While most efforts at school reform disappear after a few years, we have documented the sustainability of A+ across 8 years in a set of 24 schools. Moreover, we have documented that a high number of schools (about 10 in any given year) developed a substantive identity involving the arts and A+. Yet we want to be clear that sustaining a substantive identity requires considerable effort. Sometimes schools would experience challenges that led to schools slipping to a symbolic identity and others moving to a substantive identity. Yet many were able to maintain this identity through the 8 years. These schools were able to develop cultural beliefs about themselves as A+ and/or arts-enhanced schools that meant that when challenges came they used these beliefs to fashion responses rather than questioning these beliefs. Central to developing such deep-seated beliefs was the realization that arts were good for children and for learning. In this way, claims to being about the arts became moral claims. Such claims are unusual in schools and are all the more important because of this. The A+ schools came to believe they were doing the arts because it was the right thing to do for children. Since these schools also satisfied the demands of high-stakes testing, the moral claim became bolstered. This meant that the dilemmas of creativity versus instrumentality and top-down versus bottom-up reform were resolved not by picking sides but reclaiming education as a moral endeavor (Noblit & Dempsey, 1996). The terms of these dilemmas came to be seen not as ends in their own right but more as ways to embody doing what was right for children.

Four Benchmarks of A+ as a Reform

One of the topics we discussed in our proposal to the Ford Foundation and with Cyrus Driver in particular, was about any "tipping points" (Gladwell, 2000) there might be in the A+ reform effort. Our analyses did not show any clear "tipping points" in, for example, a school developing a substantive identity around A+ and/or the arts. As noted above, there is more complexity than the idea of "tipping points" can handle. However, we do want to project some benchmarks for arts-based school reform having better prospects of success. Benchmarks are different from "tipping points." "Tipping points" are a gravity metaphor, when forces shift sufficiently for gravity to pull a school into an identity with the arts. Benchmarks are about what is necessary for a reform of a particular type to be regarded as in place, regardless of the justification of the reform effort.

The question of how to best justify devoting this sort of attention to the arts remains, even with our analysis of the A+ Schools Program. To justify the arts' presence for their own sake is to relegate them to musty corners in the curriculum because there simply is no room to increase the number of "major" subjects, especially in this age of high-stakes accountability that seems to narrow even more what is critical for students to learn. To advocate for the arts on the basis of their contribution as tools for enhancing learning in other subjects is to place a burden on arts and education research that is too heavy for the existing literature to bear. The evidence is simply not there.

One of the problems, of course, is that empirical evidence is not likely to be forthcoming any time soon. Despite the millions of dollars spent on studying effective practice, debates still rage over the relative value of phonics versus whole language, over the effects of differences in class size, and over whether particular school reforms really work. Settling the issue of whether the arts improve learning in other disciplines or—put more crassly—increase test scores, is a long way away, if, in fact, it can ever be resolved.

Perhaps, as some (e.g. Winner and Hetland, 2000) argue, it would be best for research to concentrate on other benefits for students that accrue from participating in arts-related activities: more opportunities to express themselves creatively and in ways that suit their learning styles, enhanced interest in coming to school, greater appreciation for artistic endeavors, and the like. The comments from students, teachers, and parents in the A+ schools indicated that increased arts instruction and arts integration enhanced the learning environments in their buildings in such a manner. A+ participants, in other words, believed, based on their experiences, that students were better off for having been in schools that valued the arts. And, certainly, these beliefs played an important role in sustaining their efforts. For A+ participants, then, their hopes for improving student learning through the arts had been realized to their satisfaction.

As we demonstrated in the previous chapters, this was especially true in the schools that had managed to create a substantive role for the arts in their school cultures. Identifying the benefits of arts integration is entangled with actually integrating the arts. Our first benchmark is: *Arts integration has to be a powerful enough innovation to warrant having any expectations that there will be tangible ramifications for students.* The implication is that at least as much attention in arts-based reform movements should be devoted to the process of arts integration implementation and sustainability over time as to the educational advantages of the arts.

Advocates of arts integration must concentrate on both the educational value of arts integration and its organizational "staying power." In other words, an arts reform must demonstrate that it has a significant role to play in educating students *and* that it has a prominent and permanent place in schools' structural makeup. *Educational value* and *organizational prominence*, therefore, serve as two additional benchmarks for determining the probability that an arts-based reform initiative will manage to elevate the arts from second-class citizenship in a school's curriculum.

There is a fourth benchmark as well. This benchmark is involves the wider reform effort. Most reforms have an organization that drives or sponsors them, and A+ is no exception. What is exceptional about A+ is that the sponsoring agency was a foundation that took on school reform as a signature project. While most reform organizations are in many ways marketing a package, the Kenan Institute for the Arts took the role of sponsoring a process through which the reform initiative would be designed, implemented, and sustained. The Kenan Institute put significant funds into the effort and worked with the schools to generate grants and other funding. The Institute also ran political interference for the initiative, and conceived of the network form of organization for A+. The fourth benchmark then is *the presence of an active intermediary organization that sponsors the reform effort, develops funding, and manages the external environment to the reform, while allowing the schools and others closer to the schools to be key decision-makers.*

Our argument is that the accomplishment of a powerful arts-integration innovation, with a demonstration that the arts and arts integration promote an expansive definition of student learning, and with the arts and arts integration built into the operation of the school and its identity would indicate that an arts-based school reform is likely to have effects like we have seen with the A+ Schools Program. Clearly, other arts-based school reforms will be different from A+, but we would argue that most would benefit from considering these four benchmarks in the design and implementation of their effort.

The A+ experience is also informative about what some of the promising signs are that a school is moving down a path that will result in the arts becoming ingrained enough in day-to-day operation that it can reasonably be expected to result in educational value for students. That is, if a school appears to be heeding these signs, then the probability that it will maximize the value of the arts for students and weave the arts into the fabric of school life will be heightened. The rest of this chapter highlights some of these promising signs. It also ventures into positing similar signs that arts reformers, as well as arts reform researchers and evaluators, are acting in ways that are likely to be supportive and productive for schools and the initiatives.

Promising Signs for Educators

The Kenan Institute's well-advised emphasis on allowing, and indeed encouraging, schools to create their own versions of the A+ Program makes predicting the viability of these efforts a complicated exercise. Each school accommodated its particular mix of people, programs, politics, and resources and, thus, no two schools implemented A+ similarly. There was, and is, no A+ "model." In its place resides a commitment to integrating the arts into the school curriculum, thereby increasing students' opportunities to develop an appreciation for artistic endeavors and, equally as important, to acquire, process, and express ideas and information in creative ways that suit their learning styles.

The schools, thus, took a variety of routes to enacting their commitments to the arts. Their experiences make it reasonable to hazard some early guesses about promising developments that increase the likelihood that the arts will be able to demonstrate their educational value and to occupy an enduring place in the schools' organization. We conclude that if a school is in some way beginning to seriously pursue one of these developments, then it is likely enhancing the probability that down the road their efforts will result in something of value educationally and of permanence organizationally.

A first promising sign is that *arts integration is expected to take place in the regular classroom*. In most cases, it is unreasonable to expect the arts to have much of a role in instruction if they are limited to "specials." Regular classroom use of the arts seems to be the only way for arts integration to be a "powerful" intervention. Moreover, this expectation legitimizes teachers' ventures with new pedagogical techniques and ultimately should build capacity throughout a faculty.

Of course, integrating the arts in regular classrooms is enhanced by the presence of knowledgeable arts people in the building. A major part of "regular" teachers' discomfort with arts integration is their sense of ineptitude with the arts. Visiting artists (especially those who work with teachers in their classrooms), skilled "regular" teachers, and arts specialists have proven to be invaluable aides to teachers. Their presence is one of the few ways that teachers can enjoy the type of "guided" practice that is so essential to incorporating new strategies into their professional repertoires.

Moreover, ongoing professional development opportunities play a large role in the spread of regular classroom integration. There are two aspects to this: the extent to which a school introduces an increasing number of staff to A+ in the summer institutes and school-year meetings, and the number of school-based opportunities staff have for professional development. The latter is occurring in several ways. Some schools make sure that their visiting artists work in the classrooms with teachers; others encourage staff to seek outside-the-building arts-related experiences; and still others draw on staff expertise and devote faculty meeting time to teachers sharing this expertise with others.

Second, it is a promising sign when *a school manages to see congruence among its multiple priorities*. In other words, school staffs are able to envision the "big picture" of what they want to accomplish in their building and look for ways that the various initiatives that they are involved in can buttress, rather than bump against one another. In North Carolina, this was most plainly seen with the testing program. Schools variously saw this program as a threat, boon, or nonevent for arts integration. When schools saw the high-stakes testing program as a threat, arts integration all too often was not seen as congruent with the testing program. Yet when the testing program was seen as either a boon or nonevent in terms of arts integration, A+ and testing were more easily made congruent.

A third promising sign that the arts will eventually become organizationally prominent enough to contribute educationally is when a *school opens up the schedule to permit teachers the time and opportunity to plan cooperatively as they develop, modify, implement, and appraise arts integration*. Classroom changes of the order necessary to affect students substantially are likely to happen only when teachers are able to have these kinds of exchanges. Participating schools seem to vary widely in this regard, from having weekly and extended time for staff to work together to having almost no time to do so. It is inconceivable that any new program can be implemented and sustained without such time. Otherwise, there would be too little regular reinforcement of arts integration and a complete inability to induct new staff into what has gone on to date.

Fourth, it is promising when *there are multiple avenues of leadership for arts integration in the building*. The value of diffused leadership for any organization is well documented, and it is clear that many of the participating schools have several arts integration "champions" among their staff. This happy circumstance ensures that encouragement as well as mentoring opportunities will be abundant. A+ promoted the development of such leadership through its involvement of the principals, creation of the role of "project coordinator," and development of curriculum management teams and the various role-specific training sessions. At a minimum, having both the principal and coordinator in the school building doubles the potential for long-term programmatic leadership.

What all of these promising signs have in common is that they increase the chance that teachers will regularly "bump" into someone who is going to mention arts integration and will also have routine opportunities to advance their comfort and skill in integrating the arts. Arts integration, therefore, will become a part of the daily life of the school and will be sufficiently visible that new staff will see it as an expectation for them as well. Schools that make provisions for classroom integration, congruent priorities, multiple leadership, and collaboration will likely experience much better success in integrating the arts into their regular ways of working and thereby, increase the probability that the educational value there is to be gained from the arts will manifest itself.

There are a couple of arts-related activities that may not serve as promising signs, even though we saw them as positive developments. For example, having more arts teachers may not automatically result in deepening arts integration in school. Teachers' discomfort with the arts sometimes makes them all too willing to leave the arts to the artists. Thus, integration becomes one way, with the arts teachers adapting their instruction to accommodate the regular curriculum but not the other way around. These issues were worked out to the schools' advantage in the ones that afforded the arts a substantive role, but simply having more arts teachers did not mean that the arts would attain an organizationally prominent position. Curricular planning and coordination of schedules to allow arts integrated planning and team teaching gave arts teachers a new leadership role in the school.

Likewise, celebrating the arts through student performances (or "informances") or other productions decidedly enriched school life. Yet, again, their presence was interpreted by some staff to mean that the arts were being integrated without their having to do so in their classrooms. Although any and all of the celebratory events created awareness, among staff, students, and parents that the arts were a priority in a building and legitimized creative expression as integral to instruction, they also had less direct effects on getting the arts into classrooms on a daily basis.

Finally, most reforms—not just arts-related ones—seek to strengthen a school's ties to parents and community organizations. A+ did so as well. The schools' successes in this arena were modest for the most part. Although none of the participating sites took this to mean that their efforts were not worthwhile, it was evident that establishing these relationships was secondary to the above four signs in terms of embedding the arts into the regular routine. We would think that strong parent and community connections would be of tremendous help in encouraging the continuation of certain programs and practices, and perhaps this story will emerge as central to A+ schools over the next 5-year period.

Promising Signs for Arts Reformers and Policy Makers

The A+ Program operated at multiple layers of North Carolina education: at the school level, at the network level across schools, and at the state policy level. Kenan intentionally put in motion this complex arrangement under the assumption that actions at each level could reinforce one another, thereby engendering a broader base of support for arts integration. This proved to be an intelligent move, since—as we discussed earlier—A+ became an approved, comprehensive school reform approach in the state and a part of its annual educational budget. Kenan's specific actions at each level are illustrative of perhaps the most promising signs that arts reformers can take that will increase the likelihood that their efforts will become organizationally prominent and, eventually, result in educational value for students.

At the school level, *Kenan encouraged the schools to develop their own approaches to arts integration.* It was inevitable that each school would face a unique set of contingencies that would dictate adjustments, compromises, and rethinking. Being strapped by a detailed model rather than an acknowledged commitment to arts integration would have put a number of schools in untenable positions and perhaps would have led to their abandoning their efforts, as the dictates of the model clashed with local circumstances. Certainly the ambiguity of having to grow one's own approach presented its own set of challenges, but at the same time this approach ensured that the resulting decisions had a greater probability of navigating successfully a school's contextual situation. Kenan's refusal to be more directive frustrated many of the schools that wanted to bypass some of the time-consuming reflection and experimentation, but ultimately its avoidance of offering a "one-size-fits-all" model yielded a collection of ways to integrate the arts that meshed well within the environments in which the schools resided.

Kenan prodded the schools into developing a sense of belonging to a larger group of schools that were all connected by commitments to integration and self-direction. As members of the network, school staff jointly learned about the arts, commiserated about implementation, shared ideas, tackled problems, and initiated additional activities related to being A+ schools (such as the enriched assessment project funded by Goals 2000). As was discussed earlier, this connection gave even the schools that were having difficulty moving forward a sense that they were still A+. The network also gave the Program heightened visibility within the state.

This visibility proved to be of great benefit with the state legislature. Kenan's behind-the-scenes contacts, coupled with the public actions of the participating schools and the network, drew considerable attention to the A+ schools. Efforts on the behalf of A+ were not targeted solely at securing funding but also at making the Program an integral part of the state's educational agenda. Once the Program's goals were acknowledged as a valued part of what the state wanted to encourage in schools, the annual line of funding for the pilot was an obvious concomitant.

The events at all three levels created a synergy of support for A+. This was in contrast to many reforms that are occasionally blindsided by inadvertent actions at one level that have disruptive effects at other levels. Thus, *arts reforms that can demonstrate that they are giving substantial attention to schools' taking ownership over implementation, to encouraging a sense of shared identity across participating schools, and to shaping state policy in positive directions are setting in motion a promising set of steps that will enhance the lasting organizational prominence of the arts.*

To do this, of course, means that arts reformers and policy makers need to become politically astute about the educational-reform environments in the states and communities in which they hope to work. Arts reformers are notable for the passion they have about the arts, and they have had to be so because of the great difficulty the arts have had in gaining a foothold in school curricula. Consequently, arts-in-education supporters have concentrated their efforts on proposing justifications *for* arts integration. While we think such single-minded advocacy is admirable, it may lead also to considerable windmill tilting. It is possible that some arts-based reforms may be too arts-based. That is, they devote most of the attention to rationales for the arts with too little energy going toward organizational development. Even much of the current research on the role of the arts in education seeks to stake claims for the educational value of the arts, while glossing over what arts education and integration actually look like in practice and how schools can and should go about implementing arts-related reforms. All of this means, quite simply, that while it is a positive development for arts supporters to expand their advocacy, doing so to the exclusion of detailed insights into how to make the arts become prominent in school buildings and Statehouses will likely doom their passion to failure.

Promising Signs for Arts Researchers and Evaluators

The A+ Schools Program presumed that the pilot program had to have an evaluation that was sufficiently comprehensive to track the complexity of the reform effort and sufficiently flexible to adapt to the inevitable changes in the Program. The Kenan Institute for the Arts created a competitive request for proposals process. The review panel was faced with a set of rather different approaches to the evaluation. Some were geared to focus on impacts on test outcomes and were heavily quantitative. Others were mixed methods but clearly more qualitative. In the end, they chose one of the latter. The Kenan Institute seemed convinced that a qualitative design was more appropriate to understand a program such as A+ but also wanted sufficient quantitative data and analyses to address a policy audience that was interested "in the numbers." They also chose to award the contract to a team that had extensive research and evaluation experience in school reform rather than in the arts or arts education.

Given the nature of the A+ Schools Program, these decisions led to an evaluation very favorably reviewed in a careful analysis of studies, *Critical Links: Learning in the Arts and Student Academic and Social Development* (Deasy, 2002). While we would be the first to argue that other data analyses and theoretical perspectives would have been useful, the *A+ program did need a qualitative and flexible design to provide both formative evaluation data and to create the summative account this report represents*. The extensive local adaptation of the Program, the competing policy initiatives, and the site-specific learning that occurred severely pressed even the largely qualitative design we had proposed. Further, the A+ Schools Program was being enacted in the field of educational policy and specifically school reform. The arts were central to A+, but the stakeholders who had to be convinced were not in the arts community but were educational policy makers. *Having an evaluation team who knew and who could speak the language of school reform, even if critically, enabled the A+ Program to be articulated to this powerful stakeholder group.*

The research we conducted suggests other promising signs for arts researchers and evaluators. Understanding the effects of an arts-based reform required that we had detailed data on what actually occurred at the network, school, and classroom levels. These data enabled us to describe what the intervention actually was. The types of school identity we portrayed in this report should remind arts researchers and evaluators that variability in implementation and changes over time are key factors in the outcomes produced. This is true of any studies of school reform but may be even more important in arts reforms where creativity is valued over rote compliance to a reform agenda.

Detailed qualitative studies also allow arts researchers and evaluators to understand how elements of the reform initiative are and are not connected. For example, multiple intelligences was important to the A+ schools but less so as an instructional strategy and more as a metaphor. Without sufficient data "on the ground" in schools and classrooms, we could have mistakenly conducted analyses of the effects of multiple intelligences on instruction and student learning.

Similarly, our data repeatedly revealed that the A+ network had strong effects on schools. If we had not had data at multiple levels of analysis (individual, classroom, school, network, etc.), we could have attributed these effects to school-level data alone, again mistakenly. Finally, it was the detailed school and classroom data that led us to conclude that A+ was a "value-added" reform and would have at best only limited impact on state test results. Even with extensive data, we could not determine how arts integration, for instance, would be directly connected to scores on state tests. This led us to a different conclusion about test results that we will discuss later.

A final promising development for arts researchers and evaluators involves *creatively casting the net for student benefits.* Since tests seemed to be poor measures of student benefits, then it was essential to imaginatively search for other understandings of student benefits. This led us to use student interviews to tap into their language and its implications for A+. We also heard from teachers and principals that what they were seeing was better attendance and more enthusiasm from students. Yet the A+ schools had very high attendances before A+ began, meaning that the increases revealed in school records seemed less than dramatic.

We began to consider the form of the data that we were receiving about students and to think of the data in more cultural terms. School staffs were sharing stories about student successes. Such anecdotes played a powerful role in the evolution of arts integration efforts. Stories of previously unengaged students who had become more engaged or who had demonstrated new talents were strong justifications for increased arts-integration efforts. Test score results were also stories seen to be true as well. These stories were repeated until they took on a taken-for-granted status within the school. That is, they became seen as true. Such stories helped to shape staff members' ideas about the educational value of the arts and were shared with parents, community members, and students as well. Casting the net wide to understand student benefits seems essential to understanding how arts reforms actually impact students.

The research agenda, *The Arts and Education: New Opportunities for Research* (Arts Education Partnership, 2004), reflects the current understanding that research on arts and education is a wide and demanding field of endeavor. The promising developments that emerge from it and from this study mean that *studies have to be designed to capture the real complexity of the arts and of school reform.* This is clearly a challenge even to flexible, qualitative, and mixed-methods designs. Moreover, it also means that what is often taken to be the most important element of educational reform is not very promising.

It does not seem promising to try to focus on the effects of the arts on academic achievement, for example. Academic achievement tests are too narrowly constructed to capture the fullness of what the arts and/or arts integration can offer a student. Current tests also do not assess the key capabilities needed for the new economy. Tests focus on discrete knowledge and skills when analysts believe what is needed is "connective specialization" (Young, 1998), which involves bridging discrete knowledge domains and linking people to collectively creative new solutions. The arts may be especially relevant in this, but achievement tests are not geared to such assessments.

Finally, high-stakes testing is increasingly common and creates a predictable pattern of test results: low initial scores giving way to a few years of very high test-score gains followed by very low gains or even slight declines in scores. That is, the high stakes create dramatic test-score outcomes and make it difficult for any reform to show gains attributable to the reform. Observing this pattern in the A+ schools, we concluded that test scores were better seen as intervening variables than outcome variables. Schools took the tests each year and made changes each year for the following year. Rather than being an outcome assessment, high-stakes tests were an intervention of their own.

A Final Assessment

The A+ Schools Program has proven to be a useful, productive, value-added reform. As we have argued in this book, the schools found A+ to be a source of identity. That is, they were able to use A+ to think about what they were to teach and how to teach. A+ also gave the schools a stance from which to interpret and respond to competing reform agendas.

A+ was productive in that the schools used it to empower a set of teachers, arts teachers, and other "special" teachers, to contribute to the larger mission of the school and to the overall reform effort. It produced new lessons, new understandings of the capabilities of students, new teacher cultures, and a new definition of North Carolina's Standard Course of Study, as well as a network that evolved into the main professional development and governance mechanism for the initiative.

A+ was value added in that it broadened the experiences of teachers and students and added linkages to parents, community, and a state-wide network that previously had not existed. It also added a vocabulary about learning that conceived of students' academic strengths in more inclusive and diverse ways. Most significantly, A+ schools managed to broaden their curricula when other schools in North Carolina were narrowing them in response to high-stakes testing. Finally, A+ added value to lives of teachers and students by giving a richer, more imaginative, and more complete educational experience.

A+ reveals that the arts can play a powerful role in school reform. For example, when educators decide to include the arts, they have resources most school-reform efforts do not have. First, the arts teachers, and other "special" teachers, become part of the effort instead of remaining on the periphery of reform. Classroom teachers also gain new understandings of the curriculum and of their students. Second, the arts mean that students become engaged in noticeable ways in their education. As students come to understand themselves and their learning in new ways, they become more enthusiastic and more committed to learning. Third, for schools, the arts become a vehicle to forge links to the parents and community. This distinctive identity is attractive to many parents and allows parents to see the full range of their children's strengths. Links with the community provide both resources and legitimize the arts as integral to schooling.

Finally, the A+ Schools Program offers lessons about how to negotiate the difficult and sometimes contradictory terrain of arts-based school reform. A+ refused to choose either arts for arts' sake or art as a vehicle for other learning. By not choosing one over the other, the A+ Program allowed schools to imaginatively construct the resolutions that best fit their schools. With such local definition, schools perceive A+ as belonging to them.

School reform has vacillated between choosing top-down and bottom-up approaches. Clearly, the recent reform era that began in the early 1980s assumed that schools must be forced to reform. Yet the failure of such forced approaches has led to arguments that schools should be free to develop their own approaches to reform. A+ has been simultaneously top-down and bottom-up. Educators and schools were part of the initial planning with arts professionals and the Kenan Institute for the Arts, and this collaboration has characterized the effort throughout its existence. The Kenan Institute's metaphor of "flying a plane while building it" points to the flexibility of the reform and to the participatory aspect of defining A+ at any point in time. Not choosing one side over the other has forced schools to reconceptualize their role in reform. Taken together, this allowed A+ to be powerful, resilient, and sustainable.

Appendix
Valuing A+: The Research Strategy

Our research on A+ that provides the data for this book is based on two studies, covering a period of 8 years. First was the evaluation of the "piloting" of the A+ Schools Program. Second was the study of the sustainability of the Program.

The first study was planned to take 5 years, but it took 6 years in the end—4 years on-site and 2 years of data analysis, additional data collection, and writing. It was a formative evaluation conducted to help guide the reform process for the Kenan Institute and the A+ schools. Its primary purpose was to track and document the evolution of A+ in each of the 24 schools and in the A+ Schools Program in general. The expectation was that this would generate useful information about the roles the arts could play in schools and how schools incorporated these roles into their customary ways of working. It was funded by the Thomas S. Kenan Institute for the Arts.

To do this, the evaluation had to have an on-site presence in the schools to examine closely the internal dynamics of arts integration. Thus, the most significant piece of the evaluation design was fieldwork in the schools. In each of the 4 years of actual fieldwork, we spent about 180 total person days in the schools. Multiple visits were paid to each of the schools, with 10 schools receiving more intensive attention as case-study sites during the second and third years. These 10 schools were chosen to maximize variability in community served, levels of schooling, and ways of defining and executing the A+ experience. During school visits, we talked to building administrators, teachers, staff, and students in the schools. We interviewed community members, parents, and district administrators. We also observed classroom instruction and, while in the school, collected artifacts of student and teacher work, attended performances/special events, and sat in on planning meetings of school staff. Over the course of these visits we conducted some 2,310 interviews.

Fieldwork was not the only data collection tool used, however. Five others were drawn on as well:

1. We documented the annual *summer institutes*. This was the primary mechanism for schools to learn about the principles of the A+ Program, try out some of the curricular and instructional activities, hear from other schools about their struggles and triumphs, and figure out how to adapt what they had learned into their own school culture. Our observations of that training and identity-building process represented a crucial way to understand the evolving A+ story.

2. *Surveys* helped assess how various participants were defining the A+ experience. We surveyed students early and late in the pilot, asking them about the arts, their views on learning, and the kinds of instruction they encountered ($n = 1,725$). We also surveyed parents twice to learn about the ways they were involved in their children's education and how the schools reached out to them ($n = 3,407$) . Finally, teacher surveys provided insights into their learning priorities, issues related to A+ implementation, and the effects of A+ ($n = 602$).

3. Schools were also asked to complete *annual profiles* of their organizational structures and activities. These profiles facilitated the tracking of staffing patterns, planning schedules, and professional development activities.

4. The evaluation examined *student achievement patterns*, as measured by the required state testing program. End-of-grade tests in reading, mathematics, and writing provided individual student-level scores at the elementary and middle grades level while end-of-course tests yielded information at the high-school level. These data were analyzed for the 1994–1995 school year (the year prior to A+ implementation), and for each year of the pilot of the program (1995–1996 through 1998–1999). (We also collected these data as part of the sustainability study for the year 2002–2003.)

5. The final piece of the evaluation concentrated on *the evolution of the A+ network*. As this network strengthened, we attended regional and state-wide meetings, observed professional development programs, interviewed key local stakeholders, documented efforts to seek funding to expand network activities, and collected documents on the history of the A+ initiative.

While the evaluation's primary goal was to provide Program leaders with information that would improve the overall initiative, evaluation results were also tailored for each participating school and shared in regular feedback sessions at the end of the school year. These sessions not only informed the schools about progress, but also served as a reality check on our interpretation of what we had observed.

The evaluation produced the data for Chapters 1 through 6 of this book. Chapters 7 through 9 were based on a study funded by the Ford Foundation to examine the remarkable sustainability of the Program. While many school reforms wane over time, A+ seemed to be sustained in the original schools even as it was expanding within North Carolina and to other states. As researchers who have studied many school reforms, this was an opportunity to learn about what makes school reform sustainable and how the arts were implicated in this. The sustainability study involved four parts: a review of the data set from the evaluation of the pilot period; phone interviews with A+ school principals and A+ coordinators; case studies of substantive identity schools that had some success sustaining this identity over the 8 years as well as one school that changed dramatically and achieved a substantive identity after the pilot period; and focus group interviews with key groups of stakeholders.

Review of Existing Data

The research team thought it was necessary to review the existing data set of interviews, school and classroom observations, surveys of parents, teachers and students, test scores, and documents and other artifacts. The data set enabled us to reconsider each school and the Program itself inductively over time. Our examination of these data was important in two ways. First, it confirmed that the analysis in our evaluation reports of the role of culture in the A+ schools was essentially correct. But equally important, the review of the existing data also highlighted that schools move in and out of different cultural identities in relation to the A+ Program. While all the schools were able sustain an *affiliated* identity, *symbolic* identity seems to be highly dependent on school leadership and more vulnerable to changes in context (district leadership, accountability initiatives, etc.), and *substantive* identity schools may also move to *symbolic* identities for a period of time, but can use their cultural identity as a resource to fend off changes in context and even reduce the threat of changes in leadership.

Phone Interviews

After using the evaluation data set to confirm our school culture analysis and extending it to consider what these data indicate about sustainability, these same data were employed to identify a set of schools for new case studies with a specific focus on sustainability and the role of the arts in sustainability. However, the research team felt that since only limited data had been collected since the evaluation study, the research plan needed to fill in this gap. As a result, phone interviews were conducted with principals and school-level A+ coordinators of all the then existing A+ schools in North Carolina ($n = 34$). We also analyzed data from the state's database that included test results, attendance, disciplinary records, etc.

Case Studies

The existing data set and the phone interviews enabled the selection of schools for case studies to help us understand what the arts have to do with sustaining a school reform. While there were lessons to be learned from studying all three identity types, the research team concluded that it was best to concentrate on schools that were able to sustain a substantive identity with A+ and the arts. Within this both elementary and secondary schools were included, enabling the findings to be more broadly useful. However, in the process of doing the principal and coordinator interviews, we discovered two schools that changed their identities from affiliated to at least symbolic and potentially substantive identities. As these cases would allow investigation of the key factors in the change of school cultural identities, it was decided to pursue studies of these schools. In the end, one agreed to be studied. Thus there were four substantive identity school cases and one "regeneration" school case. The case studies were done in the spring of 2003. These case studies followed a protocol that we have used for a number of school reform initiatives. Each case study began with a phone interview with the principal to both make arrangements for the site visit and to interview her or him about where the school was with A+, the issues they were facing, and what they saw as their accomplishments with A+ and otherwise. This was followed by a 2 person-day site visit, which usually began with a school tour. Typically, six classrooms were observed including both arts and regular classrooms. Interviews were conducted with the A+ coordinator, teachers, parents, and students. The number and mix varied but typically 6–10 interviews were conducted. As with the evaluation, the case-study team ended the visit with a debriefing interview with the principal, sharing what we had learned about the sustainability of A+ and how A+ was implicated in the school's identity. The teams wrote up their field notes and drafted case summaries. These were later compared to enable a cross-case analysis.

Focus Groups

Over 2003–2004, focus group interviews were conducted with three stakeholder groups: A+ principals ($n = 24$), A+ school-level coordinators ($n = 33$), and the staff of the Kenan Institute ($n = 4$). These interviews were focused on reviewing the recent history of the Program, factors affecting sustainability, and especially the role of the arts in sustainability of the Program. These interviews were transcribed and analyzed for themes, especially those related to sustainability of reform and the role of the arts in that sustainability.

These two studies represent an unusually rich database for studies of school reform, and especially for arts-based school reform. Few studies have longitudinal data over 8 years. Even fewer studies have the volume of data we have on a school reform initiative. Taken together, these data enable a study of school reform that few can approach. From these data, we have issued a seven-volume evaluation report and an executive summary, available from the A+ Schools Program at the University of North Carolina at Greensboro. We also produced a report to the Ford Foundation that was the first draft of this book. The project has also led to a number of articles and book chapters, some of which are cited in this volume. We would refer you in particular to a special issue of *Educational Foundations* on accountability and arts-based school reform (Gertsl-Pepin, Gunzenhauser, & Noblit, 2002). The evaluation and its results were reviewed quite favorably in *Critical Links* (Deasy, 2002). We refer readers to that volume to better understand the state of research on arts and education.

Notes

Preface

1. In addition to the book authors we were assisted by a larger contingent of graduate students who did fieldwork, wrote and published from their observations, and generally kept us on our toes. Without them this work could not have been completed. Their contributions are greatly appreciated. These researchers included Amee Adkins, Catherine Awsumb Nelson, Benjamin Blaisdell, Darrell Cleveland, Sheryl Conrad Cozart, Mary Cornish, LeAnn Disla, Joanne Kilgore Dowdy, Susana Flores, Cindy Gerstl-Pepin, Carolyn Gilman, Jenny Gordon, Monifa Green Beverly, Paula Groves Price, Michael Gunzenhauser, Phillip Herman, Enrique Murillo, Paul Neufeld, Jean Patterson, Joseph Rayle, and Luis Urrieta. Monifa Green Beverly and Benjamin Blaisdell are co-authors of Chapters 7 and 8.

2 An Unusual Development

1. Twenty-five schools were originally selected for the pilot, but one school withdrew at the onset of the Program when the district superintendent found that, with the reduction in expected state funds, local funds would have to be allocated. The politics of funds to one school over the others was such that the school had to withdraw from A+. So, we will refer to the Program as having 24 pilot schools.

7 Sustaining Arts-Based School Reform

1. Monifa Green Beverly and Benjamin Blaisdell are co-authors of this chapter.
2. The schools were able to sustain an *affiliated* cultural identity. *Symbolic* identity schools though were largely able to sustain their level as well but in some cases, usually brought on by leadership changes, they fell back to an affiliated identity. *Substantive* identity schools also seemed relatively stable.
3. While there were lessons to be learned from studying all three identity types, the research team concluded that it was best to concentrate on schools that were able to sustain a substantive identity with A+ and the arts. Within this both elementary and secondary schools were included enabling the findings to be more broadly useful. However, in the process of doing the principal and coordinator interviews, we discovered two schools that changed their identities from affiliated to at least symbolic and potentially substantive

identities. As these cases would allow investigation of the key factors in the change of school cultural identities, it was decided to pursue studies of these schools. In the end, one agreed to be studied.

8 Sustaining Change: The Difference the Arts Make in Schools

1. Monifa Green Beverly and Benjamin Blaisdell are co-authors of this chapter.

References

Adelman, N. E., & Walking-Eagle, K. P. (1997). Teachers, time, and school reform. In N. Adelman, K. P. Walking–Eagle, & A. Hargreaves (Eds.), *Racing with the clock: Making time for teaching and learning in school reform* (pp. 92–110). New York: Teachers College Press.

Adkins, A. (1997). Colonial vestiges of educational reform. Unpublished Ph.D. dissertation, University of North Carolina-Chapel Hill.

Adkins, A., & Gunzenhauser, M.G. (2005). West Hollow School and the North Carolina A+ Schools Program: Integrating the arts, crafting a local agenda for reform. In W. T. Pink, & G. W. Noblit (Eds.), *Cultural matters: Lessons learned from field studies of several leading school reform strategies* (pp. 63–86). Cresskill, NJ: Hampton Press.

Arnstine, D. (1990). Art, aesthetics, and the pitfalls of discipline-based art education. *Educational Theory, 40*(4), 415–422.

Arts Education Partnership. (2004). *The arts and education: New opportunities for research.* Washington, DC: Arts Education Partnership.

Berliner, D. C., & Biddle, B. J. (1997). *The manufactured crisis: Myths, fraud, and the attack on America's public schools.* White Plains, NY: Longman.

Borman, G. D., Hewes, G. M., Overman, L. T., & Brown, S. (2003). *Comprehensive School Reform and student achievement: A meta-analysis.* Baltimore, MD: Center for Research on the Education of Students Placed at Risk.

Bracey, G. W. (1997). *Setting the record straight: Responses to misconceptions about public education in the United States.* Alexandria, VA: Association for Supervision and Curriculum Development.

Catterall, J. S. (1998). Does experience in the arts boost academic achievement? A response to Eisner. *Art Education, 51*(4), 6–11.

Century, J. R., & Levy, A. J. (2002). *Sustaining change: A study of nine school districts with enduring program.* Available from http://cse.edc.org/products/rsr/pdfs/rsr_aerapaper2002.pdf (accessed June 2008).

Clark, G. (1997). Critics, criticism, and the evolution of discipline-based art education. *Visual Arts Research, 23*(2), 12–18.

Cochran-Smith, M., & Lytle, S. L. (1999). The teacher research movement: A decade later. *Educational Researcher, 28*(7), 15–25.

Corbett, H. D., & Wilson, B. L. (1998). Scaling within rather than scaling up: Implications from students' experiences in reforming urban middle schools. *The Urban Review, 30*(4), 261–293.

Corcoran, T., & Goertz, M. (1995). Instructional capacity and high performance schools. *Educational Researcher, 24*(9), 27–31.

Csikszentmihalyi, M. (1997). Assessing aesthetic education: Measuring the ability to "ward of chaos." *Arts Education Policy Review, 99*(1), 33–38.

Cuban, L. (1990). Reforming again, again, and again. *Educational Researcher, 19*(1), 2–13.

Cuban, L. (1992a). What happens to reforms that last?: The case of the junior high school. *American Educational Research Journal, 29*(2), 227–251.

Cuban, L. (1992b). Why some reforms last: The case of the kindergarten. *American Journal of Education, 100*(2), 166–194.

Curry, B. K. (1991). Institutionalization: The final phase of the organizational change process. *Administrator's Notebook, 35*(1), 1–5.

Darby, J. T., & Catterall, J. S. (1994). The fourth R: The arts and learning. *Teachers College Record, 96*(2), 299–328.

Deal, T. E., & Peterson, K. D. (1998). *Shaping school culture: The heart of leadership.* San Francisco: Jossey-Bass.

Deasy, R. J. (2002). *Critical links: Learning in the arts and student academic and social developments.* Available from http://www.aep-arts.org/files/publications/CriticalLinks.pdf (accessed June 2008).

Desimone, L. M. (2002). How can comprehensive school reform models be successfully implemented? *Review of Educational Research, 72*(3), 433–479.

Dobbs, S. M. (1998). *Learning in and through art: A guide to discipline-based art education.* Los Angeles: The Getty Institute for the Arts.

Egan, K. (1992). *Imagination in teaching and learning: The middle school years.* Chicago: University of Chicago Press.

Eisner, E. W. (1990). Discipline-based art education: Conceptions and misconceptions. *Educational Theory, 40*(4), 423–443.

Eisner, E. W. (1998a). *Aesthetic modes of knowing.* Portsmouth, NH: Heinemann.

Eisner, E. W. (1998b). Does experience in the arts boost academic achievement? *Arts Education Policy Review, 100*(1), 32–38.

Elmore, R. F. (1992). Why restructuring alone won't improve teaching. *Educational Leadership, 49*, 44–48.

Elmore, R. F. (1995). Structural reform and educational practice. *Educational Researcher, 24*(9), 23–26.

Elmore, R. F. (1996). Getting to scale with good educational practice. *Harvard Educational Review, 66*(1), 1–26.

Fiske, E. B. (Ed.). (1999). *Champions of change: The impact of the arts on learning.* Washington, DC: Arts Education Partnership and the President's Committee on the Arts and the Humanities.

Fullan, M. G. (1991). *The new meaning of educational change* (2nd ed.). New York: Teachers College Press.

Fullan, M. G. (1993). *Change forces: Probing the depths of educational reform.* Bristol, PA: Falmer Press.

Fullan, M. G. (1994). Coordinating top-down and bottom-up strategies for educational reform. In R. F. Elmore, & S. H. Fuhrman (Eds.), *The governance of curriculum* (pp. 186–202). Alexandria, VA: Association for Supervision and Curriculum Development.

Fullan, M. G. (1999). On effecting change in arts education. *Arts Education Policy Review*, *100*(3), 17–18.

Fullan, M. G., & Miles, M. B. (1992). Getting reform right: What works and what doesn't. *Phi Delta Kappan*, *73*(10), 744–752.

Gardner, H. (1983). *Frames of mind: The theory of multiple intelligences*. New York: Basic Books.

Gardner, H. (1991). *The unschooled mind: How children think and how schools should teach*. New York: Basic Books.

Gardner, H. (1993). *Multiple intelligences: The theory in practice*. New York: Basic Books.

Gardner, H. (1999). *Intelligence reframed: Multiple intelligences for the 21st century*. New York: Basic Books.

Geahigan, G. (1992). The arts in education: A historical perspective. In B. Reimer, & R. A. Smith (Eds.), *The arts, education, and aesthetic knowing: Ninety-first yearbook of the National Society for the Study of Education* (pp. 1–19). Chicago: University of Chicago Press.

Gerstl-Pepin, C. I. (2001). *A history of the A+ Schools Program*. Winston-Salem, NC: Thomas S. Kenan Institute for the Arts.

Gerstl-Pepin, C. I., Gunzenhauser, M. G., & Noblit, G. W. (Eds.). (2002). The arts and accountability: The shifting foundations of school reform. A special issue of *Educational Foundations*, *16*(2), 108 pp.

Gibbons, M., Limoges, C., Nowotny, H., Schwartzman, S., Scott, P., & Trow, M. (1994). *The new production of knowledge: The dynamics of science and research in contemporary societies*. Thousand Oaks, CA: Sage Publications.

Gladwell, M. (2000). *The tipping point*. Boston: Little, Brown.

Goodlad, J. I. (1992). Toward a place in the curriculum for the arts. In B. Reimer, & R. A. Smith (Eds.), *The arts, education, and aesthetic knowing: Ninety-first yearbook of the National Society for the Study of Education* (pp. 192–212). Chicago: University of Chicago Press.

Greenfield, T. A. (1995). Improving chances for successful educational reform. *Education*, *115*, 464–474.

Grissmer, D., Flanagan, A., Kawata, J., & Williamson, S. (2000). *Improving students achievement: What state NAEP test scores tell us*. Santa Monica, CA: RAND Education.

Gunzenhauser, M. G. (2006). Tri-state A+ network themes. Paper presented at the A+ Schools Program National Research Conference, Greensboro, NC.

Hamblen, K. A. (1997). Second generation DBAE. *Visual Arts Research*, *23*(2), 98–106.

Hawley, W. D., & Valli, L. (1999). The essentials of effective professional development: A new consensus. In L. Darling-Hammond, & G. Sykes (Eds.), *Teaching as the learning profession: Handbook of policy and practice* (pp. 127–151). San Francisco: Jossey-Bass.

Hendricks-Lee, M. S., Soled, S. W., & Yinger, R. J. (1995). Sustaining reform through teacher learning. *Language Arts*, *72*, 288–292.

Herbert, D. (1998). Model approaches to arts education. *Principal*, *77*(4), 36–43.

Hoffman-Davis, J. (1999). Nowhere, somewhere, everywhere: The arts in education. *Arts Education Policy Review*, *100*(5), 23–28.

Jackson, P. W. (1987). Mainstreaming art: An essay on Discipline-Base Art Education. *Educational Researcher, 16*(6), 39–43.

Jehl, J., & Payzant, T. W. (1992). Philanthropy and public school reform: A view from San Diego. *Teachers College Record, 93*(3), 472–487.

Jones, M. G., Jones, B. D., Hardin, B., Chapman, L., Yarbrough, T., & Davis, M. (1999). The impact of high stakes testing on teachers and students in North Carolina. *Phi Delta Kappan, 81*(3), 199–203.

Keene, J. (1982). *A history of music education in the United States.* Hanover, NH: University Press of New England.

Kirst, M. W., & Meister, G. R. (1985). Turbulence in American secondary schools: What reforms last? *Curriculum Inquiry, 15*(2), 39–81.

Krechevsky, M. (1991). Project Spectrum: An innovative assessment alternative. *Educational Leadership, 48*(5), 43–48.

Labaree, D. F. (1997). Public goods, private goods: The American struggle over educational goals. *American Educational Research Journal, 34*(1), 39–82.

Lieberman, A., & Grolnick, M. (1996). Networks and reform in American education. *Teachers College Record, 98*(1), 7–45.

Longley, L. (1999). *Gaining the arts advantage.* Washington, DC: President's Committee on the Arts and Humanities and Arts Education Partnership.

McMillan, M. (1999). *The troubling consequences of the ABCs: Who's accountable?* Raleigh, NC: Common Sense Foundation.

Metz, M. H. (1986). *Different by design: The context and character of three magnet schools.* New York: Routledge & Kegan Paul.

Moffett, J. (2000). Sustaining change: The answers are blowing in the wind. *Educational Leadership, 57*(7), 35–38.

National Advisory Committee on Creative and Cultural Education (NACCCE). (1999). *All our futures: Creativity and education.* Warwick, England: NACCCE.

National Commission of Excellence in Education. (1983). *A nation at risk: The imperative for educational reform.* Washington, DC: U.S. Government Printing Office.

National Endowment for the Arts (NEA). (1988). *Toward civilization: A report on arts education.* Washington, DC: U.S. Government Printing Office.

Noblit, G. W., & Bettez, S. (2004). Powers of the arts in education. *The Journal of Thought, 39*(4), 7–14.

Noblit, G. W., & Dempsey, V. O. (1996). *The social construction of virtue: The moral life of schools.* Albany: State University of New York Press.

Noblit, G. W., & Johnston, B. (Eds.). (1982). *The school principal and school desegregation.* Springfield, IL: Charles Thomas.

Noblit, G. W., Malloy, W. W., & Malloy, C. E. (2001). *The kids got smarter: Case studies of successful Comer Schools.* Cresskill, NJ: Hampton Press Inc.

Noddings, N. (1994). *The challenge to care in schools: An alternative approach to education.* New York: Teachers College Press.

Oldford, R. (1998). Why institutionalization has failed. *Teacher Librarian, 29*(3), 8–15.

Olsen, B., & Kirtman, L. (2002). Teacher as mediator of school reform: An examination of teacher practice in 36 California restructuring schools. *Teachers College Record, 104*(2), 301–324.

O'Neil, J. (2000). Fads and fireflies: The difficulties of sustaining change. *Educational Leadership, 57*(7), 5–9.

Parsons, M. J. (1998). Integrated curriculum and our paradigm of cognition in the arts. *Studies in Art Education, 39*(2), 103–116.

Pelavin Associates. (1994). *Arts education research agenda for the future.* Washington, DC: U.S. Department of Education, Office of Educational Research and Improvement.

Pink, W. T., & Hyde, A. A. (1992). Doing effective staff development. In W. T. Pink, & A. A. Hyde (Eds.), *Effective staff development for school change* (pp. 259–292). Norwood, NJ: Ablex.

Pink, W. T., & Noblit, G. W. (2005). *Cultural matters: Lessons learned from field studies from several leading school reform strategies.* Cresskill, NJ: Hampton Press.

Prestine, N. A. (2000). Disposable reform? Assessing the durability of secondary school reform. *Planning & Changing, 31,* 124–147.

Rabkin, N., & Redmond, R. (Eds.). (2004). *Putting the arts in the picture.* Chicago: Columbia College Chicago.

Remer, J. (1990). *Changing schools through the arts.* New York: American Council for the Arts.

Richardson, V. (1994). Conducting research on practice. *Educational Researcher, 23*(5), 5–10.

Sarason, S. B. (1971). *The culture of school and the problem of change.* Boston: Allyn & Bacon.

Sarason, S. B. (1990). *The predictable failure of educational reform: Can we change course before it is too late?* San Francisco: Jossey-Bass.

Sarason, S. B. (1996). *Revisiting the culture of school and the problem of change.* New York: Teachers College Press.

Schmidt, S. W., Scott, J., Lande, C., & Guasti, L. (Eds.). (1977). *Friends, followers, factions: A reader in political clientelism.* Berkeley: University of California Press.

Schramm, S. L. (2002). *Transforming the curriculum: Thinking outside the box.* Lanham, MD: Scarecrow Education.

Scott, W. R. (1995). *Institutions and organizations.* Thousand Oaks, CA: Sage Publications.

Secretary's Commission on Achieving Necessary Skills. (1991). *What work requires of schools: A SCANS report for America 2000.* Washington, DC: U.S. Department of Labor.

Senge, P. (1990). *The fifth discipline: The art and practice of the learning organization.* New York: Doubleday.

Shields, P. M., & Knapp, M. S. (1997). The promise and limits of school-based reform: A national snapshot. *Phi Delta Kappan, 79*(4), 288–294.

Silverman, R. (1997). Testing the in-service hypothesis: The Getty's Los Angeles DBAE Institute. *Visual Arts Research, 23*(2), 4–11.

Slavin, R. E. (2001). Putting the school back in school reform. *Educational Leadership, 58*(4), 22–27.

Stankiewicz, M. A., Amburgy, P., & Bolin, P. (2004). Questioning the past: Contexts, functions, and stakeholders in 19th-century art education. In

E. Eisner, & M. Day (Eds.), *Handbook of research and policy in art education* (pp. 33–54). Mahwah, NJ: Lawrence Erlbaum Associates.

Stringfield, S., & Datnow, A. (1998). Introduction: Scaling up school restructuring designs in urban schools. *Education and Urban Society, 30,* 269–276.

Wakeford, M. (2004). A short look at a long past. In N. Rabkin, & R. Redmond (Eds.), *Putting the arts in the picture* (pp.81–106). Chicago: Columbia College Chicago.

Weatherly, R., & Lipsky, M. (1977). Street-level bureaucrats and institutional innovation: Implementing special-education reform. *Harvard Educational Review, 47*(2), 171–197.

White, John (2004). 20th-century art education: A historical perspective. In E. Eisner, & M. Day (Eds.), *Handbook of research and policy in art education* (pp. 55–84) Mahwah, NJ: Lawrence Erlbaum Associates.

Wiggins, G. (1993). *Educative assessment: Designing assessments to inform and improve student performance.* San Francisco: Jossey-Bass, Inc.

Wilson, B. (1997). *The quiet evolution: Changing the face of arts education.* Los Angeles: The Getty Education Institute for the Arts.

Wilson, B., & Rubin, B. M. (1997). DBAE and educational change. *Visual Arts Research, 23*(2), 89–97.

Winner, E., & Hetland, L. (2000). The arts and academic improvement: What the evidence shows (executive summary). *Journal of Aesthetic Education, 34*(3/4), 3–10.

Wohlstetter, P., & Smith, A. K. (2000). Different approach to systemic reform: Network structures in Los Angeles. *Phi Delta Kappan, 81*(7), 508–515.

Wygant, F. (1993). *School art in American culture.* Cincinnati. OH: Interwood Press.

Young, M. F. D. (1998). *The curriculum of the future: From the "new sociology of education" to a critical theory of learning.* Philadelphia: Falmer Press.

Index

Made in the USA
Lexington, KY
10 March 2014